Succession Politics in Indonesia

Also by Bilveer Singh

ABRI AND THE SECURITY OF SOUTHEAST ASIA

THE CHALLENGE OF CONVENTIONAL ARMS PROLIFERATION IN
SOUTHEAST ASIA

DWIFUNGSI ABRI: The Dual Function of the Indonesian Armed Forces

EAST TIMOR, INDONESIA AND THE WORLD: Myths and Realities

THE GARUDA AND BEAR: Soviet–Indonesian Relations from Lenin to
Gorbachev

SINGAPORE–INDONESIA RELATIONS: Problems and Perspectives (*co-editor*)

SOVIET RELATIONS WITH ASEAN, 1967–88

THE SOVIET UNION IN SINGAPORE'S FOREIGN POLICY: An Analysis

Succession Politics in Indonesia

The 1998 Presidential Elections and the Fall of Suharto

Bilveer Singh
Associate Professor
National University of Singapore

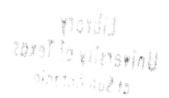

First published in Great Britain 2000 by
MACMILLAN PRESS LTD
Houndmills, Basingstoke, Hampshire RG21 6XS and London
Companies and representatives throughout the world

A catalogue record for this book is available from the British Library.

ISBN 0–333–77602–X

First published in the United States of America 2000 by
ST. MARTIN'S PRESS, INC.,
Scholarly and Reference Division,
175 Fifth Avenue, New York, N.Y. 10010

ISBN 0–312–22914–3

Library of Congress Cataloging-in-Publication Data
Singh, Bilveer, 1956–
Succession politics in Indonesia : the 1998 presidential elections
and the fall of Suharto / Bilveer Singh.
p.   cm.
Includes bibliographical references and index.
ISBN 0–312–22914–3
1. Indonesia—Politics and government—1966–1998. 2. Indonesia–
–Politics and government—1998– 3. Soeharto, 1921– . I. Title.
DS644.4.S5824   1999
320.9598'09'049—dc21   99–38753
                                                        CIP

This book is printed on paper suitable for recycling and made from fully managed and sustained
forest sources.

10   9   8   7   6   5   4   3   2   1
09   08   07   06   05   04   03   02   01   00

Printed and bound in Great Britain by
Antony Rowe Ltd, Chippenham, Wiltshire

Dedication

To my Beloved Family Members

Gurdial

Jasminder

Prabhinder

CONTENTS

LIST OF ABBREVIATIONS

ABRI	*Angkatan Bersenjata Republik Indonesia* (Armed Forces of the Republic of Indonesia)
APEC	Asia Pacific Economic Co-operation
ASEAN	Association of Southeast Asian Nations
ASEM	Asia Europe Meeting
ASPRI	*Assisten Presiden* (Presidential Assistants)
BABINSA	*Bintara Pembina Desa* (Village Development Non-Commissioned Officer)
BAKIN	*Badan Kordanasi Intelijen Negara* (National Intelligence Co-odinating Agency)
BIA	*Badan Intelijen ABRI* (ABRI's Intelligence Agency)
CIDES	Centre for Information and Development Studies

CSIS	Centre for Strategic and International Studies
DPA	*Dewan Pertimbangan Agung* (Supreme Advisory Council)
DPR	*Dewan Perwakilan Rakyat* (House of Representatives)
FKI	*Forum Kerja Indonesia* (Indonesia Working Forum)
GBHN	*Garis-Garis Besar Haluan Negara* (Broad Outline of State Policy)
GESTAPU	*Gerakan September Tiga Puluh* (30th September Movement)
GNP	Gross National Product
GOLKAR	*Golongan Karya* (Functional Group)
G-15	Group of 15
ICMI	*Ikatan Cendekiawan Muslim Indonesia* (Indonesian Muslim Intellectuals' Association)
IKD	*Institut Kajian Dasar* (Institute of Policy Studies)
IMF	International Monetary Fund

KKN	*Korupsi, Kolusi, Nepotism* Corruption, Collusion, Nepotism
KOPKAMTIB	*Komando Operasi Pemulihan Keamanan dan Ketertitan* (Operation Command for the Restoration of Security and Order)
KOSGORO	*Koperasi Serba Guna Gotong Royong* (Multipurpose Co-operatives for Mutual Assistance)
KOSTRAD	*Komando Strategic Angkatan Darat* (Army Strategic and Reserve Command)
LEMHANNAS	*Lembaga Pertahanan Nasional* (National Defence institute)
MAR	*Majlis Amanah Rakyat* (Council for People's Mandate)
MPR	*Majlis Permusyawaratan Rakyat* (People's Consultative Assembly)
NAM	Non-Aligned Movement
NGO	Non-governmental Organisation
NU	*Nahdatul Ulama*
OPSUS	*Operasi Khusus* (Special Operations)
PAP	People's Action Party

PDI *Parti Demokratik Indonesia*
(Indonesian Democratic Party)

PKI *Parti Komunis Indonesia*
(Communist Party of Indonesia)

PSI *Parti Sosialis Indonesia*
(Indonesian Socialist Party)

SAF Singapore Armed Forces

SUPERSEMAR *Surat Perintah Sebelas Maret*
(Letter of Instruction of 11 March)

UMNO United Malay National Organization

PREFACE

Politics is the exercise of state power and those who wield such powers can affect policy constructs of the state and affect lives of people living therein. In the case of Indonesia, of all the political offices, the Presidency is the single most important political office and wields the most power. Even President B. J. Habibie, the present incumbent was frank enough to admit this, arguing that 'according to the rules of the game of Indonesian politics, the President is one of the most powerful man in the country', something which the incumbent finds rather disturbing as 'this can be simply too dangerous'.* The responsibilities of the President have been enshrined in the 1945 Constitution, providing the Chief Executive with immense powers, including being the Head of State, Head of Government, *Mandataris* of the Peoples' Consultative Assembly and Supreme Commander of the Armed Forces. As an Asian country with a great political past, the actual powers of the Chief Executive are written as well as found in unwritten conventions and practices, and thus, the President is actually more powerful than can be expected. With so much at stake, the contest for the Presidency is extremely important in Indonesia, all the more since the country had, until March 1998, experienced only two 'presidential successions', and that too, during turbulent times with great loss of lives.

---

* Author's interview with President of the Republic of Indonesia, Professor B. J. Habibie on 3 October 1998.

In this study, succession refers to the way in which political power passes or is transferred from one individual to another. Narrowly, it is the orderly arrangements made for the transfer of power and how a regime manages the transition period. The ability to make transition of this kind peacefully over a period of time is taken as one of the many indicators of political stability. While in most political systems, succession can take place in the highest to the lowest office, in this study, the concern is essentially with the Presidency and to some extent, the Vice-Presidency. Succession is necessary due to the physiological existence of man – the only certainty about man is his mortality, making succession something that is inevitable, regardless of how powerful a man may be. The only unknown is when and how this will take place. Succession can come through renewal or through the forcible removal of the incumbent and where a new 'contract' would have to be worked out between the Ruler and the Ruled.

In this context, the challenge of the March 1998 Presidential elections in Indonesia was whether the process and mechanism established would be able to meet the challenges thrown up by the manifold crises confronting the country. Here, one of the key questions was what it would mean for the future of Indonesian politics in the even of Suharto's re-election to the Presidency for the seventh term. In view of Suharto's ripe age and various medical problems, on the one hand, and the immense political, economic and social problems facing the country, on the other, the key question was whether Suharto would eventually transfer power to his successor in an orderly and peaceful manner or would this be undertaken in turbulence as had been undertaken by his predecessors, especially if his re-election was opposed by various political groups.

In the end, even though Suharto was re-elected for the record seventh term, his Presidency was a beleaguered one with the contraction of the economy, unleashing political and social challenges that were to culminate in the May 1998 Revolution that ultimately forced Indonesia's 'strongman' to resign in favour of his Vice-President, B. J. Habibie. With that, Indonesia precipitously entered into the post-New Order, post-Suharto era, one full of uncertainties and crises. It is against this backdrop that this study aims to analyse the politics of succession in Indonesia and try to provide some answers as how a man, dubbed the 'best son of the soil' and elected overwhelmingly by a well-oiled political machinery, was eventually forced to resign 72 days later.

Introduction

A succession is a difficult process everywhere, more so in the Third World. In the last few years, this has been the single most important and difficult issue confronting Indonesia. Where the role of personalities, rather than institutions, is important, as in most Asian societies, only one person can drive the state car even though there are many who would like to do so. If the car has been seldom used, then, there will be great uncertainties about its driving capability notwithstanding how good it looks. If many people had died the last time someone got into the car, the tension, uncertainty and anxiety will be all the more great. Thus, the person who has been driving the state car since late 1965, namely President Suharto, has been greatly burdened in ensuring that the next driver is adequate so that he can effectively drive the car without any major mishap. Yet, there are limitations and difficulties in allowing the incumbent to dictate political transition and the pace of change, especially since the people are

1

unhappy with the regime, as was the case in Indonesia, had merely complicated the politics of succession in Indonesia in the period under study.

As Indonesia had not really witnessed a smooth succession, the question of when and who after Suharto, had become a major one, especially following the incumbent's re-election in 1993 despite his heart condition. Since Indonesia gained its independence in December 1949 (even though freedom was declared on 17 August 1945), the country had only seen one major change of political leadership. That too was immersed in bloodshed when incumbent President Suharto rode to power by suppressing a communist-led coup. Prior to this, Sukarno became President by leading the nationalist struggle against the Dutch. Both leaders came to power following tumultuous events, *albeit* of great historical importance for Indonesia. Thousands of lives were lost, either in the struggle against the Dutch from 1945-1949 or in the putsch and counterputsch from 1965-1969 that saw Sukarno removed from power and the Communist Party of Indonesia (PKI) physically obliterated at the hands of the Armed Forces of Indonesia or *Angkatan Bersenjata Republik Indonesia* (ABRI) or the ABRI-backed marauding youths of the various Muslim parties.

Since March 1993, the country had been gearing for another leadership transfer. Unfamiliarity, uncertainty and fear about the unknown and consequences of the transfer of power seemed to have unsettled the country and its political elite. The big question as to when Suharto will step down or be replaced, and what this would mean for the country and the region, remained largely unanswered until the term of the President came up for renewal in March 1998. A major reason for the growing preoccupation with succession was due to the advance age of Suharto, who turned 77 in June 1998. There was also a growing concern with his health, especially following reports of problems associated with the President's kidneys, hearts and even diabetes.

2

A number of related factors linked to make the March 1998 Presidential Election issue a major one for Indonesia and the region as a whole. First, as Indonesia is a major regional power, being the fourth largest country in the world and a major player on the world scene, especially in the Third World as well as her leadership role in ASEAN, meant that any change of leadership in Jakarta would have major ramifications for Indonesia and the region as a whole. Second, as there was no precedent of orderly succession in the past, this was closely watched, as any instability related to succession would have dire consequences for the region. Third, the fact that Indonesia's last transfer of power took place amidst great bloodshed and instability, further intensified concern with the hope that this should not be repeated and more important, that a major change in policy direction should not occur since In donesia had become closely integrated into the region. Deep down, Indonesia's neighbours feared that the restraint exercised by President Suharto *vis-à-vis* its neighbours could be changed to one of a more assertive foreign policy befitting a major regional power and this would have serious implications for the regional stability and order. Finally, with growing reports of domestic instabilities and political polarisation in the country, as evident from the student and labour unrests, reports of growing unhappiness in certain quarters of ABRI as well as the growing assertiveness of Political Islam, there were fears that these developments would have serious implications for the succession issue and any clash of these interests, either along class, ethnic, religious or ideological lines, could greatly undermine Indonesia as well as the region as a whole. Thus, there were great stakes in the succession issue, both for Indonesia and the world at large, especially as Indonesia lay astride major international waterways and is a major producer of important raw materials, such as oil and gas as well as a major market of finished products from the West and the newly industrialised countries in the Asia-Pacific.

3

Suharto's Political Architecture and Framework for Hegemony

In order to understand the issue of political succession in Indonesia and the eventual fall of Suharto, it is imperative that the political architecture of the Suharto regime be understood first. On coming to power, President Suharto created a political framework that would, by definition and necessity, support the continuity of his regime, which he saw as being largely coterminus with his life span. While he did not necessarily wanted to remain in office until death or be President for life, he nevertheless created a system that would ensure that he died in 'office' of one kind or another. Hence, in the last few months prior to the presidential elections of March 1998, he continuously harped on the theme that even though he may not be the country's President, he would continue to perform the role of a *'pandhita'*, a Javanese sage, who would have a superimposing role to advise and assist the government and its leaders. In many ways, Suharto assumed the mantle of a 'Javanese King' and where the king, in most circumstances, usually died in office unless he abdicated for one reason or another.

General Suharto rode to power in the many contradictions that were found in Indonesia. Following the collapse of Constitutional Democracy in the 1950s, Sukarno's Guided Democracy also succeeded in unleashing various political, economic, social and psychological crises in the country with national politics veering towards the Left under the influence of the mass-based PKI and the mercurial Sukarno. This was also a period of political persecution for lesser opponents and where the Masjumi, a modernist Islamic Party and the Socialist Party, the PSI, were banned by Sukarno, largely under pressure from the PKI. The country was also reeling under a severe economic crisis with all sectors badly hit and where hyperinflation was the norm. Under these circumstances, the two key political forces in the country during this period were

4

the PKI and the Army. Following the 30 September 1965 abortive coup by the PKI, which also saw the brutal murder of six senior army Generals, the Army, under the leadership of Major-General Suharto counter-attacked, culminating in the destruction of the PKI and the steady dis-empowerment of Sukarno.

The rise of General Suharto, though largely underpinned by military power, was also due to the support and endorsement the various social groups, gave to the military-dominated post-Sukarno regime, especially those that had suffered at the hands of the PKI. In the main, Suharto was able to draw support from various Islamic organisations as well as the major 'secular-oriented urban middle classes'.[1] Suharto was also the beneficiary of various sources of power inherent in the Indonesian state or innovatively mobilised as a result of various circumstances. According to Richard Robison, 'the ideological basis of Indonesian authoritarianism is the notion of the organic, or integralist state…'.[2] In such a state, in view of 'its functional concept of social structure and organisation and its view of the state as transcending particular vested interests within society', provides the 'ideal legitimation of authoritarian rule and the denial of legitimate political activity outside structures defined by the state'.[3]

In addition to the above 'ideological' basis of power, Suharto was also able to mobilise various strengths from the institutional base of the state. As President, he was largely independent from the control of Parliament, which acted more as a 'rubber stamp'. His ability to select the cabinet gave him tremendous powers of political patronage, something very important in a largely backward and conservative society. Suharto was also able to tap on the various 'extra-constitutional instruments of rule under his direct authority or that of his close associates'.[4] The key agencies in this regard were the Operational Command for the Restoration of Security and Order (KOPKAMTIB), his kitchen cabinet or inner circle of

5

key advisers, ASPRI or Personal Assistants, and the OPSUS, the special operations agency under the leadership of General Ali Moertopo. As Head of the GOLKAR's Control Board, *Dewan Pembina*, Suharto could also exercise veto power over the membership of the largest 'functional group' in the country and hence, over the membership of the national parliament and the Peoples' Consultative Assembly, which met once every five years to select the President. The President also had immense financial resources at his disposal. In addition, as the Supreme Commander of the Armed Forces, General Suharto (later, a Senior Five Star General), also had tremendous influence in determining the ABRI leadership at any one time.

In the main, a number of key structures of the political architecture of Suharto's Indonesia were identifiable. First, the bureaucracy was totally politicised and mobilised to support the political leadership. Appointments to key positions in the bureaucracy and even to regional administrative positions were totally controlled by the Centre, mainly Suharto. For instance, the appointment of *Lurahs*, *Bupatis* and Governors was primarily directed from the Centre in Jakarta. This meant that there was no way informal leaders such as Megawati Sukarnoputri, the leader of the PDI, or Dr Amien Rais, leader of the Muhammadiyah or Abdulrahman Wahid, leader of the Nahdatul Ulama, could emerge as regional leaders even though under Sukarno this was widely practised. This was so because Suharto politicised the bureaucracy and the key appointments therein so as to ensure that local leaders owed loyalty only to him and not the political system.

Second, ABRI or the Armed Forces was also heavily politicised. For long, Suharto appointed prominent Generals loyal to him to key positions in the government, be it to chair the national parliament, to lead GOLKAR, to head key agencies and government departments, as ministers in strategic ministries as well as Ambassadors in key countries of concerned. Due to the unique role of ABRI in Indonesian politics through

6

the concept of *dwifungsi ABRI* evolved since the 1945 revolution, the Armed Forces have always perceived itself as possessing a legitimate right to partake in national politics as the guardian of the 1945 Constitution, of the *Pancasila* ideology and the integrity of the state. Due to Suharto's seniority in ABRI as a revolutionary fighter, his personal charisma, his political power as well as his position as the Supreme Commander of ABRI, President Suharto has been able to shape the direction of the Armed Forces to suit his needs, including domesticating its power, once it was perceived to be emerging as a Praetorian Guard. Through selective interventions, especially in terms of promoting officers personally loyal to him, rotating the regional commander as and when the President saw fit and placing officers in strategic commands on the basis of loyalty and abiding 'conflict of interest' among the key officers so that a powerful military figure does emerge who would be able to challenge Suharto, ABRI has been moulded largely into a pliant political and security apparatus to do Suharto's bidding. Whenever Suharto saw a military figure emerging as a potential threat, the officer was likely to be 'managed' by a competing force within ABRI or worst, balanced by other agencies in the Government, such as the Special Operation Command or the State Secretariat, and later, even by the establishment of new agencies outside the Government structure, such as ICMI, which Suharto personally launched to check the growing restlessness within ABRI.

Third, political parties were uprooted at the village and regency level with the arena monopolised by the ruling party, GOLKAR. Suharto's political parties' policy at the grassroots created the 'floating masses' phenomenon which was utilised by GOLKAR to emerge as the predominant and hegemonic political party in the country. According to Michael R. J. Vatikiotis, 'the floating mass concept rested on the assumption that the vast majority of Indonesia's population was unsophisticated and prone to the ill-effects of politicking at the village level. Political parties were therefore banned from operating in the villages, and political activity was severely restricted except for brief periods close to elections. The idea behind the 'floating mass' concept was to 'depoliticise the Indonesian population'.[5] The village level politics was totally dominated by GOLKAR through the BABINSA, the ABRI Sergeant who co-ordinated and controlled all village politics on the instructions of the Centre. The BABINSA manipulated village-level politics for the benefit of GOLKAR and made it impossible for the other political parties to penetrate the village level political arena.

Fourth, and related to the Suharto's policy on political parties, was the deliberate efforts aimed at preventing the rise of political parties in the country that could perform the role of interest articulation and political mobilisation. This was mainly due to ABRI and Suharto's perception of the political parties as a negative force in national unity and where more than fifty political parties, in the period of Liberal Democracy from 1950-1959, competed with one another on the basis of ethnicity and primordialism. This party system was mainly responsible for political instability as governments rose and fell within a very short period. Hence, even though political parties were legally and organisationally present, their functions and activities were largely restricted and where they were compelled to function according to the 'rules of engagement' drawn up by Suharto's and where, more often than not, these parties were viewed as being dysfunctional to the national cause as defined by Suharto. This, in many ways, represented Suharto's operationalisation of Sukarno's 'Guided Democracy' under the guise of the 'New Order'.

In this connection, Suharto 'simplified' the political process by sanctioning the existence of only three political parties, namely, GOLKAR, the Indonesian Democratic Party (or the PDI) and the United Development Party (PPP) even though ten political parties participated in the 1971 general elections.

While GOLKAR emerged as an umbrella organisation set up by the Army leadership to combat the political challenge posed by the PKI in 1964, the PDI was created through the fusion of three secular-national political parties and the PPP through the fusion of a number of Muslim parties. These parties were formally launched in 1973 following the Political Parties and GOLKAR Bill and have dominated Indonesia's political landscape of Suharto's Indonesia between 1973 to 1998. Even though the PDI and PPP were granted a legal and political existence, under all circumstances, they were 'junior partners' and their role greatly marginalised. This was, in part, due to the internal contradictions within both the PPP and the PDI. In the PPP, the traditional Muslim groups were in conflict with the modernist Muslims while in the PDI, the nationalists could not agree with the Christians and Catholics.

By sharpening the practice of 'management through conflict', Suharto succeeded in keeping both the PPP and PDI weak and divided, and thus largely peripheral in national politics. The legislation introduced in 1983, requiring all political parties to adopt *Pancasila* as their sole ideology was also damaging for the PPP and PDI, especially the former as it prevented it from championing the cause of Islam and its values. Even though GOLKAR emerged as the ruling party following the 1971 general elections, technically it was not a political party but only a functional group. It was an umbrella organisation and what kept GOLKAR together as a powerful political force was due to the direction and powers given to her by its sole political leader, Suharto. In many ways too, GOLKAR was part of the political architecture only by virtue of Suharto's decision to use it as a source of political legitimacy for his rule. Otherwise, GOLKAR was nothing more than a political instrument of Suharto and by manipulating various elements of the political architecture, Suharto was able to ensure the longevity of his rule since power was transferred to him through the *SUPERSEMAR* instrument on 11 March 1966.

9

The point to note is that GOLKAR did not behave as a typical political party as in other political systems. Through various devices, President Suharto ensured that GOLKAR would always be relatively weak and divided, and where it could not make key decisions without Suharto's involvement. On that basis, GOLKAR was not directly an autonomous part of the country's political architecture but more an instrument of Suharto to control the political system he had created. In this regard, GOLKAR was also often irrelevant and invoked only when it was needed, especially symbolically. It was like a 'shirt' which was worn when someone needed to dress up: otherwise, it was kept in the 'wardrobe'. Thus, in essence, Suharto created a political system, in many ways, feudal in character and which depended on him for its effectiveness and control. In this connection, Suharto developed a political system based on loyalty to a political personality, Suharto, and not the institution. This was the crux of Suharto's political credo. All politics led from and to Suharto. There was nothing in between and if anything did emerge which threatened the Suharto's political system, it was quickly neutralised or destroyed. Thus, the political system was custom-made for Suharto.

Here, the observations of Richard Robison are worth noting: 'the real basis of Suharto's power is the institutional arrangements and political alliances he has constructed … These are elements of power that would not automatically be transferred to any successor'. Thus, 'whoever replaces him will inherit only a fraction of his real political power. It is therefore unlikely that the configuration of power will remain the same. New alliances in which the position of the President is less dominant and more accountable are probable'.[6]

It is against this backdrop that this study aims to analyse the 1998 Presidential Elections in Indonesia and how 'succession politics' were played out in that key country of Southeast Asia. As the outcome had serious implications for Indonesia, the Southeast Asian region and the world as a whole, the value of such a study is self-explanatory and self-evident. In this endeavour, the study will examine the various 'succession debates' and scenarios that were discussed in the period 1993 to early 1998, the importance of the 1997 General Elections and the various changes in the ABRI leadership and their implications for the Presidential Election, the various political maneuvers undertaken by the key political actors in the country, especially President Suharto himself, prior to the Presidential Elections, the course of the all-important 1–11 March 1998 MPR Session which elected the President and finally, the post MPR post dynamics that led to the fall of Suharto and the institution of a new political regime in the country.

NOTES

1 See Edward Aspinall, 'The Broadening Base of Political Opposition in Indonesia', in Garry Rodan (Ed.), *Political Oppositions in Industrialising Asia*, (London and New York: Routledge, 1996), p. 216.

2 See Richard Robison, 'Indonesia: Tensions in State and Regime', in Kevin Hewison, Richard Robison and Garry Rodan (eds.), *Southeast Asia in the 1990s: Authoritarianism, Democracy and Capitalism*, (Sydney: Allen and Unwin, 1993), p. 42.

3 *Ibid.*

4 *Ibid*, p. 47.

5 Michael R. J. Vatikiotis, *Indonesian Politics Under Suharto: Order, Development and Pressure for Change*, (London: Routledge, 1993), pp. 94-95.

6 Richard Robison, 'Indonesia: Tensions in State and Regime', in Kevin Hewison, Richard Robison and Gary Rodan (eds.), *Southeast Asia in the 1990s: Authoritarianism, Democracy and Captialism*, (Sydney: Allen and Unwin, 1993), p. 49.

1

The 'Succession Debates' and Scenarios in Indonesia, March 1993-March 1998

INTRODUCTION

For long a taboo topic, the succession issue in the past had only arisen incidentally after elections when the *Majelis Permusyawaratan Rakyat* (MPR) or the People's Consultative Assembly, was expected to elect, in effect, rubber-stamp, a President. As President Suharto had been elected uncontested since 1971, this had tended to be a merely formality. The reason for this was not difficult to find as Suharto has been the source of all power and authority in the country since October 1965, when he led the crushing of the PKI-instigated putsch against the army leadership, more so, since the *SUPERSEMAR*[1] transferred executive powers to Suharto from Sukarno in March 1966. Suharto's control of all constitutional and extra-constitutional sources of powers and authority made him the most powerful man in the country bar none.[2]

12

As age caught up President Suharto and with the country having undergone fundamental economic, political and social changes, the time seems to have arrived for the succession question to be addressed once and for all. All the shadow play (*Wayang*) about this question had to be put aside as the entire country's future, including that of President Suharto and his family, appeared at stake. This became all the more so as even the President broke tradition and begun talking about the succession question more candidly. Following the May 1997 General Elections, which the ruling GOLKAR won resoundingly and the onset of the economic crisis in late 1997, which hit Indonesia hard, in the process, undermining President Suharto's legitimacy and posing the most serious challenge to his leadership yet, the March 1998 Presidential Elections took on a new importance, as this had fundamental bearings on the role and future directions of Indonesia both internally and externally.

THE FIRST DEBATE

Interestingly, a full-blown succession debate has taken place on two occasions, both ironically, following the election of Suharto as President, first in 1988 and second in 1993-94. This is not to say that there have been no pressures on Suharto to step down. Throughout the 1970s and 1980s, such pressures were manifest, indicating that some form of power struggle, related to succession, was in vogue. In the mid-1970s, some senior figures in ABRI were believed to have pressured Suharto to step aside in favour of another ABRI general. In 1980, the Petition of 50 (*Petisi 50*) group, which also included many senior and popular Generals, including Nasution, Dharsono and Ali Sadikin, criticised Suharto for using *Pancasila*, the state ideology, as an instrument to silent and coerce his political opponents. Throughout this period,

13

there continued to be intermittent student and labour unrests, which had the object of undermining Suharto.[3]

However, the succession debate only broke into the open after March 1988, following Suharto's election as President for the fifth term. In late 1988 and early 1989, the country was hit by students' unrest, apparently backed by some ABRI factions, calling on Suharto to step down.[4] Two related events fuelled the succession debate. The first was a statement by Admiral Sudomo, the then Co-ordinating Minister for Political and Security Affairs and a close confidant of the President, stating that the country should develop a national consensus for the coming 1992 elections. As part of this national consensus, one of the many ideas forwarded was the possibility of two to three candidates for the Presidency.[5] Despite Sudomo's public apology to Suharto, the Admiral had claimed that the President had proposed the idea to him to be relayed to the public.[6] President Suharto was even credited for encouraging the 'responsible discussion' of the possibility of multiple candidates for the Presidential election and where he did not publicly disagree with the proposal, as was forwarded by Admiral Sudomo.[7]

The second event to fuel the succession fires in 1989 was a telling statement in Suharto's autobiography, *Soeharto: My Thoughts, Words and Deeds*, released in early 1989. It stated, *inter alia*, that 'By the time I will have completed my term of office (1988-1993) I will be 72 and retire from the Presidency. Considering that the average life span of Indonesians is...56, then 72 is well above average and can be regarded as rather old. So it seems no exaggeration to say that 'my inauguration as President and Mandatory of the MPR on 11 March 1988 was the last time for me'[8] This was interpreted by most Indonesians to mean that Suharto did not want to stand for elections again in 1993 and hence, the ensuing succession debate.

However, for those who became over-enthusiastic and when the President became uncomfortable with the prospects of him being considered a former President sooner than Suharto thought he was ready, he immediately issued a warning in September 1989: 'I might die on my feet.... Perhaps that is what they want so I can be replaced. But if they want to replace me with someone else using unconstitutional means, I will clobber (*gebuk*) them no matter if they are politicians or Generals'.[9] This sent most critics scurrying for cover and put paid to the succession debate for the next three years except when raised by Suharto himself. However, on a number of occasions, Suharto did broach the succession issue. This was best recorded in the works of Professor Donald W. Wilson. In 1988, Suharto is said to have asked Donald Wilson the $1 billion question: 'Tell me how much longer you believe I should serve?'[10] Later, President Suharto remarked to Wilson that:

> ...many people would rather speculate than to believe the truth.... People argue that I do not want the question of succession to be discussed. This is not true. I am not President for life. The people have elected me, and it is they who will decide how long I should continue. I serve at their call; and when they choose, I will step down. What I do not like is irresponsible speculation that tries to pit one side against another by advancing the name of this person or that person and suggesting that people should align themselves with one or another of these individuals. By doing this they would try to destabilise the political environment in Indonesia.[11]

For many concerned Indonesians, silencing the succession debate did not end or solve the problem. This was primarily due to the fear that succession will be accompanied, as in the past, by bloodshed. That this was stated by none other than the then Defence and Security Minister, General Benny Moerdani, lent credence to this concern. In an interview with the weekly *Editor* on 4 February 1989, General Benny warned that a flare-up could break out in the period between the step-ping down of one leader and the emergence of another. He went on to argue that 'if we consider it rationally, a thousand death will not mean much. Don't it be up to a hundred mil-lion.... A thousand death, compared to the 170 million popu-lation of Indonesia is nothing'.[12] Thus, the underlying concern with stability and security remained uppermost among the po-litical elite even though it was not publicised as far as the is-sue of succession was concerned.

THE SECOND DEBATE

An even more intense debate broke out in late 1993, barely nine months after President Suharto was sworn in as President for his sixth term. This time, it was initiated by a leading Is-lamic scholar, Professor Amien Rais, who later became Chair-man of the 28 million strong Muhammadiyah. He argued that it was necessary to decide on the criteria that should be used in selecting the country's next President so that succession can proceed smoothly.[13] The ruling *Golongan Karya* (GOLKAR) party refused to discuss the issue with its Chairman, Harmoko, dismissing it as being unethical to do so until nearer the time in 1998.[14]

The President was, however, prepared to join in the issue and made a number of telling statements between February and April 1994 that would have important implications for the way the succession debate and ultimately, the manner actual succession, could played out. First, he argued that there was no need to discuss the matter any further as the country al-ready had a mechanism in place to take care of the problem.[15] This referred to the General Elections which elected represen-tatives for the MPR and *Dewan Perwakilan Rakyat* (DPR) or House of Representatives, and where finally, the MPR would elect the President and Vice-President. Second, Suharto stated that 'we have to abide by the established procedure that we have been using. Don't make your own rules because this might spawn friction and disputes'. He was convinced that the 'MPR will not hit snags in the process of electing the new President as long as the assembly carries out its tasks in conformity with the Constitution'.[16] Suharto said that he would step down on time and that he was not President for life.[17] He also felt that the country would be able to find someone to succeed him from among the 200 million Indonesians. He denied that he was grooming a successor.[18] He also dismissed the idea of resigning midway through his term. He argued that if he did, it would mean that 'I break the Constitution and does not uphold it. I am obliged to fulfill the Presidency according to the mandated term of office'.[19] He also made it known that he would not want to be reelected for President when his term expires in 1998. This is because 'the law of nature prevails and must be taken into consideration and I have considered it'.[20] He also made known his intention of continuing to be involved in state matters by lending a guiding hand while staying in the background. At the same time, he said that 'people should not exaggerate a Presidential candidate's shortcomings. Instead, they should focus on his strengths. So people should throw their weight behind whoever is elected by the MPR as President to succeed me when I step down at the end of my current five-year term in 1998'.[21] Since then, the President has broadly maintained these positions with the issue of succession having been superceded by other more pressing concerns.

If one were to follow the remarks of President Suharto closely, these indicated that he was determined to step down on completion of his term in March 1998, with even the armed forces leadership anticipating this development. Thus, General Edi Sudradjat, the Minister for Defence and Security, said at a military seminar in Jakarta on 3 March 1994 that ABRI must be prepared to ensure that a smooth transfer of power took place. He added that 'whatever happens, the national leadership succession process must get underway because the time has come for that'.[22] This was the clearest indication that the military leadership was preparing for the likelihood of Suharto relinquishing power by March 1998. Suharto's statement also implied that he was certain to leave office by 1998.

Until then, whether President Suharto's statement of leaving office was tactical or otherwise remained to be seen as he had also made an similar commitment in his Autobiography. At that time, he implied that he would not stand for re-election in 1993 but he proved his critics wrong by becoming the President for the sixth term. Whether Suharto's March 1994 statement was meant to deflect criticisms and to end the succession debate launched by Amien Rais remained to be seen even though in early 1998 he accepted GOLKAR's nomination for the post, proving that his denial was more tactical than real. However, President Suharto must, however, be given the benefit of the doubt as his statement not to stand again in March 1994 was made in a largely stable environment. He may have reconsidered this due to the onset of the economic crisis in September 1997 and since this needed a strong and tested hand, President Suharto may have calculated that he had no choice but to stay on and put the situation right, among others, to help his country regain the confidence that has been lost since late 1997. The President may want to leave the political scene with a positive legacy rather than a country whose economy is on the brink of collapse.

SUCCESSION SCENARIOS
(MARCH 1993 TO MARCH 1998)

In the light of the 'second succession debate' launched by Professor Amien Rais, various questions relating to succes-

18

sion have been asked. Among others, the following are the pertinent ones: Is President Suharto grooming a 'crown prince'? Who are the likely candidates to take over when Suharto steps down? Will the established mechanism be able to work and are the ground rules for succession clearly established? Will there be a single or multiple candidates for the job? Will the present indirect system of election where the MPR elects the President be continued or would direct Presidential elections be introduced? Will the new President have restrictions placed on the number of terms he can serve? All these questions can only be answered depending on how and when power is transferred from Suharto to his successor. This in turn will depend on the options that are opened to President Suharto. In the period 1993 to 1997, a number of scenarios were discernible.

SCENARIO ONE

President Suharto Remains as President as he is Unwilling or Unable to Step Down

This scenario argued that despite President Suharto's disavowal since 1988 that he was not President for life, there was nothing to suggest that he could run for another term. Even though he would be 77 years old in June 1998, he was still considered healthy for his age. Even though he kept repeating that he had no intention of suffering from the '*TOPP* Syndrome'[23] – T, *Tua* (old), O, *Ompong,* (toothless), P, *Peot,* (hollow cheeks) and P, *Picun,* (senile), there was nothing to suggest that he was prepared to abdicate his top power position. His prime concern was to know how much longer he could remain in power and alive, and if possible, he would like to make them conterminous. In other words, he wished to die in office. Also, the manner he had structured the power equation made

19

it clear that the whole system would collapse if he was forcibly removed. He was in the centre of the power structure and without him, it would be meaningless. This was typically Javanese.

In Javanese history and practice, power is the essence of everything.[24] Thus, when power is transferred from one person to another, it usually tends to be traumatic. It is easy to ritualistically legitimise those already in power. However, this is a different question when power is being vested in a new person. As the Javanese believe that power is a force that can be owned by individuals and that it comes from God, the question of legitimising the possessor of the *Sinar* (light), *Cahaya* (radiance) and *Wahyu* (mandate) is very problematic. This can take time. The Javanese also believe that this can be passed from one person to another and can be housed in objects like *pusakas* (heirlooms) such as krisses and spears as well as the fact that this can be developed through spiritual practices. As power is unitary, in the sense that it comes only from a single source, it becomes all the more important to identify who has it, as only a good leader can possess it. This is all the more important as power is not answerable to the people but to God alone. Identifying such a leader or person with power can thus become problematic.

Since President Suharto is believed to have it, it would be far easier to continue the system rather than attempt to change it as this may bring about unknown ramifications. President Suharto is, thus, behaving in a typically Javanese manner by not naming a successor. While in the past, where dynasties were present, this passed from father to son, to the person who has been identified by the power holder in the first place, such a system cannot be practiced in a modern polity. This is in part to prevent a 'nominated successor' from challenging the incumbent as had happened in historical Java. However, the role of the power holder is still important and can make the difference. Thus, as long as President Suharto continues to withhold support from a candidate to his office, there is unlikely to be a clear competitor to him. This could be, in part, to deny any legitimacy to such a candidate as he would in fact be competing with Suharto for the *Wahyu*. Javanese, however, believe that an incumbent always grooms a candidate privately as usually this comes from someone who is two echelon down. Also, there is the belief that since President Suharto realises that the three leading political parties, GOLKAR, PPP and PDI will be unable to reach a consensus on a candidate and would object if ABRI attempts to foist its candidate on the system, this would in actuality mean President Suharto's ability to continue to hold office by default due to the inadequacy of the system to reach consensus on the new leader.[25]

There is also the question that Suharto is not just unwilling but also unable to step down. Other than being against Javanese practices, there is the perennial threat to the security of his family, which has benefited much and some say, rather unfairly from the President's rule.[26] President Suharto may also fear the consequences of losing power and what it would mean for him personally. Hence, the Javanese description of President Suharto as 'riding a tiger' and where to dismount meant being devoured. The circulation of *Primadosa*, which also accused Suharto of engineering the 1965 PKI coup, was just one tell-tale of what dismounting the tiger may cost. Also, as Asian societies tend to settle the issue of political accountability after a leader had stepped down, as happened in South Korea and the Philippines, and with President Suharto being accused of many political, economic and even security improprieties, this may well deter him from stepping down.

SCENARIO TWO

President Suharto Steps Down Mid-term

While this was repeatedly denied by President Suharto, for

some, it made good political sense for him to step down mid-term as this was the best course of action available to him. By doing so, especially after 1995, Suharto would have secured his place in Indonesian history on two counts. First, would be his role as the 'historical President' to preside over the 50th anniversary of the country's political independence, 30th anniversary of GESTAPU, 20 years of national campaigns and most important of all, the third year as the Chairman of the Non-Aligned Movement (NAM), marking the pinnacle of Suharto's Presidency. As President Suharto was very conscious of his role as a world leader and to that extent, the NAM chairmanship marked his greatest feat as an Indonesian President, stepping down after that appeared to make sense for some political analyst.

More important, by stepping down after 1995, probably in 1996, which marked his 30 years of rule since the *SUPERSEMAR*, President Suharto would be able to operationalise a system of political succession in the country, where constitutionally, his Vice-President will be elevated to the Presidency. In addition to giving the Vice-President hands-on experience of the top job, it would also establish a system and precedent of succession, where none existed. This would institute a degree of predictability about the nature of political change in the country and this would have had a great stabilising effect not just for Indonesia but also for the ASEAN region. The need for stepping down mid-term would have been brought about by the realisation that Suharto would have reached the height of his power as President and there would be nothing higher that he could aspire. In view of the various pressures from within, it would have been the best, to step down while he was still in control of many power structures.

Thus, even if Vice-President Try Sutrisono became President in 1996, went the argument, he will still be wearing Suharto's mantle. Any challenger to Try must possess higher moral authority, political appeal and support. This would have allow

Try to develop a working relationship with the MPR. So far, the MPR has been choosing a President in a situation of no contest. Many wondered whether the MPR would be able to take the pressures of an open challenge if there were more than one Presidential candidates. The point had to be registered that the MPR had never acted as a normal parliamentary body in choosing a leader in a competitive situation as no such political culture or precedent existed. If the parliamentary history of the 1950s was invoked and if that was any guide to go by, then Indonesia could be expected to be paralysed by full-blown parliamentarism. Thus, there were many advantages for President Suharto to step down before 1998 even though few thought that this would happen, as among others, it would have meant the President backtracking from his earlier stance of wanting to complete his full term in 1998.

SCENARIO THREE

President Suharto Steps Down On Completion of his Term and 'Vanishes' Politically

Many also argued that President Suharto would step down on completion of his term in March 1998, an option which the President stated in 1994 which he personally preferred. This would also be the least costly, most natural and face-saving method of exit for the President. Citing old age and having served the people as their leader for more than thirty-three years, the President had stated publicly that at the age of 77 in 1998, he would be too old to lead a young country of 200 million. President Suharto's children and key confidants have also admitted that the President was 'too tired' and wanted to step down to do things that people normally do. This view argued that this made it highly likely that the President would step down on completion of his term in March 1998.

23

It is due to this factor that he had consistently denied any intention of stepping down mid-term. While this scenario would pre-empt pressures on him to step down before his term expired, it would also ensure that he completed his five year term. This also solved the question as to when the leadership change will take place but not the question of the successor. This scenario assumed that President Suharto would leave office and disappear from the political scene altogether, something which many think is unlikely to happen unless he is afflicted by some incapacity.

SCENARIO FOUR

President Suharto Steps Down But Continues to Dominate the Political Scene from the Rear

While much pressure was exerted by various forces and groups for a change of leadership, the last scenario assumed that a change would take place but would mean little in reality. For many, all indications tended to suggest that the period March 1993 to March 1998 would be Suharto's last term as President, and this partly explained the intense jockeying for power in anticipating of the leadership transition. Yet, it was also clear that Suharto would not disappear from the political scene. While Suharto may not be prepared to be nominated for his seventh term, the argument went, he would, however, continue to direct affairs of state as a *Begawan*, Wiseman. Being an avid fan and believer of Javanese *Wayang Kulit*, the Shadow Play, the role of the *Begawan*, who guides state affairs from the rear, is one that interests Suharto the most. Suharto believes very strongly in the Javanese practice of leadership, where a leader can rule through three methods: requiring one to set example when one is in leadership position from the front, to stimulate when in the middle, and to support

24

when at the rear. On stepping down, Suharto intends to practice *tut wuri handayani,* to guide state affairs from the rear.

Just as he has directed ABRI to practice this art of leadership for the period 1993 to 1997, best seen by the nomination of a civilian to head GOLKAR, Suharto would himself play this role when he steps down in 1998. While Mr Lee Kuan Yew played this role formally through the post of a Senior Minister in Singapore while remaining in control of some key organisations (such as the Government Investment Corporation), Suharto will most likely perform this role more informally. This would imply that whoever takes over from Suharto as the next President, will have to be approved by Suharto even though the President has denied that he was grooming a 'crown prince' as he believed that a constitutional mechanism was in place to elect a new leader. By stepping aside but not down, Suharto would be able to allay fears of chaos and revenge even though many really wondered how effective such a system would be if it led to a situation of a lameduck Presidency. There would also be the possible problem of identifying who is in possession of the *Wahyu* (Guidance) and a likely conflict could occur between Suharto and whoever becomes the next President as each of them would want to be the sole possessor of absolute power *a la Java.*

SCENARIO FIVE

President Suharto is Forced Out of Office, either by a Military Coup or a Peoples' Power Revolution

While this was something that was in the minds of many people as an academic option, it was never publicly discussed, due mainly to the fear of inviting retribution from the President and his security apparatus. This option argued that just as former President Sukarno was forced out of office due to tumultuous events that led to the President losing control of the situation, a replay of a similar scenario was always possible, forcing the military to take power or the President being overthrown a *la Marcos* by a Peoples' Power movement. While this was privately discussed as a possible scenario, very few people gave much credence to it due to the all-powerful position of the President and his near total control of the country, especially the key political, economic, social and security apparatus.

In a seminar at the Institute of Southeast Asian Studies on 28 November 1995, Dr Afan Gaffar, a leading political scientist from Gadjah Mada University put forward a number of scenarios as far as succession was concerned as follows:[27]

The Constitutional Arrangement

This argued that if the President was healthy, there was a very great chance that he would stand again for the highest office and would be re-elected again in March 1998. Not only had many political groups started pledging support for this but it was also due to the fact that 'there is no other leader that have the same capacity such as the President'.

The Crown Prince Scenario

This view argued that the President was grooming an individual to take over his duties and post as President and this would be transferred to the anointed individual when the time came. Afan argued that Suharto's daughter, Siti Hardiyanti Rukmana and his son-in-law, Prabowo Subianto, were possible candidates for this scenario.

26

The Democratic Scenario

This argued that President Suharto would step down and re-linquish his power but instead of transferring it to an anointed individual, he would allow the political community to decide the choice of the next President. Here, the three key political parties would decide the outcome even though Afan thought that this was 'the least possible' scenario as the 'Indonesian political community, both at the elite and at the mass level, is not ready for democracy'.

The Almighty God Scenario

This predicates that the President dies in office and this will be followed by a contest for national leadership. It could be solved by the constitutional mechanism, with the Vice-President taking over or by intervention by other forces, such as the military, which could directly take over, as in 1965 or place its candidate in power but calling the shots from the rear.

Conclusion

Despite the discussion of various scenarios by political pundits and analysts, what became increasingly clear by late 1997, was that barring something unfortunate happened to the President until March 1998, in terms of death or physical incapacity, power was likely to remain concentrated in his hands. Despite various reports of challenges to President Suharto from various quarters and constant outbreak of demonstrations, all the key political aces remained lodged in the President's hands. President Suharto continued to have dominant influence and control over GOLKAR, ABRI, the MPR, DPR, and the key political, economic and social organisations. The deference to President Suharto was almost complete. The Javanese also continued to be influenced by principles of respect for authority. For instance, the Javanese believe in *Sabda Pandhita Ratu*, meaning that 'the King should not be challenged'. As President Suharto is largely regarded as the modern-day 'Javanese King', mainly out of respect for his great achievements, there is also a great reluctance to challenge him. Thus, politically, militarily, economically, socially, culturally and even psychologically, President Suharto has remained unchallengeable, notwithstanding attempts by some Muslim and Democratic politicians to embarrass him. Thus far, every major challenge has been ruthlessly put down, best evident in the manner the PDI challenge was dealth with in July 1996.

In this connection, all attention was focussed on 1995 and 1996. 1995 was Indonesia's Year of Celebrations, marking the height of Suharto's Presidency. He won national and international accolades for his achievements and the progress he brought to his country. It was, however, wishful thinking to expect him to step down after this. Instead, the President's energies were directed towards two key tasks. First, it was to prepare GOLKAR for the 1997 General Elections. The ruling party, under a largely civilian leadership, was expected to face stiff competition from the PPP and PDI even though these parties were unlikely to dislodge GOLKAR as the ruling party, all the more so, since both parties were afflicted by internecine conflicts. Second, there was the need to prepare ABRI's leadership for the dawn of 1998. This was to witness the most number of top-level reshuffles in the armed forces since 1965 and by February 1998, a new group of military leaders were in place to see the country through for the next five years, with key loyalist holding all strategic positions in the armed forces.

28

NOTES

1   *SUPERSEMAR* is an acronym for *Surat Perintah Sebelas Maret* or Letter of Instruction of 11 March. It contained written instructions issued by President Sukarno, giving General Suharto powers to take action to restore security and order in the country.

2   See Richard Robison, 'Indonesia: Tensions in State and Regime', in Kevin Hewison, Richard Robison and Garry Rodan (eds.), *Southeast Asia in the 1990s: Authoritarianism, Democracy and Capitalism*, (Sydney: Allen and Unwin, 1993), pp. 41-47.

3   See Michael R. J. Vatikiotis, *Indonesian Politics Under Suharto: Order, Development and Pressure for Change*, Revised Edition, (London: Routledge, 1994), pp. 139-141; Also see, David Jenkins, *Suharto and His Generals: Indonesian Military Politics, 1975-1983*, (Ithaca: Cornell Modern Indonesian Project, 1987), pp. 53-156.

4   Michael R. J. Vatikiotis, *Op cit*, p. 143.

5   'Calon Presiden Mendatang Tidak Harus Calon Tunggal', *Suara Karya*, 13 April 1989; 'More Candidates for Presidency Will Be Allowed', *The Jakarta Post*, 13 April 1989.

6   'Menko Polkam Sudomo Minta Maaf Kepada Presiden: Sehubungan Ucapannya Tentang Konsensus Nasional', *Kompas*, 13 April 1989.

7   See Donald W. Wilson, *The Next 25 Years: Indonesia's Journey Into the Future*, (Jakarta: Yayasan Persada Nusantara, 1992), p. 123.

8   See *Suharto: My Thoughts and Deeds: An Autobiography* (as told to G. Dwipayana and K. H. Ramadhan), (Jakarta: PT Citra Lamtoro Gung Persada, 1991), p. 474.

9   See M. Vatikiotis, 'Succession Scenarios', *Far Eastern Economic Review*, 28 September 1989, p. 31.

10   Donald Wilson, *Op cit*, p. 29.

11   *Ibid*, p. 30.

12   Cited in Amien Rais, 'Keterbukaan Dan Suksesi', *Editor*, No. 45, 15 July 1989, p. 30.

29

13   At a Muhammadiyah meeting in Surabaya in December 1993, Professor Amien Rais argued that succession must take place in 1998 and that it was necessary for the country to begin discussing the various criteria that would be needed to select the next President. For elaboration of the various themes on the issue, see *Editor*, No. 23, 3 March 1994, pp. 64-70 and *Forum Keadilan*, No. 23, 3 March 1994, pp. 85-86.

14   Harmoko argued that the discussion on the issue should be undertaken in 1997 in line with the Constitution and by the MPR. See 'Perlukah Membicarakan Suksesi Sekarang?', *Ibid*, pp. 56-57.

15   'Succession, No Problem: Suharto', *The Jakarta Post*, 24 February 1994.

16   *Ibid*, 21 March 1994.

17   'President Suharto's Wish', *Ibid*, 22 February 1994. Also see, 'Not Grooming a Successor', *Ibid*, 16 March 1994.

18   Suharto asked publicly, 'Why should I groom a 'crown prince' to succeed me since we already have the system and mechanism that regulate it in line with the Constitution. After all, I am not a King'. *Ibid*.

19   *Ibid*.

20   'The Succession Issue', *Ibid*, 17 March 1994.

21   *Ibid*, 21 March 1994.

22   'Military Must Be Ready to Ensure Smooth Succession', *Ibid*, 4 March 1994.

23   *Ibid*, 22 February 1994.

24   See Benedict R. O. G. Anderson, 'The Idea of Power in Javanese Culture', in *Language and Power: Exploring Political Cultures in Indonesia*, (Ithaca, New York: Cornell University Press, 1992), pp. 17-77.

25   In an interview with the author, Dr Amir Santoso, a leading Political Scientist from the University of Indonesia, 'Indonesia is a heterogenous society and its political parties are not sophisticated enough to carry out an orderly succession through open competition'. He predicted 'a total mayhem if each of the three political parties nominated different candidates for the Presidency'.

26   These allegations are clearly laid out in Wimanjaya's *Primadosa*, a three volume collection of articles and analysis that has not been published.

27   See Dr Afan Gaffar, 'Trends in Contemporary Indonesian Politics: Preparing for Succession'. Paper presented at the Seminar conducted by the Institute of Southeast Asian Studies, 28 November 1995, Singapore.

2

The May 1997 Indonesian General Elections and Changes in ABRI Leadership in the Context of the Presidential Elections

INTRODUCTION

When Indonesians went to the poll on 29 May 1997, there was little doubt that the ruling party, GOLKAR, would win. Months before, GOLKAR's Chairman, Harmoko had predicted that his party would chalk up 70.02 percent of the votes, an improvement over the 1992 results when the Party suffered a dip with its votes going down to 68 percent. Yet, when the results of the 1997 hustings came, it surprised every one, possibly even GOLKAR, with the ruling party winning 74.51 of the votes (see Table 2.1). The result was endorsed by all the three parties contesting the election, namely, GOLKAR (Functional Group), PPP (United Development Party) and PDI (Indonesian Democratic Party) on 23 June 1997.

Table 2.1
Final Results of the 1997 General Election

Party		No. of Seats		Share of Votes	
	1992	1997	1992	1997	
GOLKAR	282	325	68.10	74.51	
PPP	62	89	17.00	22.34	
PDI	56	11	14.89	3.07	

Source: Compiled by the Author

OUTSTANDING FEATURES OF THE ELECTION

Both the conduct of the general election and the accompanying results had a number of features worthy of note. Compared to the previous hustings under the New Order, this was the most violent election, with nearly 400 people having died, either the result of riotings, accidents or in the case of East Timor, attacks by the insurgents challenging the province's integration into Indonesia.

Second, the one-month campaign was highly charged with many youths joining the campaign trail, more often than not, to protest against government's policies. In this connection, the 'greening' of the Major cities throughout the country, especially in the politically sensitive and important island of Java, was obvious. 'Greening' refers to the large turnout for the rallies of the Muslim-PPP, which was a major winner in the 1997 election, partly brought about by the disaffection with the ruling GOLKAR and partly the result of crossovers from the strife-torn PDI, resulting in the increase in appeal of the PPP. This was also responsible for the high turnout at the general election with nearly 90 percent of the eligible voters casting their votes.

Third, unlike the past, the 1997 election was marred by charges of irregularities. Even though all the parties, in the end, endorsed the election results, both the PPP and PDI accused the ruling party of undertaking various electoral violations, including vote-rigging. This was the major reason for the wide-spread riot on the island of Madura, where the PPP had been influential. For instance, in the Sampang regency, the ballot boxes were burned by the rioters. This led to, for the first-time ever in the history of the New Order for a re-vote even though it was only limited to the Sampang in Madura.

THE RESULTS

GOLKAR won a landslide victory, breaking previous records and established itself as the dominant and hegemonic party in the country. It won 325 of the 425 seats contested for the House of Representatives winning 84,187,907 votes of the total votes cast. It had a clean sweep of seats in Jambi, Bengkulu, Bali, North Sulawesi and Southeast Sulawesi. The seats won by the various parties by provinces can be gleaned from Table 2.2.

This was GOLKAR's best performance since elections were first held under the New Order in 1971 and where GOLKAR had won all the previous elections. Not only did GOLKAR improved its overall tally, it also enhanced its majority in some of the more prestigious and politically importance constituencies with the number of its seats increasing in North Sumatra by 3, in Jakarta by 10, in West Java by 6, in Central Java by 8, in East Java by 4, in Bali by 2, in West Nusa Tenggara, East Nusa Tenggara, North Sumatra and South Sumatra by 1. Overall, GOLKAR's seats in parliament increased from 282 in 1992 to 325 in 1997, a whooping increase of 43 seats, partly brought about by the additional 25 seats which were contested in the election, given up by the Armed Forces.

34

Table 2.2
Seats by Provinces

PROVINCES	GOLKAR	PPP	PDI
Aceh	7	3	0
North Sumatra	18	3	2
West Sumatra	13	1	0
Riau	7	1	0
Jambi	6	0	0
South Sumatra	2	2	0
Bengkulu	4	0	0
Lampung	0	1	0
Jakarta	12	6	0
West Java	10	10	1
Central Java	40	17	2
Jogjakarta	4	3	2
East Java	40	22	2
West Kalimantan	6	1	1
Cental Kalimantan	5	1	0
East Kalimantan	4	2	0
South Kalimantan	7	3	2
Bali	9	0	0
West Nusa Tenggara	7	1	0
East Nusa Tenggara	12	0	1
East Timor	3	0	1
South Sulawesi	21	2	0
Central Sulawesi	4	1	0
North Sulawesi	7	0	0
Southeast Sulawesi	5	0	0
Malaku	5	0	0
Irian Jaya	9	0	1

Source: Compiled by the Author

35

Of the two remaining parties, the PPP performed credibly, improving its total number of seats in parliament from 62 in 1992 to 89 in 1997 even though the expectation was that it would be even better. This was mainly because of the disarray in the PDI even though the PPP did see a number of its voters in central and eastern Java swinging towards GOLKAR as a result of the aggressive 'yellowisation' campaign launched by Harmoko and GOLKAR's Vice-Chairperson, Mbak Tutut, Suharto's eldest daughter.

However, the most startling results involved the PDI, a party that had been on the rise since the early 1980s. In the 1982 election, the PDI secured 24 seats, dropping from its 29 it won in the 1977 hustings. In 1987, it won 10.87 percent of the total votes, increasing the number of its seats to 40. In 1992, the share of the PDI's votes went up to 14.49 with the number of seats secured increasing to 56. However, in the 1997 election, the party suffered a 'free fall' with the number of its seats dropping to 11 and its share of votes plunging to only 3.07 percent, the worst performance ever by the party. The decimination of the PDI will have dire consequences for the politics and party system in Indonesia in the years to come.

EXPLAINING THE RESULTS

As GOLKAR has been the ruling party since 1971, it was in an advantageous position from all points of view and thus, the overwhelming mandate given to her was not that surprising. In addition to almost unlimited resources at its disposal, it was also able to establish the 'rules of engagement' which again benefitted her, such as the conduct of the campaign, etc. Like other hegemonic parties in Southeast Asia, be it the ruling United Malay National Organisation (UMNO) in Malaysia or the People's Action Party (PAP) in Singapore, the longevity of rule also advantaged the ruling party as it has been able to contest the election from the position of strength, in having establish a credible track record, in having the most credible candidates and finally, in a position to co-opt the best and if this proved difficult, to use the law to manage the advantage of the ruling party. What helped to entrench GOLKAR further was its ability to project itself as the party of the future and mobilise the 'Big Family', namely, the Armed Forces, the Bureaucracy, various Mass Organisations as well as the business community. In the face of this political juggernaut, it was unlikely that either the PPP or the PDI could dent the power of GOLKAR.

At the same time, while the PPP performed credibly well, mainly due to the largely united leadership and operating in a largely Islamic environment, it was able to take advantage of religious sentiments to its benefit. Yet, it could not compete with GOLKAR nationally. On the other hand, the fractious PDI, where, in many ways, the internecine conflict within the party was more significant than its competition with the other two parties, led to its being mauled with its leadership badly humiliated and humbled. For the first time, the Chairman and Secretary-General of the party failed to win a seat in parliament, signposting very clearly the misfortune that has afflicted the party once dubbed as the 'rising star' of Indonesia politics.

MEANING OF THE 1997 GENERAL ELECTION RESULTS

While the victory of GOLKAR was never in doubt, the scale of its victory, however, has merely confirmed its entrenched position in Indonesian politics. This victory will provide the entrenched ruling elites of GOLKAR, especially President Suharto with a free hand to mould the political system and thus affect the future direction of Indonesian politics for the coming years, especially as the country prepares itself for the 21st century.

More immediately, President Suharto, as the unchallenged

leader of the country since 1966, will most likely be re-elected for the unprecedented seventh term in the coming Presidential Election which is scheduled for March 1998. With the House of Representatives dominated by 325 GOLKAR members, together with 75 members nominated from the Armed Forces and with the additional 500 nominated members, together constituting the 1,000-strong People's Consultative Assembly or MPR, which selects the President and the Vice-President, Suharto will have no problem securing the nomination for the Presidency.

Here, the key question would be as to whom the President will choose as his vice-presidential running mate and from the time the election results were announced in June 1997 until the March 1998 MPR Session, this would be the most critical question of discussion and analysis. This is so as the next Vice-President is likely to play a more important role in government than the previous office holders due mainly to the age of President Suharto who turned 76 on 8 June 1997 as well as lingering questions with regard to his health. As to whether the appointment of the next Vice-President would tantamount to the implementation of the 'succession *a la Indonesia*' is also another issue that needs to be watched.

A number of candidates have been mentioned as potential candidates for the Vice-Presidency with the strongest among them being the incumbent Vice-President, Try Sutrisno, Professor Habibie, the Minister for Research and Technology, K. Ginandjar, Chairman of the State Planning Board and recently retired General Hartono, the former Army Chief. In this connection, one of the immediate actions taken by the President may have some bearings and may be an indicator of things to come with regard to the all important MPR Session of March 1998. In an unprecedented move, on 6 June 1997, Harmoko, the GOLKAR Chairman and one mainly credited for GOLKAR's excellence electoral performance, was named Minister of State with Special Assignments and his cabinet post of

Minister of Information given to General Hartono, who was retired as the Chief of Army. Harmoko will remain in cabinet until the end of September and from 1 October onwards become the Chairman of the House of Representatives. While he has been tasked to prepare the elected legislators for the 1998 MPR Session, what this also means is that he is out of contention for the Vice-Presidency. Hartono, on the other hand, is still a possible contender even though he would have been moved out of the Armed Forces, probably the country's most influential political organisation, thereby weakening his 'power base' if any.

While the political elites will be embroiled with the 'unfinished business' of the election, namely, the selection of the country's next President and Vice-President, what may be over-looked is the unintended consequences of the election results. First, the decimation of the PDI almost called into question the structure of the political system as it is predicated on the need for all the three political parties to be directly involved and represented in the eleven commissions of the House of Representatives and fortunately, through a last minute arrangement, the PDI won its eleventh seat. It would have been interesting for the current political system if the PDI had secured anything less than the required eleven seats.

Second, more by default rather than design, and lost amongst the victory celebrations of GOLKAR and to some extent, PPP, is the fact that Indonesia may well be on track for the emergence of a two-party system and this will call into question the whole nature of political arrangements that has been put into place since 1973. The question to raise is that will Indonesian politics in future be polarised between the secularists led by GOLKAR and Islamists led by the PPP? This is an important question for a country like Indonesia that is nearly 90 percent Muslim and yet, professes adherence to *Pancasila*, where one of the pillars is the belief in one God, but not necessarily Allah.

At the same time, what will happen to the PDI? Will it split

39

into two, with some joining the PPP and others, GOLKAR, as its membership did during the recent voting? What about the new political parties that have emerged but have not been allowed to participate legally in the political system, such as Bintang's PUDI and the banned PRD, alleged to be a front for the discredited PKI? These are fundamental questions that needs to be closely monitored as the results of the 1997 general election have the potential to put into place a totally new political system and as this also coincides with the transition into the post-Suharto era, anything is possible in the fourth largest country in the world which is also the largest Muslim nation on earth.

While President Suharto continues to keep everyone guessing about what he may have in mind and has kept all the key cards close to his chest, the 1997 election results would certainly have a bearing on the moves that he may have in mind. What is certain is that the political party of which he is the leader has been returned to power with even a bigger majority and to that extent, it has strengthened his legitimacy and provided him with another mandate to rule the world's largest archipelagic state. This will also legitimise whatever moves he may make from now until March 1998, by which time the political directions of Indonesia would be made transparent as the country prepares for the post-Suharto era and for the next century.

CHANGES IN ABRI LEADERSHIP AND ITS MEANING FOR THE 1998 PRESIDENTIAL ELECTIONS

Changes in the Indonesian Armed Forces or ABRI are not new. Changes in the past have been explained as being routine, undertaken following the completion of an individual's tour of duty. These changes are usually effected twice per year, either in April or October. Yet, the changes that have been set in motion since 1995 have been different in two main ways. First, they have taken place outside the usual period of

April or October and second, the sheer numbers and frequency involved have indicated that these changes are more than simple tour of duty transformations. Some individuals have barely even taken up their new posts when they have been re-assigned.

Between January 1995 and April 1996, there were 9 'promotion' rounds outside the April and October period, involving among others, changes at the highest levels of ABRI. At the same time, rising stars such as Susilo Bambang Yudhoyono, saw themselves shifted from one post to another even before they could take up their new posting. For instance, Colonel Bambang, from the class of 1973, who was then the military commander of Jogjakarta (*Danrem 043/Pamungkas*) was promoted to the rank of Brigadier-General on 4 December 1995, the first person of his batch to receive the one star He was appointed as the Head, Military Observer Group in Bosnia. Three months later, in early March 1996, he was appointed as Deputy Assistant of Operation at ABRI Headquarter at Cilangkap. But within two weeks of that appointment, he was posted out as Chief of Staff of the politically sensitive Jakarta Command.

The promotions in the period 1995-1996 basically saw the generation of the 1965-67 being entrenched in power in ABRI. Except for General Raden Hartono who was from the Class of 1961, the other armed services were in the hands of those from the class of 1965-67. For instance, the new Air Force chief was Marshal Sutria Tubagus from the class of 1967, the Navy Chief was Admiral Arief Kushariadi, also from the class of 1967. The exception was with regard to the Police Chief, Lieutenant-General-General Dibyo Widodo, who was from the class of 1968. In general, the key positions in ABRI Headquarters was in the hands of those Generals who graduated in the period 1965-67, especially those from the Army. Among these were: Lieutenant-General Suyono, the KASUM ABRI and Lieutenant-General Sofyan Effendy,

41

the Commandant of LEMHANNAS. Two other prominent members from this class were Major-General Theo Syafei and Major-General Imam Utomo, respectively as Regional Commanders. Lieutenant-General-General Syarwan Hamid, Major-General A. Rivai and Major-General Tayo Tamadi, all from the class of 1966 also held important posts. Syarwan was KASOSPOL ABRI, with the other two appointed as Regional Commanders. If anything, all the key Regional Commands were in the hands of the Generals from the 1965-1966 batch except for the Trikora Command in the hands of Major-General Dunidja, from the class of 1967, the Jakarta Regional Command in the hands of Major-General Sutiyoso from the class of 1968, the KOSTRAD Command in the hands of Lieutenant-General Wiranto from the class of 1968 and the KOPASSUS (Special Forces Command) in the hands of Major-General Prabowo Subianto from the class of 1974. By the time of the 1997 round of promotions, two younger officers, Major-General Agum Gumelar and Major-General S. B. Yudhoyono also became regional commanders, with the former taking charge of the Wirabuana Command and the latter, of the Srivijaya Command.

In general, by 1997, the officers to watch were those from the post-1965, 1966 and 1967 batches. There were 466 graduates from the 1968 batch. The stars of this batch were as follows: a Lieutenant-General Wiranto (an ADC to the President from 1989 to 1993, Chief of Staff of the Jakarta Regional Command in 1993, Commander of the Jakarta Regional Command in 1994 and Commander of the KOSTRAD Command in March 1996); Brigadier-General T. Nurdin Yusuf, (Chief-of-Staff of the KOSTRAD Command); Major-General Sutiyoso, (Commander of the Jakarta Regional Command); and Brigadier-General Amir Syarifuddin (KAPUSPEN ABRI).

There were 437 graduates from the 1970 batch. The key star of this batch is Lieutenant-General Subaygo Hadi Siwoyo, the former ADC to the President, the former Com-

42

mander of KOPASSUS and the Diponegero Command in Central Java. Another prominent member of this group is Major-General Jhony Lumintang, the present commander of the Trikora Command. There were 329 and 395 graduates from the 1971 and 1972 batches respectively. The key stars from the 1971 batch are Major-General Kivlan Zein, Major-General Ismed Yuzairi and Major-General Zacky Anwar Makarim. The key star from the 1972 batch was Brigadier-General Abdul Rahman Gaffar, the former Danrem of Jogjakarta. However, it was the 1973 and 1974 batches that attracted most attention with the movement of Bambang Yudhoyono from the 1973 batch and Prabowo Subianto from the 1974 batch being watched closely as they were likely to be the two individuals who would fill ABRI's key posts in the near future.

LEADERSHIP CHANGES IN ABRI

Prior to the general elections, President Suharto had put in place a military leadership that was to ensure that the elections were held with minimum disturbances. That ABRI's mission became '*mengsukseskan Pemilu*, to ensure the success of the general elections, was enough of a signal that the Armed Forces would deal with any individual or group that tried to disrupt the peaceful conduct of the hustings. Despite this, the 1997 elections were one of the most violent ever and had the Armed Forces not played a more active and decisive role, the probability of the security situation becoming worst was always there. Despite the high toll in terms of casualties, the victory of GOLKAR at the election was also largely due to the role of the Armed Forces which not only provided the largely secure environment for voting to take place but also did its best to support the ruling party, largely due to the historical ties between GOLKAR and ABRI forged in the early 1960s in its effort to combat communism. To the extent that

43

President Suharto put in place a military leadership that was to ensure the success of the general elections, the ABRI leadership performed extremely well, especially under the leadership of the army commander, General Raden Hartono, an avid supporter of GOLKAR. The key personalities in this line-up were as follows: General Feisal Tanjung as Commander-in-Chief of the Armed Forces, General Hartono as the Commander-in-Chief of the Army, Lieutenant-General Tarub as the KASUM ABRI, Lieutenant-General Syarwan Hamid as the KASOSPOL ABRI, Lieutenant-General Wiranto as the Commander of the KOSTRAD Command, Major-General Sutiyoso as Commander of the Jakarta Regional Command, Major-General Prabowo Subianto as Commander of the Special Forces (KOPASSUS), Lieutenant-General Moetojib as Head of BAKIN, the Co-ordinating Agency for Intelligence and Major-General Farid Zainuddin as Head of BIA, the Armed Forces Intelligence Agency.

However, the changes instituted in ABRI in 1997 were mainly aimed at serving two key purposes: to ensure that the generational change took place according to plan and to ensure that the March 1998 People's Consultative Assembly meeting, which selected the country's President and Vice-President, proceeded smoothly. In this endeavour, wide-ranging changes were made to the Armed Forces leadership. On 6 June 1997, even before the full results of the general elections were known, it was announced that General Raden Hartono would be retired, relinquishing his post as Army Chief. Surprisingly, in a rare cabinet reshuffle, Hartono was made Minister of Information while the incumbent, Harmoko, who was also Chairman of GOLKAR, was made Minister of State with Special Duties and this mandate was to last until 1 October 1997. The new Army Chief was General Wiranto. Promoted to four stars together with Wiranto were the Navy Chief-of-Staff, Admiral Arief Kushariadi, Air Force Chief-of-Staff, Marshal Sutria Tubagus and National Police Chief,

General Dibyo Widodo. Wiranto's KOSTRAD Command was taken over by Major-General Soegiono, then Commander of the Presidential Security Guards. Promoted to the rank of Lieutenant-General, Soegiono, from the class of 1971, was among the first from his batch to gain the third star. Soegiono's post was taken over by Major-General Sutarto, then, one of Hartono's key assistants. In this round, President Suharto also appointed and promoted Major-General Subagyo, then Commander of the Diponegero Command, to the post of Deputy Chief-of-Staff of the Army, replacing Lieutenant-General Sudjasmin, who was earlier retired. Subagygo's command was taken over by Brigadier-General Mardjinto, then deputy Governor of the Armed Forces Academy in Magelang.

Barely six weeks later, another extensive reshuffle took place in ABRI involving nearly 300 high-ranking officers in the Army, Navy, Air Force and Police. General Feisal Tanjung signed the decree on 14 July 1997. This reshuffle saw major changes in the structure of the Armed Forces with the Navy, Air Force and Police establishments being provided with the post of a Deputy Chief-of-Staff, just as in the Army. Vice-Admiral A. S. Widodo was the new Deputy Chief-of-Staff of the navy, Vice-Marshall S. Djamiko the new Deputy Chief-of-Staff of the Air Force and Lieutenant-General Lutfi Dahlan the new deputy National Police Chief. It was also announced that Rear Admiral Suratmin would be the Armed Forces' Inspector-General. Major-General Yusuf Kartanegara, the assistant for intelligence affairs to the Armed Forces Chief of General Affairs was to be replaced by Commodre Yuswaji. Major-General M. Yunus Yosfiah, the Commandant of the ABRI's Staff and Command School was promoted to Lieutenant-General and named as the new ABRI's Chief of Socio-Political Affairs, replacing Lieutenant-General Syarwan Hamid. Related to this, an important change was the announcement of Major-General S. B. Yudhoyono, the Commander of the Sriwijaya Commander, as the new Assistant to the Armed Forces Chief of Socio-

45

Political Affairs. He replaced Major-General Budi Harsono. Major-General Muzani Syukur took over as Commandant-General of the National Military Academy while its incumbent, Major-General Purwantono joined the Army's Kartika Eka Paksi Foundation.

ABRI's spokesman, Brigadier-General Slamet Supriadi took over as deputy assistant for intelligence affairs to the Armed Forces' Chief of General Affairs. Major-General Nurdin Yusuf, the Deputy Commander of the Army Strategic and Reserve Command (KOSTRAD) took over as Army's Inspector General. Equally important, was the appointment of new regional commanders. Brigadier-General Suadi Atma, the deputy Commander of the Trikora Regional Military Command took over as Commander of the Srivijaya Regional Military Command. Major-General Djamari Chaniago, the Chief-of-Staff of KOSTRAD's second division, took over as Commander of the Siliwangi Regional Military Command. Brigadier-General Djadja Suparman, the Deputy Chief of the Sriwijaya Regional Military Command took over as the Commander of the Brawijaya Regional Military Command. Brigadier-General P. R. Muhdi, the Deputy Chief-of-Staff of the Brawijaya Regional Military Command took over as Commander of the Tanjung Pura Regional Military Command. Brigadier-General M. S. Syahrir, the Deputy Chief-of-Staff of the Udayana Regional Military Command took over the post left vacant by his boss, Major-General Rivai. Brigadier-General Rizal Nurdin took over as Chief of the Bukit Barisan Military Command. Major-General Luhut Panjaitan, the commandant of the Infantry Weapons Centre became the Chief of the Army's Traning Centre, replacing Major-General Achfas Mufti. Similar wide-ranging changes took place in the Navy, Air Force and the Police Force.

In addition to propelling a new generation of leaders to the helm of the Armed Forces, with the army leadership essentially in the hands of the class of 1968 to 1974, President

Suharto also strengthened the Armed Forces' presence in the national parliament. With 75 seats reserved for the Armed Forces, Lieutenant-General Syarwan Hamid, was appointed as the deputy chairman of the MPR/DPR and was to lead and represent the Armed Forces' voice in the national legislature, where through the concept of '*dwifungsi ABRI*' or ABRI's dual function, it was to impact on the direction of national politics. The army alone would have some 25 Generals, from the rank to Brigadier-General to Lieutenant-General in the house. Of the 75 ABRI members, 40 are new members. Some of the new faces included, in addition to Lieutenant-General Syarwan, Major-General Budi Harsono, Syarwan's former deputy, Major-General Tarigan, (the former SESKOAD Commander) as well as five former regional commanders, namely, Major-General H. A. Rivai (Udayana), Major-General Tayo Tarmadi (Siliwangi), Major-General Sedaryanto (Bukit Barisan), Major-General Imam Utomo (Brawijaya) and Major-General Nanuri Anun (Tanjungpura).

The 'train' of changes continued for the next few months. The Commander of the Armed Forces Military Intelligence, BIA, Major-General Farid Zainuddin, relinquished his post on 1 September 1997 and was replaced by Major-General Zacky Anwar Makarim, one of the best intelligence officers in the country. However, it was in February 1998, barely two weeks before the General Session of the MPR that the key leadership change was announced, putting in place a number of younger officers that were to lead the Armed Forces in the next few years and an army leadership that was to ensure that the March 1998 MPR Session was conducted with minimal interference.

On 12 February 1998, it was announced that General Feisal Tanjung would be stepping down as the Armed Forces Chief. He was replaced by General Wiranto, then the Army Chief. Wiranto's post was taken over by Lieutenant-General Subagyo Hadisiswoyo, who was promoted to a four star general. The Chief-of-General Staff, Major-General Tarub was retired and was replaced by Major-General Fachrul Razi. The Chief of Socio-Political Affairs, Lieutenant-General Yunus Yosfiah was retired, with his deputy, Major-General Bambang Yudhoyono taking over and promoted to a three-star general. The KOSTRAD Commander, Lieutenant-General Soegiono became the new Deputy Army Chief, replacing Lieutenant-General Subagyo. Major-General Prabowo relinquished his KOPASSUS Command and took over as Commander of KOSTRAD and was promoted to the rank of a three-star general. The new KOPASSUS Commander was Major-General Muchdi, the former regional commander of the Tanjung pura district with the Commander of First Division of KOSTRAD, Brigadier-General Suwisma, taking over the Tanjung Pura Commander and promoted to a two-star general.

What the changes meant was that the Armed Forces leadership was in the hands of a younger generation. The 51 years old Wiranto, a graduate of the 1968 batch, became the leader of the train. The other key officers were much younger. Subagyo and Fachrul Razi were graduates from the 1970 batch, Soegiono from the 1971 batch, Bambang Yudhoyono from the 1973 and Prabowo from the 1974 batch. Another key feature of the new leadership was the fact that they had all served the President directly in one capacity or another. Wiranto and Subaygo had served as adjutants to the President. Soegiono had been Commander of the Presidential Security Guards. Prabowo was the President's son-in-law. Only Bambang Yudhoyono and Fachrul Razi were 'outside' the circle of being close confidants to the President. This would mean that the key commanders, especially those commanding critical forces, including the Commander of the Jakarta Command, who had been the President's bodyguard, were regarded as highly loyal to the President and this would also mean that President Suharto entered the March 1998 fray with loyalists holding key positions in the Armed Forces, thereby making ABRI as one of his key pillars of support.

48

Equally important, the changes reflected President Suharto's effort to keep the Armed Forces divided and amenable to him as a new balance of power was established. Now, there was an uneasy balance between the Wiranto and Prabowo 'factions', something that was to unravel later and affect the balance of national politics as a whole as well as ABRI's general standing as a whole.

3

Political Manoeuvres Prior to the Presidential Elections and the March 1998 MPR Session

INTRODUCTION

As it has been a traditional practice, the President read-ied the ABRI leadership just prior to the 1–11 March 1998 MPR Session. The new military leaders were placed in their respective strategic positions by mid-February, with General Wiranto formally taking over as the Armed Forces Chief on 16 February 1998. By this time, the new Army Chief, General Subagyo was also in position. Also, Lieutenant-General Prabowo Subianto, Lieutenant-General Bambang Yudhoyono, Major-General Fachrul Razi, Major-General Muchdi Purwopranjono and Major-General Suwisma were promoted and slated to take over their new posts follow-ing the MPR Session.

However, unlike the past Presidential Elections, the 1998 elections were particularly important as this took place against the backdrop of Indonesia's worst economic crisis since 1965.

Since August 1997, value of the Indonesian Rupiah nosedived dramatically and this created a serious crisis of confidence in the country's political and economic future. As such, the issue of the election of the new President and Vice-President became directly linked with the issue of recovery from the country's economic crisis, or as some have argued, opponents of President Suharto conveniently used the economic crisis, or even worst, engineered the economic crisis, to bring pressure to bear on the President so that he could, either be toppled or compelled to undertake political reforms in such a manner that would suit these 'groups'. Whatever was the truth of these allegations, in a nutshell, the March 1998 Presidential Elections took place against a backdrop of a major crisis, raising in the process, the stakes of the elections.

POLITICAL MANOEUVRES INVOLVING THE PRESIDENTIAL ELECTIONS

Since Professor Amien Rais raised the issue of Presidential succession, especially in 1995, many groups had come forward to nominate the incumbent, President Suharto for the post of the President, making it the seventh time he would be leader of the country. This intensified following GOLKAR's resounding victory at the polls in May 1997. As the ruling party controlled more than two-third of seats in the Parliament and the consultative assembly, Suharto's re-nomination was largely regarded as a mere formality. However, more important were the various manoeuvres and decisions launched by the President and other key players in anticipation of the March 1998 MPR Session.

Even before the full results of the 1997 General Elections were announced, President Suharto shocked the nation by appointing Harmoko, the then Minister of Information, and Chairman of the victorious GOLKAR, as the Minister with

Special Duties, a post Harmoko was expected to hold until 1 October 1997. Harmoko's cabinet post was given to General R. Hartono, the KSAD, who was retired and the post of Chief of Army given to General Wiranto. The changes in the cabinet and the Armed Forces were largely anticipatory moves preceding the MPR Session.

Following the rare cabinet reshuffle, on 9 August 1997, President Suharto suggested to the nation's legislators that TAP MPR 88 should be reactivated, in the light of the various crises confronting the country. By this law, the President could act, in the name of the MPR, to take any measure to ensure national development and stability. This suggestion was diligently taken up by the two Working Committees of the MPR, established to prepare for the March 1998 MPR Session. The First Working Committee, handling GBHN matters, was headed by General R. Hartono, with Major-General Bambang Yudhoyono as his deputy. The Second Working Committee, handling non-GBHN matters was headed by General Wiranto with Akbar Tanjung as his deputy.

The appointment of General Wiranto as Chairman of the Second Working Committee was politically significant, signaling Suharto's attempt to contain Hartono's rising powers. Not only did it show that the President did not fully trust Hartono, who had been catapulted to the key position as a result of Tutut's lobbying, but more important, the President wanted the Chairmanship of the Second Working Committee, in the hands of someone who was more trustworthy and sound. Wiranto's Committee was to evaluate the list of candidates for the Presidency and Vice-Presidency. By this appointment, Suharto also signaled that Wiranto was far more important, reliable and trustworthy than Hartono, thereby posing a new challenge to the former KSAD from ABRI itself.

While these meetings and manoeuvres took place against the backdrop of the country's worst economic crisis, Siswono Yudohusodo, the Minister for Transmigration, suggested that the term of the President's tenure be limited to ten years in the post-Suharto era after 2003 even though the proposal did not gain much support with President Suharto himself stating that the country's Constitution had already delineated the matter.[1]

However, the most important development to take place between the May 1997 General Election and the period prior to the MPR Session was with regard to the nomination of the Presidential candidate. The fact that President Suharto would be 77 years in June 1998 and that he was rumoured to be afflicted with various illnesses, especially following his enforced 'ten days medical rest' following his overseas trip in October 1997, raised various questions as to how long President Suharto could effectively rule the country or worst, for how long more would he live, all the more, as the country was in a crisis situation.

Prior to February 1998, notwithstanding the very strong political position of President Suharto, various groups began to openly support or oppose President Suharto's nomination for the Presidency. In August 1997, the Chief of GOLKAR's Fraction in the DPR, Moestahid Astri, publicly for the first time called for President Suharto's re-nomination to the Presidency. By October 1997, it was clear that GOLKAR's sole candidate for the Presidency would be Suharto. At GOLKAR's thirty-third anniversary reception on 19 October 1997, GOLKAR's Chairman, Harmoko announced that "the nation's best son, who fulfills all the criteria as President for the 1998-2003 term is Haji Muhammad Suharto".[2] However, speaking as the Chief Patron of GOLKAR, the President urged the ruling party to reconsider their nomination. He argued that the party leaders should recheck with the people that the re-nomination was what the people wanted. He argued that the people must not be forced to do so. Among others, he said that "I hope their trust is not a pseudo one because if so I could be accused of being someone who is obstructing succession, an obstacle to the regeneration process. I could also be accused of being a complacent GOLKAR cadre, accused of being dissatisfied with being a President for six terms and now wanting a seventh term".[3]

Even more interesting, for the first time, President Suharto also suggested various succession scenarios and the future role he could play in the country's politics. In an off-the-cuff speech, he stated that even if he was no longer leading the country, in view of his experience, he could still help the people and the future government by being the *Pandhita*. He said in Javanese that he would *lengser keprabon madeg pandhita*. In the Javanese shadow play, the *Pandhita*, as a sage, was regarded as the spiritual leader and was regarded as a key helper of the *Prabu*, the real ruler. Earlier, the President has also advised the people not to turn him into a cult figure. Not surprisingly, when Harmoko named Suharto as GOLKAR's sole candidate for the Presidency on 19 October 1997, he also stated that "the decision to re-nominate the incumbent President, reached at the just concluded GOLKAR leadership meeting , is by no means an act to turn Suharto into an individual cult. Instead, it is the manifestation of the people's aspirations and will". [4]

Following this, GOLKAR's consistency in naming Suharto as its Presidential candidate was maintained right through to the MPR Session in March 1998. For instance, during GOLKAR's thirty-third celebrations in Ponorogo, East Java, Harmoko argued that GOLKAR would stick to its decision arrived at the 19 October 1997 GOLKAR meeting of naming Suharto as its candidate.[5] On 14 December 1997, Harmoko reiterated his party's stance and that it 'will continue with its nomination of Pak Harto'. He said that GOLKAR will remain steadfast in its support for President Suharto's re-nomination to another term of office despite concerns over the President's ailing health. [6]

GOLKAR's need to repeat its support for its sole candidate was in part prompted by the growing number of individuals and groups that called on President Suharto to step down. In addition to Amien Rais and Megawati Sukarnoputri, who expressed their willingness to challenge Suharto for the Presidency, a number of youth groups called for the rejection of Suharto's re-nomination for the Presidency. On 2 December 1997, the Communication Forum of Jakarta Youths and Students opposed the re-nomination of Suharto for the Presidency on grounds that it would discourage others with the potential to lead the country to emerge and do their part for the country.[7] Earlier, on 18 October, the Association of Indonesian Law Students Council also opposed Suharto's re-nomination. These opposition voices gained some strength following Siti Hardiyanti Rukmana (affectionately called Mbak Tutut), Suharto's eldest daughter stated in Semarang that as a daughter and for the sake of the family, she would prefer that her not be re-nominated for the Presidency. On 7 January 1998, the Foundation for the Unity for the National Brotherhood or YKPK nominated Try Sutrisono, the incumbent Vice-President for the Presidency. At the same time, student demonstrations and protests broke out in many cities in the country, especially in Jakarta and Jogjakarta, the two politically sensitive points in the country and where the common theme was for Suharto not to be re-nominated.

In the face of these demonstrations and opposition, due to the nature of the political process, by mid-February 1998, it became clear that Suharto would be the sole candidate for the Presidency. This was because all the factions in the MPR, namely, GOLKAR, ABRI, the Regional Representatives, the PPP and PDI, nominated Suharto as the candidate for the Presidency and this meant that any other nominee stood no chance whatsoever in this contest. By the time the MPR Session began on 1 March, there was no other candidate for the top political post, ensuring Suharto the seventh term of the Presidency. On 8 March 1998, all the key factions in the MPR approached Suharto for the nomination and the incumbent formally accepted the nomination to be President for the period 1998 to 2003. On 10 March, the MPR formally elected Suharto as the country's President and he was sworn in accordingly.

POLITICAL MANOEUVRES INVOLVING THE VICE-PRESIDENTIAL RACE

In view of the various difficulties involved in Presidential selection and most important of all, the all-powerful position of President Suharto, the race in the Presidential elections was a non-event. Instead, the Presidential elections was in essence a 'Vice-President's race'. This was because of the manner the Vice-President's selection was instituted as well as the importance attached to the post. For the first time since 1965, the post of the Vice-President was viewed as a strategic one due to the age and health conditions of the incumbent President. This strategic significance raised the stake of the Vice-Presidency and in many ways, all the key political manoeuvres in the country since the May 1997 General Election was linked to this issue.

Unlike the single candidature for the Presidency, there were various names put forward for the Vice-Presidency. The contest for the Vice-Presidency was further intensified by the fact that President Suharto did not appoint a special team to select the Vice-President, as has been the practice in the past. For instance, in 1978 and 1983, there was a Team of Eleven, in 1988, a Team of Nine and in 1993, a Team of Eleven. No similar team was named on grounds that the 'democratic mechanism' was in place and that it was up to the MPR to decide on the matter.[8] This represented a break with tradition even though supporters of the new procedure argued that the appointed Vice-President would be selected from a broader base and thus be more democratic in nature. According to the

56

new procedure, the various Fractions in the MPR were to decide on the candidate and then consult with the elected President. The need for consultation with the President was provided for by MPR Law Number 11, 1978 as it stated that the elected Vice-President must be able to work with the President. This, in effect, gave the President the ultimate veto over the choice of the Vice-President even though right up to the very last minute the President refused to publicly mentioned whom he wanted as his running mate. If there was any guide as to the candidature, it was MPR Law Number 11 of 1973 which provided fifteen criteria which must be met by any Vice-President.

By the time the MPR Working Committees went into session in October 1997, there were fourteen names which were mentioned as potential candidates for the post as follows:

- Try Sutrisno, the incumbent;
- Harmoko, the Chairman of the MPR and DPR;
- B. J. Habibie, the State Minister for Research and Technology;
- Ginandjar Kartasasmita, Head of the State Planning Agency;
- General R. Hartono, the Minister of Information;
- General Edi Sudradjat, the Minister of Defence and Security;
- Siti Hardiyanti, a Senior GOLKAR official and Suharto's eldest daughter;
- General Feisal Tanjung, the Commander of the Armed Forces;
- Sultan Hamengkubuwono, the leader from Jogjajakarta;
- General Wiranto, the Army Chief and later, Commander of the Armed Forces;

- Amien Rais, leader of the Muhammadiyah;
- Ismail Matereum, leader of the PPP; and
- Baharuddin Lopa, a member of the Human Rights Commission.

By late 1997, the Vice-Presidency race was narrowed to a number of candidates: Try Sutrisono, Harmoko, B. J. Habibie, Hartono, Ginandjar and Wiranto. In addition to Try's popularity, the appointment of Harmoko as Chairman of the MPR/ DPR while retaining his position as Chairman of GOLKAR, the appointment of Hartono as Head of the MPR Working Committee on GBHN matters, Wiranto's appointment as Head of the MPR Working Committee on non-GBHN matters, Ginandjar's appointment as Head of the GOLKAR Fraction in the MPR and Habibie's appointment as the Co-ordinator of GOLKAR's Board of the Patron vented these expectations. However, attention was focussed on two main candidates, the incumbent, Try Sutrisono and Habibie. The incumbent's advantage was that he had been a close associate of the President for nearly twenty-four years, as a former Commander-in-Chief of ABRI, was believed to have the support of the military, was a Muslim and a Javanese. He was also believed to be non-controversial and was seen to be in a position to reconcile the major political fractions in the country even though certain Muslim groups did accuse him of being involved in various anti-Islamic activities, especially the Tanjung Priok Incident in 1984. Habibie, as the father of the technological movement in the country, was also said to be strong, among others, due to his close personal ties with the President, his vision for the country as well as his strong support among the Muslim intellectuals, and where Habibie was the Chairman of ICMI. From October 1997 to mid-February 1998, there was a tug of war between the two candidates and it was difficult to discern as to who would emerge as the key

58

candidate for the Vice-President's post. When a number of key associates of Habibie were not elected to the MPR in October 1997, many viewed this as an indication of the depressing political fortunes of Habibie.

However, on 20 January 1998, when the Big GOLKAR Family, constituting of GOLKAR, ABRI and the Bureaucracy leaders saw President Suharto and successfully solicited Suharto's accent to stand for the Presidency, it was also announced that in addition to existing fifteen criteria, there would be an additional fourteen criteria which must be met by the Vice-President candidate. These criteria were developed by GOLKAR from an initial five criteria which the President suggested to GOLKAR as follows:

- Be acceptable to all groups;
- Be able to lead the country in the era of globalisation;
- Be a visionary and have knowledge of industry and technology;
- Be able to assist in overcoming the country's economic crisis; and
- Be acceptable and known internationally.

The additional fourteen criteria stated that the Vice-President must be:

- Able to preserve national unity and cohesion;
- visionary;
- Has proven loyalty to the nation;
- Has mastery of science and technology;
- Able to assist the President in solving national problems;

- Be consistent and supportive of the New Order;
- Understands the Nation's struggle;
- Be able to assist the President in the International Forums;
- Has a comprehensive understanding of the people's conditions;
- Has a good access to and is well known in international forums; and
- Has strong leadership qualities and wisdom.

What was clear from these criteria, especially point four and five, was that the one person that was being directed as the most likely candidate by these new defining features was Habibie. This led some to argue that the fourteen new criteria were aimed more at eliminating the bulk of the contending candidates and narrowing the list to just a few with Habibie as the front runner.

On 11 February 1998, GOLKAR named two candidates for the Vice-Presidency, Harmoko and Habibie even though its Chairman, Harmoko had announced earlier that the ruling party would only propose one name, as it had with the Presidential candidate. This would indicate that the GOLKAR bodypolitic was divided on the issue. It is believed that when GOLKAR met on the issue, Harmoko was named as the Vice-Presidential candidate through acclamation and it was only later that Habibie's name was included as a compromise. The other affliates of GOLKAR such as SOKSI, MKGR and KOSGORO were also divided on the issue. SOKSI named Harmoko and Hartarto as its candidate, MKGR named Try Sutrisono and KOSGORO named Try as its main candidate.

On 15 February, the PPP named Habibie as its candidate for the Vice-Presidency. On the following day, Harmoko withdrew from the Vice-Presidential race on grounds that he would like to concentrate on his MPR duties. On the same day, GOLKAR and the PDI named Habibie as their candidate for the post. On 17 February, the Regional representatives also threw in their support for Habibie. On 18 February, Try Sutrisono, the incumbent and the key challenger for Habibie announced that in line with the tradition of a one term Vice-President, he would not like to be considered for the post. On the same day, ABRI announced its support for Habibie for the post. This meant that by 18 February, all the key fractions in the MPR had only one candidate for the Vice-Presidency and this also meant that for all intents and purposes, the 1–11 March 1998 MPR Session was expected to be a mere formality as all the key and outstanding issues had been resolved by then.

The choice of Habibie for the post was not surprising in view of a number of interventions from the President. These signals were important as Presidential accent is absolutely necessary for any one to be selected for the number two post in the country. Among others, these signals included the five criteria which were stated by Suharto to the key members of the Big GOLKAR Family, Suharto's favourable mention of Habibie in his interview with the Japanese daily *Nikkei* and the appointment of Habibie to the strategic post of Co-ordinator of GOLKAR's Board of Patrons. That Habibie has been a Minister since 1978, had strong ties with Suharto since 1950, has been his trusted confidant for many years and had important duties to look after the country's strategic industries as well as ICMI were good indications of Suharto's confidence in Habibie and his future role in the country's politics.

However, as Habibie emerged as the key contender for the Vice-Presidency, a number of former officials or the wives of these officials began campaigning for Emil Salim, a former minister, for the Vice-Presidency. Even though Emil stood no chance as Habibie had the support of all the key fractions in the MPR, the Emil phenomenon was viewed by some as a shadow play, to overcome the embarrassment of the fact that Habibie was already assured of his post even before the MPR Session or by others, as a protest in the manner Habibie's selection was engineered by Suharto and his supporters.

THE 1–11 MARCH 1998 MPR SESSION

The eleven day 1–11 March 1998 MPR Session[9] involving 1,000 legislators, costing US$ 5 million, was convened to receive the President's accountability statement, to debate and approve the State Policy Guidelines (GBHN) for the next five years as well as to select the country's President and Vice-President for the period 1998 to 2003. By most counts, most of the key pressing issues had already been settled before even the MPR Session was convened and to that extent, the MPR Session was largely expected to rubber stamp most of the decisions which had already been agreed upon prior to the Session.[10] It was to a large extent a known affair and to that extent too, was expected to be a non-event even though the PPP MPR Fraction Leader, Jusuf Syakir warned that the various 'agreements were made by 90 members of the Assembly working committee. I believe a lot of debate will still mark the upcoming General Session because of the presence of another 910 members. The State Policy Guidelines draft, although it has been approved already, is not the final product. It needs a second look.'[11]

Yet, unlike the past, the 1998 MPR Session was held against the backdrop of a severe economic crisis as well as rising political restlessness among the populace, especially students and workers. Reports of food shortages in different parts of the country had led to rioting and demonstrations. The authorities attempted to clamp down on protest movements and attributed the upheavals to 'irresponsible groups' seeking to disrupt and undermine the MPR Session.[12] What made the government particularly wary about these demonstrations was the key singular demand that political reforms be instituted to save the country, something the political leadership appeared somewhat loathed to undertake, as this would signal that it was crumbling under public pressure. All these developments led to heavy security with some 25,000 personnel being deployed to safeguard the General Session, under the leadership of Major-General Syafrie, the Commander of the Jakarta Garrison.

The President's Accountability Address

In a nutshell, President Suharto stated that developments in the last few months preceding the MPR Session have exposed the internal weaknesses of the country and threatened to undermine the country's hard built development. The President argued that until the advent of economic turmoil in the last few months of the MPR Session, the country's economic progress was proceeding smoothly with major development targets being met and even surpassed. However, "since the second half of last year [1997], when the monetary turmoil struck, it seems that every thing we have built with great difficulty, sometimes with pain and sacrifices, was all of a sudden undermined". This was best evident by the rate of economic growth. In the period 1993 to 1996, the average economic growth for the country stood at 7.1 percent. However, it dropped to 4.7 percent for 1997. While the President maintained that the country's fundamentals were still strong, the economic crisis, nevertheless, had exposed the major weaknesses of Indonesia. According to President Suharto, 'apparently, our economic resilience was not strong enough to withstand external blows. Apart from external influences, some of the hardship we are suffering today is also due to our internal weaknesses'.

Aside from the economic crisis, the President noted that many of the targets set out in the Sixth Five Year Development Plan (REPELITA VI) had been reached or nearly achieved. Among these, the President outlined as follows:

- economic growth rates of 7.3 percent, 7.5 percent, 8.2 percent and 8.0 percent from 1993 to 1996;

- per capita income rose from the 1993 level of US$842 to US$ 1,155 in 1996;

- poverty alleviation programmes have reduced the number of poor from 25.9 million in 1993 to 22.5 million in 1996;

- life expectancy has increased from 62.7 years in 1993 to 64.2 years in 1997;

- mortality rates have sharply declined from 58 per 1000 births in 1993 to 52 in 1997;

- maternal mortality has declined from 425 per 100,000 in 1993 to 390 in 1994;

- gross mortality has been reduced from 7.9 per 1000 inhabitants in 1993 to 7.5 in 1997;

- the number of simple and very simple houses constructed under REPELITA VI was 550,000, far in excess of the targetted 500,000.

The President, however, only made a fleeting reference to political development in the country, acknowledging that 'the political climate was quite tense' prior to the May 1997 general elections. This was, however, blamed on 'people who were not yet mature enough to put democracy into practice and misued freedom and openness'. The President also criticised the critics of Indonesia's political system arguing that nine out ten eligible voters exercised their voting right and that this was 'far higher than in other countries which have enjoyed hundreds of years of political tradition'. In this connection, the President reserved special praise for the country's Armed Forces, commending its work and dual function, which he argued had made meaningful contribution to national stability and political life.

In his accountability speech, the President also called on the International Monetary Fund (IMF), which was organising a US$ 43 billion rescue package, to do more to stabilise the country's currency and economy, directly implying that the international body had failed to solve Indonesia's problems thus far. It was due to this that President Suharto argued that he was 'carefully and cautiously contemplating the possible adoption of a Currency Board System'. Arguing that he did not see any improvement in the situation in the short run, he said that he has asked 'the IMF and other heads of government to assist us find a more appropriate alternative', something which the President referred to as the 'IMF-Plus' formula, even though the new Finance Minister, Fuad Bawazier, later indicated his willingness to abandon the idea, mainly to placate the IMF and the United States.

While GOLKAR, ABRI and the Regional Representatives accepted the President's accountability speech, the minority parties present in the General Session, the PPP and PDI, stated openly that the speech was incomplete. Ismail Hassan Matareum and Soerjadi, the Chairman of the PPP and PDI respectively stated that certain strategic issues, including the need for political reform in the country were missing from the speech. Ismail argued that 'what has been achieved in the political sector in far below our expectations'. Two other PPP legislators, Hamzah Haz and Muhammad Buang were even

65

more stronger in their criticisms. They argued that the 'President's accountability speech was focussed on economic reform only while economic problems cannot be separated from politics'. Also, 'economic reform should go hand in hand with political reform'. Similarly, Soerjadi argued that 'the account was incomplete because it discussed mostly the country's success in development programmes. The account did not touch on government officials' corruption and collusion or business monopolies'. Supporters of President Suharto, however, viewed the speech differently. Hasan Basri Durin, the Chairman of the Regional Representatives argued that the 'accountability speech was sincerely, objectively and straight forwardly prepared by President Suharto. My faction will accept it unconditionally'. Hari Sabarno, the Chairman of the Armed Forces faction said that 'we have re-nominated Pak Harto for the Presidency. Why would we reject his account?'. Two days later, the PDI accepted the President's accountability speech and on the following, the PPP followed suit. This ended one major concern of the 1998 MPR Session.

The Debate Over the State Policy Guidelines (GBHN)

The GBHN was drawn up by the General Session Working Committee One headed by General R Hartono, then Minister of Information. These were supposed to be broad guidelines by which the President was to rule the country and achieve the targets for the period 1998-2003. As with the President's Accountability Speech, the dominant and minority factions differed on the matter. Both the PPP and PDI demanded that the next government take concrete steps to end the widespread corruption in the bureaucracy and monopolistic practices which they blamed for the widening disparity that was said to have caused the economic crisis in the country. They also argued that unless the government undertook a major po-

66

litical overhaul, together with the economic reforms prescribed by the IMF, there was no chance of recovery. The minority parties also argued that the GBHN drawn up by the working committee was too optimistic as it was finalised before the full effects of the crisis had become apparent.

MPR Passage of the Draft Decree

While MPR General Session Working Committee One headed by Hartono handled all matters related to the GBHN, the Working Committee Two headed by General Wiranto handled all non-GBHN matters, especially the matters related to various decrees to be passed by the MPR General Session. Here, in addition to the Assembly's internal rules and the two decrees on Presidential and Vice-Presidential elections, the novelty as far as decrees before the 1998 General Session was concerned pertained to special powers being granted to the President, who would act, on behalf of the MPR, in certain circumstances.

During the General Session, GOLKAR and ABRI argued that the next President should be given special extra powers to deal with potentially new problems. In particular, the President should be given the necessary powers to take the necessary measures to safeguard the continuation of development programmes as well as national security. The General Session had first passed a similar decree in 1966, then allowing the acting President, Suharto, to take the necessary action to restore order following the abortive coup by the PKI in 1965. The General Assembly retained the decree for the next four General Sessions in 1973, 1978, 1983 and 1988. It was, however, never actually applied. The 1993 General Session dropped the decree. In August 1997, however, in a briefing to 500 legislative candidates, President Suharto suggested that the decree be revived in order to pre-empt future challenges to developmental programmes, the state ideology of *Pancasila* and even the nation's survival itself. Even though there were concerns expressed about the rise of absolute power of the President, General Wiranto argued that 'there are certain legal procedures the President will first have to meet if he wishes to execute the powers, including consultation with the House of Representatives in advance and a report to the Assembly delivered in his or her accountability speech. So, what sort of absolutism will the decree generate?', he enquired. Notwithstanding some concern, especially by the minority parties, all the draft decrees were passed on 9 March 1998.

The Presidential Election

The election of President Suharto for the seventh term was never in doubt since all the factions in the 1998 MPR General Session only had one candidate, namely, Suharto. However, there was still the need to go through the political ritual and this was undertaken according to constitutional requirements and procedures. On 8 March 1988, the leaders of all the factions, led by ABRI, called upon Suharto and formally asked the incumbent to accept the re-nomination for the Presidency. The five delegations met Suharto in the following order: ABRI, GOLKAR, PDI, PPP and the Regional Representatives. The PPP factional leader, Jusuf Syakir for instance stated that 'He [Suharto] is prepared to be re-nominated, although he admitted that the country is facing its toughest challenge ever, particularly due to the prevailing economic crisis'. Similarly, Lieutenant-General Yunus Yosfiah, the leader of the Armed Forces faction stated that 'He [Suharto] told us that he was already 77 years old, older than Prophet Muhammed when he died at 63 years of age.... but with a fighting spirit and adherence toward Indonesian soldiers' oath. He was prepared to devote his soul, not to mention possessions, to the country'.

68

On the following day, 9 March, the Speaker of the General Assembly, Harmoko and his four deputies, Lieutenant-General Syarwan Hamid, Abdul Gafur, Fatimah Achmad and Ismail Hassan Matareum met President Suharto at the State Palace to confirm the re-nomination for the Presidency. According to regulations, this was the last preliminary step before Suharto could be re-elected. Following the meeting, Harmoko declared that 'the re-nomination of Suharto as Indonesia's Presidential candidate is said to have met all the requirements'. On the following day, 10 March, the 1,000 member People's Consultative Assembly re-elected Suharto for a seventh five-year term.

In his inaugural speech, President Suharto called upon the people to stand behind the government in its effort to overcome the various crises that was being confronted. 'I plead' said Suharto, 'for support from all groups, any circles, women, men and generations'. The President admitted that the country was undergoing an extremely difficult test and trial, brought about by the economic crisis and it also meant that the people will not be able to enjoy the good life they had for the last 25 years. He said that 'as a nation, we must tighten our belt. As individuals, as a group, some of us may lead affluent lives. But as a nation, we can no longer afford to lead an extravagant life. During the present hardship, we need a stronger solidarity, a sense of sharing the same fate and destiny'. Showing an olive branch to various critics, he argued that 'I have fully and broad-mindedly listened to all subtle and veiled or strong, blunt criticisms.... These criticisms constitute valuable inputs for the improvement of my government in the coming years'. At the same time, the President dismissed pundits who argued that the newly elected President may step down mid-term. In his inaugural speech, he stated that 'in five years time from now, God willing, I shall stand on this rostrum to present the accountability of my leadership before the Indonesian people's representatives'.

69

The Vice-Presidential Election

As in the re-election, or rather selection of the President, the various faction leaders paid a visit to the President to ascertain his view on the candidate. Officially, there was also only one candidate for the post, B. J. Habibie despite the 'unofficial' challenge posed by Emil Salim. The different faction leaders sought Suharto's view on his running mate as one of the criteria required that the Vice-President must be able to work with the President. When on 10 March 1998, Ginandjar Kartasasmita, the leader of the GOLKAR Faction in the MPR met the President, the latter said that Habibie was 'an appropriate assistant for him as the country is striving for industrialisation, which requires strong technology support'. The President also said that Habibie met all the criteria put forward for the Vice-President. The Armed Forces faction, which met the President earlier stated that the latter argued that 'it will be a big mistake if the nation does not take advantage of one of its best sons, who has an excellent mastery of science and technology'. President Suharto also underlined that 'Habibie had a vision on national and international affairs. With support from the President and endorsement from all the five factions in the MPR, Habibie was sworn in as the country's Vice-President on 11 March 1998.

The Suharto Government, 1998-2003

Following the March 1998 MPR Session, the President announced that restoring the currency stability of the country was the new government's most immediate priority. The followed President Suharto's earlier statement in his inaugural address that 'the country was going through extremely difficult test and trials. We are being subjected to very hard economic and financial turmoil'. The President also, very quickly,

70

announced his new cabinet, on 14 March, so that the business of running the country could move on. The Seventh Development Cabinet was constituted by the following officials:

Suharto	—	President
B. J. Habibie	—	Vice-President
Gen. Feisal Tanjung	—	Co-ordinating Minister, Political and Security
Ginandjar Kartasasmita	—	Co-ordinating Minister, Economy, Finance and Industry/ Chairman of National Development Planning Board
Hartarto Sastroseonarto	—	Co-ordinating Minister, Development Supervision and State Adminstrative Reform
Haryono Suyono	—	Co-ordinating Minister, People's Welfare and Poverty Eradication/ Chairman of National Family Planning Board
Gen. R Hartono	—	Minister of Home Affairs
Ali Alatas	—	Minister of Foreign Affairs
Gen. Wiranto	—	Armed Forces Chief/ Minister of Defence and Security
Muladi	—	Minister of Justice

M. Alwi Dahlan	—	Minister of Information
Fuad Bawazier	—	Minister of Finance
Mohamad Hasan	—	Minister of Trade and Industry
Justika S.Baharsjah	—	Minister of Agriculture
Kuntoro Mangkusubroto	—	Minister of Mines and Energy
Sumahadi	—	Minister of Forestry and Plantation
Rahmadi B. Sumadhijo	—	Minister of Public Works
Giri Suseno Hardihardjono	—	Minister of Transportation
Abdul Latief	—	Minister of Tourism, Art and Culture
SubiaktoTjakarwerdaja	—	Minister of Co-opertives and Small Enterprises
Theo L. Sambuaga	—	Minister of Manpower
Lt. Gen. Hendropriyono	—	Minister of Transmigration and Resettlement of Forest Nomads
Wiranto Arismunandar	—	Minister of Education and Culture
Farid Antara Moeloek	—	Minister of Health
Quraish Shihab	—	Minister of Religious Affairs

Siti Hardiyanti Rukmana	—	Minister of Social Services
Saadilah Mursjid	—	State Minister/State Secretary
Rahardi Ramelan	—	State Minister for Research and Technology/ Chairman of Agency for Assessment and Application of Technology
Sanyoto Sastrowardjoyo	—	State Minister for Investment/Chairman of Investment Co-ordinating Board
Maj. Gen. Ary Mardjono	—	State Minister of Land Affairs/Head of National Land Board
Akbar Tanjung	—	State Minister for Housing and Settlements
Juwono Sudarsono	—	State Minister for Environment/Chairman of Environmental Impact Management Agency
Haryanto Dhanutirto	—	State Minister for Food, Drugs and Horticulture

Tanri Abeng	—	State Minister for Empowerment of State Enterprises
Tutty Alawiah	—	State Minister for Women Affairs
H.R Agung Laksono	—	State Minister for Youth and Sports Affairs
Soedjono C. Atmonegoro	—	Attorney General
Sjahril Sabirin	—	Governor of Bank Indonesia

CONCLUDING ANALYSIS

Suharto's seventh cabinet had a number of unique features. First and foremost, it was in many ways, a crisis cabinet, designed to overcome the country's economic crisis. In this endeavour, it had a number of leading professionals who are leaders in their respective fields who were included in the cabinet, such as Ginandjar, Hartarto, Fuad Bawazier, Rahardi Ramelan, Tanri Abeng and Sanyoto Sastrowardjoyo, to turn around the economy. The inclusion of Muladi and Juwono Sudarsono, to oversee justice and environment respectively, can be seen from the same perspective. Second, Muhamad Bob Hasan became the first ethnic Chinese in more than thirty years to hold a cabinet post under the New Order. Third, the inclusion of Siti Hardiyanti Rukmana or better known as Tutut, who is also Suharto eldest daughter, also marked a major departure for the first time that the President had included his own sibling in the cabinet. Fourth, also noticeable was the reduced number of personnel from the military in the cabinet. This time round, excluding Suharto, there were only six individuals with military backgrounds in the cabinet, representing the lowest representation from the miitary in the cabinet in the last thirty years, indicating clearly that Suharto was subtly but surely undertaking a process of 'civilianisation' of the country's politics. With GOLKAR and the Vice-President in the hands of the civilians, two posts which since the birth of the New Order had largely in military hands, merely confirmed the momentum of this trend. Finally, what was also most noticeable was the increased powers given to the Vice-President.

The choice of Habibie as Suharto's running mate created some controversy, partly due to the extrovert nature of Habibie, his reputation as a free spender in strategic industries, and who had been tasked with enhancing the country's technological capability since 1978. In the last cabinet, Habibie was known as the 'super minister' due to his ability and success in placing individuals from ICMI into the cabinet. This time round, what has made Habibie's position important and noticeable is the fact that he is strategically placed both politically and constitutionally to takeover the Presidency should anything untoward happen to the President or even if the former decides to transfer power to his running mate.

Next, the fact that the President has empowered the Vice-President, by clearly designing a number of areas as part of the Habibie's responsibility is also a clear signal that the Vice-President would continue his high profile in domestic and international politics. For the first time under the New Order, the Vice-President was given a wide-ranging global brief as well as the special task of overseeing industrial development at home. When the President announced his cabinet line-up on 14 March 1998, the President also stated that 'I give the duty to the Vice-President to help in global geopolitics through various world organisations'. More specifically, the President asked Habibie to deal with the United Nations, the Non-Aligned Movement, the Asia-Pacific Economic Co-operation, the Organisation of the Islamic Conference, the Group of 15, the Group of 8, the Asia-Europe Meeting and ASEAN. These

75

eight international forces are among the most important foreign policy pre-occupations of Indonesia and Habibie has been designated to deal with them, making him effectively the 'real foreign minister of Indonesia'.

NOTES

1   *The Jakarta Post*, 30 August 1997.

2   *Ibid*, 20 October 1997.

3   *Ibid*.

4   *Ibid*.

5   *Suara Pembaruan*, 20 November 1997.

6   *The Jakarta Post*, 15 December 1997

7   *The Jakarta Post*, 3 December 1997.

8   See *TIRAS*, 31 December 1997, p. 90.

9   Historically, the dates of the MPR Session are important, especially from the point of view of President Suharto. On 1 March 1949, Lieutenant-Colonel Suharto launched a six hour attack on Jogjakarta, showing up the weakness of the Dutch. As for 11 March 1966, General Suharto had power transferred to him to take over the country.

10 The leader of the PPP fraction in the MPR described the MPR Session as a political ritual: 'Of course, the General Session will serve as merely a ceremony, but should it matter to us? It is like a preparation for a wedding service. We have to pass a set of traditional and religious procedures. They may take us a long time although the wedding service itself may last just one minute'. *The Jakarta Post*, 1 March 1998.

11 *Ibid*.

12 *Ibid*.

4

Post-MPR Politics and the Fall of Suharto

INTRODUCTION

In his now famous but rather premature acceptance speech as the country's President for the seventh term, on 10 March 1998, Suharto declared that, 'God willing, I will be in this same forum five years from now to deliver my accountability speech'.[1] While most political analysts even argued that the Indonesian President had consolidated his political power[2], despite the worst political and economic crises confronting the country, barely 72 days later, President Suharto resigned as the country's political leader and Indonesia's much awaited political transition into the post-Suharto era took place, for most, rather precipitously and unexpectedly. How was a political giant like Suharto brought down? Was it really the consequences of a 'peoples' power movement' as was the case in the Philippines twelve years earlier? Or did a political conspiracy bring Suharto down? Even more important, what was the meaning for Indonesia, the Asia-Pacific region, especially Southeast Asia and the world at large, of the ushering of the post-Suharto era?

Following the swearing in of President Suharto and his deputy, B. J. Habibie, it was generally agreed that the key challenge facing the new Indonesian government was to show results in terms of overcoming the country's economic and financial crisis. Otherwise, the emergence of a bankrupt economy, stoked by hyperinflation, something Suharto, as the 'father of development' was supposed to be immune from, was expected to fuel political anger of the restless people to a point where the Suharto regime was likely to be blamed for all the troubles and where there was a possibility that this anger could be easily harnessed by the anti-Suharto forces to bring the regime down.

However, every passing day since 11 March 1998, President Suharto and his Government were bogged down by crisis after crisis. As was argued by John McBeth, 'Behind the façade of political stability is the risk of internal rot, with the economic crisis nibbling away at the President's political support. Disturbing symptoms of the downbeat are apparent: growing middle-class resentment, a deepening rift within the elite, more than a quarter of the workforce either unemployed or underemployed, and a seemingly reborn student movement – gathering strength in a nation where lack of organisation has so far stymied political opposition'.[3] What made President Suharto's response to the burgeoning economic crisis somewhat half-hearted, especially in term of assistance from international financial agencies such as the IMF and World Bank was his general suspicions of these agencies as having a political agenda as far as Indonesia was concerned. Thus, after the President signed a 50-point agreement with the IMF Chief Michel Camdessus in January 1998, the situation of the Indonesian Rupiah did not improve. Suharto felt humiliated and it was then that the idea of a Currency Board, floated by American economist Steve Hanke, was being discussed as a quick-fix effort to help the country's economic recovery. In many ways, this further exacerbated the confidence problem Indonesia was facing. As was pointed out by an astute observer of Indonesia, 'the signs are that the President is searching for a simple solution to that problem, one that stabilises the rupiah without tackling the structural problems of the economy, such as a surfeit of banks and a corporate sector handcuffed to crony interests'.[4] Even though Jakarta backed away from the risky plan to peg the Rupiah to the US dollar through the currency board, in many ways, the dye was cast.

Yet, Suharto continued to believe that the external agencies such as the IMF and World Banks and their sponsors, such as the United States Government, were not keen on helping Indonesia to recover economically but were using the economic tragedy to undermine and threaten his political position. As an official in the new Indonesian Government confided, Suharto 'knows that he is the target of people in the US Congress. He sees a conspiracy to get rid of him'.[5] According to an Indonesian official in Washington, Jakarta was increasingly 'looked on as the Iraq of economies'.[6]

The single most important constituency which applied pressure unendingly on Suharto and his Government were the students. Even though historically since the onset of the New Order, which ironically came to power at the back the students demonstrations which brought Sukarno down, the student movement has been badly factionalised into two main groups of 'moderates' and 'revolutionaries' by ideological, personality and campus differences, the students succeeded in maintaining their anti-Suharto momentum. While the student demonstrations began as criticisms against government policies, especially economic policies, by mid-March the students became bolder and began to call for Suharto's resignation.

79

This represented a major departure from the past and with the number of students joining the demonstrations increasing day by day, between March and May 1998, Indonesia witnessed its largest student demonstrations in thirty years. After the March MPR Session, the students were joined in by University administrators, faculty members and alumni leaders. At the same time, unlike the past, the co-ordination among the student movements in the various campuses improved, with many student groups even reaching to other sectors of society, such as the workers, etc, and it was this momentum which gave the anti-Suharto forces the character of a 'peoples' power movement'. By April 1998, all the major campuses in Indonesia in all the major cities were involved in demonstrations of one kind or another, be it in Jakarta, Jogjakarta, Solo, Bandung, Surabaya, Semarang, Ujung Pandang and Medan.

A number of related events further boosted and gave substance to the student demonstrations and demands for Suharto to step down. First, was the charge that the new cabinet announced on 14 March 1998 was nothing more than 'cronyism' at its best. The fact that the cabinet included the President's eldest daughter, Siti Hardiyanti Rukmana, and a close friend and golfing partner, Mohamad (Bob) Hassan were viewed as 'adding salt to injury'. The new Finance Minister, Fuad Bawazier, was also known as a confidant of the family. Many have argued that bulk of the cabinet members were largely handpicked by Suharto eldest daughter, leading an outgoing minister to describe the cabinet selection process as 'a very private affair'.[7]

Second, there seems to be no abatement whatsoever as far as the economic crisis was concerned. All the economic policies and IMF packages seem to have no effect on the value of the Indonesian Rupiah and confidence in the country. This led many to conclude that the problem was not the Indonesian economy *per se* but more had to do with the Indonesian political leadership. Until and unless this problem was addressed

80

there was no hope whatsoever of improving the national economy. This further boosted the students' anti-Suharto cause.

Third, in the midst of the national political and economic crisis, the government began to harass a number of its political opponents. Of particular importance was the police investigation of a prominent local businessman, Arifin Panigoro, who was closely linked with Amien Rais and his group, for plotting to topple the government.[8] On 5 February 1998, in a Jogjakarta seminar chaired by Amien Rais, Arifin was alleged to have called upon the former to activate a 'people's power uprising' against the Suharto government. Some argued that the government's investigation against Arifin was meant to warn local businessmen to keep their distance from opposition groups and activists especially at a time when the government was having difficulties in managing the various crises confronting her. Also, in this particular case, it was far easier and safer to investigate Arifin, a self-made millionaire than Amien Rais himself, as the latter was head of the 28-million strong Muhammadiyah and who was in a position to unleash his masses in an anti-government campaign. Nevertheless, the government's action of investigating Arifin and trying to frighten opposition activists were viewed as a provocation, and this forced the students to vent their anger all the more against the regime.

Fourth, the students were provided with moral support from a most unusual source, middle class Indonesian mothers protesting against the price of milk. The protest movement was led by Karina Laksono, a well-connected business executive, and in March 1998, nine female activists were arrested at gun point by the Police in North Jakarta.[9] This was a clear indication of the growing unhappiness with the government's economic policies and the state of suffering the people were going through. In situations such of these, it was not difficult to mobilise people for an anti-government cause.

Fifth, what gave the students a further boost in their anti-government demonstrations was the shocking testimony by a number of political activists that they had been kidnapped, held for many weeks and tortured by the security forces.[10] On 27 April 1998, Pius Lustrilanang, the Secretary-General of SIAGA, went public, despite a death threat, that he was kidnapped, held in a detention centre and tortured by the security forces. He also disclosed that he had seen a number of the political activists who had been reported missing. Since the anti-government demonstrations erupted in full swing in February 1998, some 24 activists had been reported missing. SIAGA is a loose alliance of supporters of opposition leaders, Amien Rais and Megawati Sukarnopurtri. According to Pius, his abductors were interested in knowing more about SIAGA's activities. While the true identity of his abductors was not immediately known, the Armed Forces were immediately the prime suspects, with many even arguing that there may be 'rogue' elements within ABRI undertaking this. Whatever the motivations, the abductions provided the necessary catalyst to 'breathe more fire into the increasingly vigorous anti-government student protests countrywide'.[11]

Finally, what the students lacked all these years was a symbol of unity. Questionable government's policies and the general economic downturn provided the convenient opportunity with Suharto as the single target against whom the students vented their wrath. Even more important, for the first time in many years, the students were actively supported by key political figures and in this connection, the students came to see Amien Rais as one of their leading supporters. Throughout the period of student demonstrations, Amien spoke highly of the political education the students were giving the country. Amien argued that 'I think the students will become the vanguard of the people's aspirations. Because the students do not have vested political interests, they speak out what is in their hearts'.[12]

While the students kept up the pressure and called for

wide-ranging reforms and for the President to step down, on 1 May 1998, President Suharto announced that fundamental reforms must wait until 2003, that is, when Suharto term as President expired. In line with IMF guidelines, on 4 May, the government announced cuts in fuel subsidies. A direct result of this was the outbreak of violent riots in Medan. On 9 May, the President flew to Cairo, Egypt to attend the G-15 Summit. In the meantime, the student demonstrations became increasingly co-ordinated and what was most ominous for the Suharto regime was the fact that it began to attract support from other segments of society, especially the disaffected elite. In his absence, the country went through a radical transformation, in a way, marking the crescendo of the anti-Suharto movement that had been taking place in the country since the onset of the economic crisis since August 1997 and this was to usher in the post-Suharto era.

'The May 1998 Revolution' and the Fall of President Suharto

Between 12 and 20 May 1998, Indonesia experienced a 'revolution' of a kind that was to culminate in the transfer of power from President Suharto to his Vice-President, B. J. Habibie. When Suharto cut short his trip to Cairo and returned home on 15 May, he returned to a different Indonesia. A major trigger in this 'revolution' was the peoples' reaction to the shooting of four Trisakti University students by security forces on 12 May. While the true identity of the culprits remain disputed and as to whether the military high command did give instructions for the shooting to take place, the students and the anti-government forces took it as a provocation and an attempt to frighten the opposition into silence. In response, following the burial of the dead students on the following day, Jakarta witnessed its worst riots in thirty years.

83

This continued for the next two days and thousands of buildings and shops, especially owned by the ethnic Chinese and people associated with the Suharto family, were torched. Reportedly, more than 1,000 people were killed in Jakarta alone with the ethnic Chinese targeted for 'ethnic cleansing' as the attacks on them and their properties, were undertaken in an organised fashion. In Cairo, President Suharto announced that if the people wanted him to step down, he was prepared to do so as long as this was undertaken constitutionally: 'If I am no longer trusted to lead the country, I will become *Pandhito*, a sage and endeavour to get closer to God. I will spend my time to guide my children so that they become good people, guide the community and give advice. I will do *tut wuri handayani* (guide from behind)'.[13] The President also said that he would not defend his position with military force.[14]

President Suharto returned to Indonesia at dawn on 15 May and one of the first statements he made was to deny that he has offered to step down. Earlier, Ali Alatas, the Foreign Minister, who accompanied the President to Cairo, offered a 'correction', arguing that 'he (Suharto) has said on several occasions before, that if the people do not have trust in me anymore, then of course, that is their right, and he would not oppose it as long as it is done constitutionally. I repeat, as long as it is conveyed and decided upon...through our elected representatives in the consultative assembly'.[15] In many ways, this statement, uncompromising as it may be, set the tone for developments in the next four days. In the meantime, the unrest spread to the rest of the country, with the main focus being in the key cities of Java. The government's response to the proliferation of nation-wide riots was to announce on 16 May a cut in fuel and electricity prices, arguing that the people's anger was due more to the cuts in subsidies rather than anything else.

On 16 May, the MPR and GOLKAR Chairman, Harmoko, and accompanied by his deputies, Lieutenant-General Syarwan Hamid, Ismail Hassan Matereum, Abdul Gafur and Fatimah Achmad, called on the President. Apparently, the parliamentary leaders told Suharto that there had been a paradigm shift in the people's mood and that what was being demanded was that either the President stepped down voluntarily or his fate would be decided by a special session of the MPR. While little has been exposed of the meeting, leaked information has maintained that 'the President suggested that the parliamentarians put it to a debate in the House of Representatives and if all factions agreed that he should step down, then he would'.[16] Publicly, however, Harmoko stated the President had promised to accelerate reforms, as demanded by the people as well as to give priority to the reestablishment of law and order. In order to actualise these goals, the President also promised to reshuffle the cabinet, as a strong team was needed while at the same time, conceding to the demands of the students.[17] On the same day, the President also met with the leaders of the University of Indonesia in order to ascertain the students' demands. Following the meeting, the Vice-Rector of the University of Indonesia stated that 'if people want him to resign and this can happen anytime, he will *lengser keprabon* (abdicate)'.[18]

On 17 May, calls for Suharto resignation mounted. Of particular importance was the increasingly organised and co-ordinated nature of the 'Quit Suharto Movement' even though the '*dalang*' (mastermind) of the movement was unseen. What became apparent following the Trisakti shooting was that Indonesia's long-suppressed opposition groups seized the opportunity to organise themselves in what appeared to be their first real chance to bring Suharto down. One of the most important organisation established in this endeavour was the *Majelis Amanah Rakyat* (MAR) or Council for People's Mandate, established on 14 May in Jogjakarta under the leadership of Amien Rais. Purportedly its members included Adnan Buyung Nasution, Ali Sadikin, Frans Seda, Sumitro Djojohadikoesoemo, Siswono Yudohusodo and Arifin Panigoro. In a statement read by Amien Rais following MAR's launch, it argued that 'for the sake of this nation and for a smooth and peaceful reform toward democracy, we call on President Suharto to step aside'. Amien also called on the students to work towards restoring normalcy to the country.[19] On the following day, another alliance of civilian leaders, the *Forum Kerja Indonesia* (FKI) or Indonesia Working Forum was established to apply pressure on Suharto to undertake large-scale reforms, including Suharto stepping down from the Presidency.[20] On the same day, that is, 16 May, the Co-ordination Body of Muslims, grouping eleven key Muslim organisations in the country was established. Equally significant was a special press meeting organised by several prominent Muslim scholars on 17 May, including Emha Nadjib and Nurcholish Majid, at Hotel Wisata, Jakarta which called on the government to quicken the pace of political reforms, calling for general elections in 2000, three years before Suharto Presidency ended.[21]

In the midst of the call for reforms, Suharto return from Cairo also seemed to have enhanced the divisions within various groups, especially those that were calling on Suharto to resign. First, there appeared to be a rift in ICMI. This followed remarks made by ICMI's Executive Chairman, Achmad Tirtosudiro and Secretary-General Adi Sasono that their organisation supported calls for an extraordinary session of the MPR and a cabinet reshuffle as a means for political reform. Both Achmad and Adi also released a written statement calling for total political reform, arguing that the government's reform proposals were 'vague, too little and too late'.[22] The Vice-President, B. J. Habibie, then still Chairman of ICMI, denied that the statements of Achmad and Adi reflected ICMI's position, of which he was still Chairman. Rather, the Vice-President argued that the remarks of the two top ICMI officials were made in their 'personal capacity' even though both Achmad and Adi refused to retract their statements.[23]

Another source of division among opponents of Suharto was the one between MAR and FKI. Appearingly, MAR represented a coalition of civilians who were '*Santri*' in orientation while FKI was much more '*Abangan*' in thrust. More important, during the launch of FKI, Amien Rais was absent even though it was announced that he was one of the three key leaders, the other two being Megawati and Abdurrahman Wahid. At the same time, Abdurrahman Wahid criticised MAR for claiming that it represented all Indonesians. He argued that 'many groups in society are not represented at MAR'.[24]

Among the Muslims, another divide was between activists aligned with Amien Rais and Adi Sasono, on the one hand, and the others, who considered themselves as moderates. Here, Muslim intellectuals such as Emha Nadjib and Nurcholish Madjid had clear differences with the Amien-Adi group and these were made transparent when the former argued that even though they supported what Amien was doing, they disagreed with the way this was done. Nurcholish stated that 'Amien Rais is my *imam* (teacher). I admire him but I wish he would co-ordinate better, talk to us, so we can really help'.[25] Similarly, Emha argued that 'we support him but he should recognise us. Don't be like a locomotive that run forward by itself, leaving the coaches behind in confusion'.[26]

Added to these divisions were the burgeoning divisions within ABRI and which were surfacing in the light of the political-economic crisis, and which to many, was the undercurrent of an emerging power struggle and where the key factions in ABRI were trying to position themselves in anticipation of Suharto's resignation or overthrow. As ABRI prided itself as being a 'people's army' there were also speculation that an important source of divide was the inclination of some officers to loyally defend President Suharto at all cost while another was unwilling to shoot at the people and were inclined to pressure the President to step down. While factionalism within ABRI was not new, the single most divide in ABRI during this period was between two key powerful groups, one led by the ABRI Chief and Defence Minister, General Wiranto and the other by Lieutenant-General Prabowo Subianto, the Commander of the Army Strategic Reserves.

In the light of the intense politicking in the country, especially in the capital, there were strong rumours that the security situation would worsened, in part, due to the split in the Armed Forces. Following Suharto's return from Cairo, one of the first things he did was to consult with the senior officers in the capital so that they could present a picture of unity to the country. In this endeavour, on 15 May, Lieutenant-General Prabowo Subianto, publicly denied that there were divisions within ABRI. He stated that there was 'no dual leadership' in ABRI. ABRI, he said, was 'very solid and united' under the leadership of General Wiranto. General Prabowo argued that the rumour about a split in ABRI 'is only an issue created to look as if there is a division within the Armed Forces' and this is part of an effort by certain groups to weaken ABRI and the country.[27]

In the midst of these divisions and growing pressure for Suharto to resign, on 18 May, Parliamentary Speaker and Chairman of GOLKAR, Mr Harmoko, after consulting his parliamentary colleagues, made a public statement which signalled that the endgame of Suharto Presidency was being played out. At 3.00 p.m. Jakarta time, Mr Harmoko told the press that he and his colleagues have studied thoroughly the increasingly volatile situation, including the demand for reform, the holding of an extra-ordinary session of the MPR and the resignation of the President: 'In response to this situation, the Speaker and his deputies hope that the President will act wisely and with wisdom and will step down for the sake of the unity and integrity of the nation'.[28] Yet, barely five hours later, General Wiranto, the ABRI Chief, told the press that 'the statement made by Harmoko is an individual statement, even though it is made in a collective manner. According to the Constitution, it does not have legal power'.[29]

What was equally interesting, the different factions in the House of Representatives also began to look at the different options that were available to the President in the light of the worsening situation. Irsyad Sudiro, the leader of the GOL-KAR faction in the House of Representative stated that his party had identified five main options as follows:

- Persuading Suharto to resign and appointing the Vice-President, B. J. Habibie as the new President without convening an extraordinary MPR Session;

- Persuading both the President and Vice-President, Suharto and Habibie, respectively to return their mandates to the MPR;

- Allowing the President to remain in office to carry out total reform as was proposed by him on 19 May 1998;

- Replacing the President and the Vice-President with a Triumvirate Council comprising the Minister of Foreign Affairs, Minister of Home Affairs and the Minister of Defence and Security; and

- Holding an extraordinary Session of the MPR to select a new President and Vice-President.[30]

At the same time, Saadilah Mursjid, the Minister/State Secretary, was very much attracted to the ideas put forward by Nurcholish Majid and friends at their 17 May press conference at Hotel Wisata, especially since the views forwarded did not require Suharto's immediate resignation as was being pushed by other groups. On 18 May, at 3.00 p.m., when Harmoko announced to the press his colleagues' decision calling on the President to resign, Nurcholish Majid was invited by Mursjid to his office at the State Secretariat to discuss the ideas mentioned earlier. Accompanying Nurcholish were Fahmi Idris and Utomo Damanjaya. Impressed by the reasonable demands of the moderate Muslims leaders, Mursjid promised to convey the ideas to the President.

That day, after a discussion with the President, at 7.00 p.m., Saadilah invited Nurcholish and his two friends to Suharto's residence to further develop the proposals. Only Nurcholish was able to make it as Fahmi was affected by the worsening security situation and Utomo was uncontactable. At 8.30 p.m., Nurcholish met Suharto who was accompanied by Mursjid and Probosutejo. At the meeting, Nurcholish made clear that public pressure had reached a point where they were demanding nothing short of Suharto's resignation, to which Suharto replied that he had no problem: 'Sure, from the very beginning I have said that I am prepared to step down'.[31] Following this, the President thought that it was best he met up with key Muslim leaders and this was to take place at 9.00 a.m. the following morning.

On 19 May at 9.00 a.m., the President met nine leading Muslim leaders at his office, including Abdurrahman Wahid, the leader of the 30-million strong NU, Nurcholish Majid, Emha Ainun Nadjib, Yuzril Mahendra, KH. Ali Yafie, KH. Ilyas Rchiyat, Anwar Harjono and Malik Fadjar but not Amien Rais, the Muhammadiyah Chairman, leading the anti-Suharto student demonstrations and calling for the President's immediate resignation.[32] Discussed at the meeting were the reforms that the President needed to undertake in order to meet the growing demands for change on conditions that the participants in the meeting would not be members of the various bodies that were being proposed.[33]

Following the meeting with the '*Walisongos*', in the press

conference that followed, the President promised to undertake a number of measures to accommodate the demands for change. He said that 'the question of me stepping down is not a problem'. However, for the sake of national unity, he would continue as President and would lead the reform process as soon as possible. In this endeavour, he promised to undertake the following measures:

- Set up a reform committee whose members would include leaders and experts from Universities.
- Enact a law on general elections, political parties, the composition of the House of Representatives, People's Consultative Assembly and regional councils, an anti-monopoly law, an anti-corruption law, etc in line with the people's wishes.

- Hold general elections as soon as possible based on the new election law.
- Hold a general assembly of the People's Consultative Assembly following the election to establish the state guidelines, elect a President and Vice-President and establish further regulations. 'With this, I say that I a.m. not willing to be nominated again to become the President'.

- To undergo this heavy task, because of the crisis in the economic, legal and political areas, I will re-shuffle the Cabinet and the new Cabinet will be called the 'reform Cabinet'.[34]

This would mean that the President had deliberately opted for the third option, namely, to stay on as the President and to carry out total reform. President Suharto offered a peaceful transfer of power on his terms and it was not acceptable to many of his opponents. Thus, in the name of avoiding further bloodshed and instability, the President saw the need to hold on to his office while preparing for his graceful exit. The leaders of the 'Quit Suharto Movement' were, however, unimpressed and they continued to intensify the pressure on the President. At 11.00 a.m., Harmoko and other Parliamentary leaders held a five hour meeting with the leaders of the different fractions and a conclusion demanded that the President should resign according to the constitution. This was conveyed to Suharto in writing at 5.00 p.m. Amien Rais, to sustain the pressure, threatened to despatch one million people on the streets the following day, 20 May, which was being celebrated in Indonesia as the National Awakening Day. This raised the political temperature in the capital to an all-point high and the worst was being anticipated.

ABRI, however, deployed 78,000 soldiers throughout the capital and all key points were blockaded with barb-wire barricades in order to prevent the protest march. Due to the strengthened security situation in the capital and fearing a 'second Tiananmen' in Jakarta, in the early hours of 20 May, Amien Rais called off the planned 'one million people's power demonstration'. In a statement read over all radio stations, he said that 'to prevent this violence I am calling on the population to cancel the commemoration of the day of action towards reforms. I know you must all be disappointed but I am even more so'. He argued that 'the head of the Jakarta military command has clearly said that his side will take fire actions. I am worried that victims might fall among both the people and the military, and this will only endanger our campaign for reform'.[35] Having failed to organise the 'people's power protest march' in Jakarta, most of the protesters congregated at the parliamentary complex and continued their calls for Suharto to step down.

In the meantime, President Suharto and his key advisers tried to establish a National Committee for Reform, as was promised by the President in his press conference following his meeting with Muslim leaders on 19 May. Saadilah Mursjid, announced that the President would be issuing an executive order establishing the committee and this would include public figures and experts from the universities. Some of the possible candidates in the committee mentioned were Megawati Sukarnoputri, Amien Rais, Abdurrahman Wahid, General Wiranto, Ichlasul Amal (Rector, Gadjah Mada University), Liliek Hendradjaya (Rector, Bandung Institute of Technology), Ali Yafie (Deputy Chairman, Indonesian Council of Ulemas), Sudharmono (former Vice-President) and Anas Urbaningrum (Chairman, Indonesian Muslim Student Association).[36] Unfortunately by late evening on 20 May, Suharto and his key advisers, were unable to establish the reform committee, as the people approached, refused to be associated with the committee.[37] To make things worse, on the evening of the fateful day, Suharto was informed that 14 of his key ministers, majority of them handling the economic portfolios, were unprepared to be re-appointed as members of the 'Reform Cabinet'. Sensing that the market, streets, parliament, intellectuals and cabinet had deserted him, the President decided that it was time to step down. It was then that he instructed his key advisers to prepare for his resignation for the following day. The main officials involved were Saadilah Mursjid, his deputy, Bambang Kesowo, special assistant to the State Secretary, Sunarto Sudarmo, Yasril Djakob, the Military Secretary and Yusril Ihza Mahendra, the legal specialist from University of Indonesia.

On 21 May at 8.30 a.m., the entire parliamentary leadership gathered at the State Palace and at 8.50 a.m., Suharto met them. He told them that 'in order to comply with the wishes of the parliamentary leadership and that of the different fractions in the DPR, I have decided to actualise Article 8 of the

1945 Constitution. Gentlemen, please wait here while I inform the public of this decision'.[38] At 9.00 a.m., President Suharto, in the presence of the nation's leading judges and a number of selected officials, made the historic announcement of transferring power to his vice President, B. J. Habibie:

> During these recent times, I have been following carefully the development of our national situation, especially the aspirations of the people for reforms in all sectors in the life of our nation and state. Based on my deep understanding of these aspirations and prompted by the conviction that these reforms need to be implemented in an orderly, peaceful and constitutional manner for the sake of maintaining the unity and cohesion of the nation, and the continuity of the national development, I declared a plan to form the committee for reform and to change the composition of the Seventh Developmental Cabinet. But the reality to date has shown that the said Committee for reform cannot be materialised because there was no adequate response to the plan to form that Committee. In the wish of implementing these reforms in the best manner possible, I deem that faced with the impossibility of forming the committee, changes in the composition of the Seventh Developmental Cabinet are no longer necessary. Considering the above development, I am of the opinion that it would be very difficult for me to implement in a good manner, duties in governing the State and in development. Therefore, in line with Article 8 of the 1945 Constitution and after earnestly taking into consideration the views of the leadership of the Peoples' Consultative Council and the leadership of the factions in it, I have decided to declare that I have ceased to be the President of the Republic of Indonesia as to the time I read this on this day, Thursday, May 21 1998.

> In line with Article 8 of the 1945 Constitution, the

Vice-President of the Republic of Indonesia, Professor Doctor Engineer B. J. Habibie is the one who will
conclude the remainder of the presidential term,
holder of the Mandate of the MPR, for 1998-2003.[39]

As part of the resignation speech, President Suharto also
stated that 'for the assistance and support of the people while
I led the nation and state of Indonesia, I express my thanks
and I seek forgiveness if there were any mistakes and shortcomings'. He also said that 'because conditions do not allow
the taking of oath in front of the People's Consultative Council, to prevent a vacuum of leadership in implementing the
government of the state, the Vice-President should now take
his oath before the Supreme Court of the Republic of Indonesia'.[40] It was following this that the Vice-President, B. J.
Habibie, took the oath of office as Indonesia's third President
since independence before Chief Justice Sarwata. Following
this, General Wiranto, the ABRI Chief made the following
statement: 'I, as the military chief, as Minister of Defence,
would like to make a statement. First, with regard to the situation and development of recent times, ABRI, the military,
honourably accepts the withdrawal of Mr Suharto and, in
keeping with the Constitution, we assent to the appointment
of Vice-President Habibie as President. Standing united,
ABRI invites and exhorts society to accept the wishes of Mr
Suharto... in keeping with the Constitution'. General Wiranto,
then went on to assert that 'ABRI will protect the safety and
dignity of all former presidents, including President Suharto
and his family'.[41] The former President then returned to the
room where the key Parliamentary leaders were assembled, including Harmoko, Syarwan Hamid, Abdul Gafur, Ismail Hasan
Matereum and Fatimah Achmad and parted with the following
words to them: 'Friends, I am no longer the President. I hope
the DPR will look after the people and the State'.[42] With that,
Indonesia was ushered into the post-Suharto era.

95

NOTES

1   *The Jakarta Post*, 11 March 1998.

2   See John McBeth, 'Indonesia: Suharto's Way', *Far Eastern Economic Review*, 26 March 1998, p. 18.

3   *Ibid*, 16 April 1998, p. 19.

4   *Ibid*, 26 March 1998, p. 18.

5   Cited in *Ibid*, p. 19.

6   *Ibid*.

7   *Ibid*, p. 20.

8   See John McBeth, 'Indonesia: A Warning Shot', *Ibid*, 2 April 1998, p. 23.

9   Michael Vatikiotis, 'Consumers Caught in the Middle', *Ibid*, 9 April 1998, p. 15.

10   See Margot Cohen with John McBeth, 'Indonesia: The Vanishings', *Ibid*, 7 May 1998, p. 24 and 'A 'Disappeared' Speaks Out and His Testimony Implicates the Armed Forces', *Asiaweek*, 8 May 1998, p. 22.

11   Cited in *Far Eastern Economic Review*, 7 May 1998, p. 24.

12   See Margot Cohen, 'Indonesia: Campus Crusaders', *Ibid*, 26 March 1998, p. 26.

13   Cited in *The Jakarta Post*, 14 May 1998.

14   See *The New Paper*, 14 May 1998.

15   Cited in *The Jakarta Post*, 15 May 1998.

16   See John McBeth and Michael Vatikiotis, 'Indonesia: The Endgame', *Far Eastern Economic Review*, 28 May 1998, p. 15.

17   *The Jakarta Post*, 17 May 1998.

18   *Ibid*.

19   *Ibid*, 15 May 1998.

20   *Ibid*, 16 May 1998.

21   *Ibid*, 18 May 1998.

22   *Ibid*, 8 and 10 May 1998.

23   *Ibid*, 10 May 1998.

24   *Ibid*, 16 May 1998.

25   *Ibid*, 18 May 1998.

26   *Ibid*.

27   See *The New Paper*, 16 May 1998 and 'No Split within ABRI', *The Sunday Times*, 17 May 1998.

28   *The Jakarta Post*, 19 May 1998.

29   *Ibid*.

30   See *Megapos*, Vol. 1. No. 4, 28 November – 5 December 1998. pp. 2-3.

31   See 'Detik-detik Yang Menegangkan', *Gatra*, 30 May 1998, p. 28.

32   According to Nurcholish Majid, when the list of the people to attend the 'special meeting' with the President was being discussed, he asked, 'How about my classmate?' When the President asked, 'who?' and Nurcholish replied, Amien Rais, Suharto, said, 'Hold on' and that was how Amien was excluded from the '*Walisongo*' meeting. See *Ibid*.

33   *Ibid*.

34   See *The Straits Times*, 20 May 1998.

35   *The New Paper*, 20 May 1998.

36   *The Jakarta Post*, 21 May 1998.

37   At 9.00 p.m. on 20 May, Quraish Shihab, the Religious Affairs Minister is reported to have approached Nurcholish Majid to chair Reform Committee. Then that was turned down, the President is to have said,

'I better resign. If a moderate like Cak Nur do not want to be a member of the Reform Committee, I have no chance but to resign.'

38   See *Gatra*, 30 May 1998, p. 28.

39   The full text of the Suharto's resignation speech can be found in *The Australian*, 22 May 1998.

40   *Ibid.*

41   See *The New Paper*, 21 May 1998 and *The Jakarta Post*, 22 May 1998.

42   See *Gatra*, 30 May 1998, p. 28.

5

Contending Explanations of Suharto's Fall: A People's Power Revolution or a Political Conspiracy?

INTRODUCTION

How did a man in the position of President Suharto, who only 72 days earlier, was overwhelmingly elected by the MPR for his seventh term for the Presidency, fall so unexpectedly and in many ways, in such a precipitous manner? Many have argued that it was a 'people's power movement', led by the students, that brought him down.

In particular, the Western media and many of their supporters in Indonesia, have attempted to project Suharto's fall as a consequence and end product of growing democratisation with the rise of 'people's power', the true of sovereign in any polity, deciding that the 'strongman' must go. The West, since the onset of the post-Cold War era, has been championing the cause of democracy and human rights, and in this context, the strongman rule of Suharto had been viewed as an anathema and bad example that should be eradicated. In addition, there were many in the West that had attempted to ascribe to Indonesia the Huntingtonian 'civilisational paradigm' and where the simple Islam-Christianity divide had been invoked. Here, Indonesia as the largest Islamic country in the world, had been a natural target for vilification and in order to prevent the 'minorities' [read, Christians] from being persecuted, it was necessary that the 'Islamic dictator', Suharto, who had been mobilising Islamic-oriented groups, best evident by his sponsorship of ICMI, be checked. What the above 'thesis' had tried to imply was that President Suharto was a 'victim' of his own developmental policies. With the rise of the Indonesian middle-class and other concerned with the politics of 'democratisation' as well as due to the ramifications of 'globalisation', there was no way Suharto could have continued to sustain his 'authoritarian regime' and his fall was the consequence of the rise of the 'third wave' of democratisation that had engulfed the country in the last few years.

Attractive and convincing as the 'thesis' may appear, when one analyses the developments in Indonesia in the period after the March 1998 MPR Session, especially between 12 and 20 May, then the 'people's power' thesis can be easily dismissed as being somewhat simplistic, even naive. This is because what actually transpired was an intense power struggle between different elite groups in Jakarta, with Suharto's fall as one of many consequences of this power play. In this regard, one can agree with Father Sandywan Sumardi of the Jakarta Social Institute that the struggle for power was the key to understanding the mid-May 1998 looting and rapes, and the earlier incidents of violence, including the fatal shooting of four demonstrators at Trisakti University, and the abduction and torture of more than 20 pro-democracy activists. He dismissed the 'May Revolution' as a 'spontaneous explosion caused by long-smouldering resentment over economic disparity'. Rather, in his view, 'the orgy of organised violence stemmed from a conflict among key Indonesian power-holders that drew on racial hatred. This was not about ethnicity. It was an inter-elite conflict that needed victims'.[1] On 22 July 1998, *The Straits Times* (Singapore) editorial argued, in response to the growing anti-Chinese pogroms in Surabaya, East Java, that 'their [the Indonesian Chinese in May] suffering bore mute witness to the unspeakable consequences that follow when laws governing human behaviour are suspended, even tempo-rarily. The attacks, which were targeted at some of the most vulnerable members of the community, were all the more hei-nous because they are suspected to have been organised by certain individuals to secure specific ends during the mayhem that culminated in President Suharto's fall from power'.[2]

In the same vein, Emha Ainun Nadjib, one of the nine *Walisongos* whom President Suharto met on 18 May 1998, stated on 25 June at a gathering of students from Mamba'ul Ulum Islamic College in Solo, Central Java, that 'the recent resignation of former President Suharto was engineered by people who had carefully conspired to topple the long serving leader'. According to him, President Suharto wanted to end his five-year term in 2003 on a good note but certain groups managed to force him to quit. While not identifying the indi-viduals or groups involved, he argued that 'in their efforts to oust Suharto, the groups attacked the character of the former President's protégé and son-in-law, Lieutenant-General Prabowo Subianto by accusing him of masterminding the highly publi-cised cases of kidnapped activists and slaying of protesting students'. Emha argued that 'naturally these ploys damaged the reputation of Suharto, especially when they were backed up by press reports from unclear sources such as the Internet'. According to Emha, 'mass riots erupted in Jakarta on May 13, sparked by the fatal shooting of four students at West Ja-karta's Trisakti University a day earlier. The unrest prompted Su-harto to cut short a trip to Egypt, and despite his efforts to remain in power, he soon resigned at the behest of public pressure'.

However, according to Emha, 'there was more than public

101

pressure that caused the national leader to step down. Prabowo, who served as Chief of KOSTRAD and was former head of the Army's elite KOPASSUS force, was Suharto's most reliable security affairs man. Prabowo was the fastest rising star in ABRI, gaining promotion after promotion. Critics said that nepotism was clearly the reason for his rapid ascendancy through the ranks'. However, Emha argued that Prabowo was 'a quality military official and others simply could not compete with his career'. According to Emha, 'Prabowo was targeted because other officers were jealous of his good military career and because he is close to Muslims and has always refused to collude with wealthy Chinese businessmen. In this case, Prabowo would certainly become a threat to other high-ranking officers who are engaged in practices of collusion with ethnic Chinese persons'. Hence, the rumour mill in Jakarta alleged that Prabowo ordered the kidnapping and deaths of certain activists as well as the Trisakti shootings. A power struggle between Prabowo and Defence Minister/ABRI Commander, General Wiranto was also said to be taking place'. Emha argued that the apparent rift between Wiranto and Prabowo had been entirely contrived in order to mislead the public into thinking that Prabowo was working alone'. He also maintained that 'it was the unidentified groups who are behind the kidnappings and most responsible for the Trisakti shootings. If KOPASSUS were the perpetrators, they would not have kidnapped small time activists like Haryanto Taslam and Pius Lustrilanang', he argued. Emha also dismissed the charge that Suharto had ordered Prabowo to kidnap the activists in a bid to quell protests against the former President.[3]

Despite the temptation to describe Suharto as an 'evil genius' and the *dalang* behind most of Indonesia's misery, including being the principal 'engineer' behind the 1965 GESTAPU abortive coup, in reality, the achievements of Indonesia under Suharto and the New Order cannot be discounted. In addition to 'saving' the nation from the scourge of Communism in

1965, Suharto also succeeded in maintaining national unity and bringing about economic development. Prior to the onset of the 'Asian meltdown' in July-August 1997, Indonesia achieved economic success after success with economic growth reaching 8 percent per year, including some US$30 billion a year in foreign direct investments. Indonesia was expected to become the world's fifth largest economy by the year 2020.

In this connection, despite the Suharto regime being described as one overwhelmed by KKN, corruption, collusion and nepotism, yet, historically speaking it made a number of achievements. President Habibie, in an interview with the author on 3 October 1998 stated that the most important achievements of former President Suharto was in the area of human resource development. The Suharto's administration succeeded in transforming the largely 'random mentality' of the people to one which was largely developmental and programme-oriented. In this connection, the New Order succeeded in building up a generation of talented cadres and skilled individuals, in turn, which enhanced competition, including in the political arena and which may have inevitably brought about Suharto's downfall.[4]

In the same vein, the Minister of Co-operatives and Small Business, Adi Sasono, told the author that President Suharto and his government did chalk up some very impressive achievements. He argued that, "in my opinion, Suharto has done a lot of good deeds for the country". There were four main achievements in particular, he argued. First, he established a good and developed economic infrastructure and made much progress in the traditional and informal economic structure of the country, such as in fishing and traditional farming. This helped to create a new economic culture, in turn, allowing the economy to takeoff at a later stage, until it was 'hit' by the Asian economic crisis. In this connection, Suharto did introduce modern management system and allowed new ways to be introduced in tackling economic problems.

Second, Suharto's policies allowed a new middle class to emerge and this was due mainly to the successes of the New Order in the area of education. When Suharto took power in 1966, the literacy rate was only 20 percent and by 1998, it had soared to more than 90 percent, a commendable achievement by any standards. Third, Suharto and his government also succeeded in tackling the problem of absolute poverty. In 1966, the figure stood at 65 percent and just before Indonesia was hit by the economic crisis, this was reduced to only 11 percent, a "great achievement indeed", argued Adi. Finally, Adi argued that Suharto was primarily responsible for introducing an "open sky policy" for the country since 1984 and it was these policies that led to the rise of massive social consciousness in the country, including values such as human rights, democracy, equality, justice and equity. In many ways, it was due to these 'achievements' that later, "Suharto became a victim of his own success" as he could not keep up with the changes around him, largely brought about by his own policies in the last fifteen years or so.[5]

In an attempt to present a balanced assessment of Suharto's fall, three main 'explanations' would be adopted in an attempt to understand this historic event, which has and will continue to have great ramifications for Indonesia, its immediate neighbours and the region beyond.

THE THREE KEYS TO SUHARTO'S FALL

In view of this, it is necessary to look anew and deeper to understand the circumstances that brought Suharto down. Here, a number of questions need to be answered? First, why did the President seek re-election in March 1998 despite repeatedly stating that he was prepared to step down? What made the President believe that he was still wanted, respected and trusted by the people and that he could hang on to the Presidency for another term? Even though he asked the GOLKAR leadership in late 1997 to 'recheck' his endorsement by the people, why was Suharto still nominated as the sole candidate for the Presidency even though later, it was reported that the people were rejecting him? Was it simply a make-belief creation by some officials and trusted aides who wanted to hasten Suharto's exit and that the only way possible to remove him from office was through 'people's power' rather than persuading him to do so? Or, were these officials only keen in having Suharto around so that they could continue to benefit from his presence due to their official vested interest and stakes in the system? Why did Suharto agree to remove fuel subsidies even though the IMF was prepared to delay implementing that part of the package for fear of sparking unrest in the country? Why did the President leave for Cairo even though the political, economic and security situation in the country had already deteriorated? Was Suharto advised to do so or did he do these on his own volition? Why did ABRI react so slowly to the worsening security situation in the Jakarta and more important, why did General Wiranto and his key officers choose to attend a military ceremony in Malang, Central Java, even though the riots were raging in the capital? Was Suharto totally out of touch with reality, not realising the gravity of the situation the country was in or was he cajoled into that position so that someone or some group could take advantage of the situation to overthrow the Suharto regime and come to power? In order to answer these questions, the following explanations would attempt to shed some light.

EXPLANATION ONE:
THE CONSEQUENCE OF SUHARTO'S POLITICAL ARCHITECTURE

In a way, there were two sets of factors inter-reacting with each other, culminating in the downfall of Suharto. The first pertained to the political architecture which Suharto constructed to remain in power. As alluded earlier, the 'Suharto system' entailed a number of pillars: politicisation of the bureaucracy, politicisation of the Armed Forces, uprooting of political parties at the local level and preventing political parties in general from performing their legitimate and proper function of representing the voters through the expression and articulation of their interests within and through the different political parties. At the same time, Suharto, using constitutional and extra-constitutional means, succeeded in gaining control of all the levers of power in the country so much so that nothing significant could operate without Suharto's agreement or affirmation. If the President was opposed to it, the chances were that it would not take off. At the same time, the President tried to give a gloss of legality and constitutionality to all his levers of control in the political system and it became almost *de rigueur* for Suharto to comment, in his last few years in power, that any change was possible, including his stepping down, as long as it was legally and constitutionally undertaken.

Thus, Suharto's control system could be seen in the President's control and veto power in the administration of the MPR, DPR, GOLKAR, ABRI, the bureaucracy, the economy and mass organisations in general. By manipulating the various elements of the 'political architecture', through a policy of 'divide and rule' and 'management through conflict', Suharto was able to ensure the continuity of regime from 1966 to 1998. In the end, however, due to the nature of the structure which Suharto created, his ability to manipulate further was constrained and limited, mainly due to the rise of the new political situation in the country. The political architecture was such that only he and no one could manipulate it. Once he could no longer so do, in part, due to his declining health and physical prowess, Suharto became less vigilant, especially as he lost many of his key and able lieutenants and surrounded himself with mediocre and incapable advisers and ministers. This was especially following the death of his wife, Ibu Tien. As his capacity to manipulate the rigidly structured architecture declined, the political system weakened and eventually collapsed. In many ways, Suharto became a victim of his own system. He was brought down, not so much by the economic downturn, riots or students demonstrations as much as by the fallout of the political system which he created. Once he failed to police and control the political system that controlled every aspect of the political life in the country, its collapse was a foregone conclusion. What is even more significant is that the political system was customise and personal to him, and once the situation was beyond him, he had no choice but to surrender power.

At the same time, there were many 'wrongs' in the system, which over time, had the cumulative effect of signalling that the President was simply incapable, or worst, uninterested, in managing the country. This further undermined and weakened Suharto's political architecture of control. What were these wrongs and failures?

Failure to Solve the Economic Crisis

Since July 1997, the country's currency was under attack by speculators and until Suharto's fall in May 198, he had failed to solve the problem, something which even his successor has continued to grapple with in the first few months of his Presidency. Suharto was forced out of office in disgrace to the extent that he left behind a shattered economy brought about by the currency crisis and where he had no answer to the problem. The woes of the economic crisis in Indonesia is best evident from the fact that the per capita income in the country has plummeted down to about US$200, representing a drop of 80 percent from the mid-1997 level and where more than 50 percent of the people are said to be living below poverty level.

Symbol of Corruption, Collusion and Nepotism

A major reason Indonesia's economy was in a shattered state was due to the unsound fundamentals on which it was premised. By the time Suharto resigned, the acronmy *KKN* came to personify him and his regime and where K stood for *Korupsi*, corruption, *Kolusi*, collusion and N *nepotisme*, nepotism.

Failure to Overcome Poverty and Drastic Income Disparities

One of the lasting negative legacies of the Suharto era was the fact that despite the rapid economic development which the country experience from the late 1960s onwards, the distribution of the wealth was extremely uneven, and what was worst, where there was a direct co-relation between wealth and ethnicity. Suharto's policies of corruption and collusion permitted the ethnic Chinese, who were the major engine of growth in the country, to accumulate immense wealth and it was this massive income gap which became a major sore point as Suharto came to be viewed as a leader bent only for creating wealth for the ethnic Chinese. Thus, even though Suharto oversaw the rapid growth of the country GNP and per capita income rose from US$60 in 1965 to US$1000 in mid-1997, what was also clear was that the 3.5 percent ethnic Chinese owed nearly 80 percent of the country's private wealth. This also helped to explain the general anti-Chinese sentiments in the country, which came to a head in the May revolution.

Remained in Power for Too Long and Appeared to be Out of Touch with People's Aspirations

By being in near absolute power since 1966, especially through the mid-1970s to the mid-1990s, Suharto was credited for all the major achievements in the country, especially in terms of economic development, political stability and educational upliftment of his people. In good times, he was reveredly referred to as the 'Father of National Development'. At the same time, due to the longevity of his rule, he also became the sole depository of all ills that faced the country, especially with regard to the economic downturn and the attendant social problems that followed. By staying in power for too long, especially his decision to contest the Presidency in March 1998, he avail himself as a convenient target for all critics and opponents to the system, and if anything, what united the opposition was only a single issue, 'down with Suharto and his policies', and when this was largely achieved, the political opposition dissipated.

Failed to Institute a System of Political Succession

Related to staying too long in power was Suharto key mistake of failing to institute a system of political succession that would not have required a 'revolution' to take place and where the President was literally forced out of office. Arguing that there is a constitutional mechanism and that it would take care of the problem was not good enough. In the end, even though Suharto should be credited for stepping down and handing over power to his Vice-President, in accordance with the constitution, yet, it took many weeks of instability and many lives to force the President out of office, with Indonesia's 'succession' history being recorded with bloodshed every time it has taken place.

Fallout from Natural and Man-made Disasters

Suharto was also unfortunate that his last few years were marked by all kinds of disasters. The country was hit by the haze crisis which affected Malaysia, Singapore, Brunei and Papua New Guinea, by massive floods, earthquakes, prolonged drought, causing massive starvation and loss of lives. In the last few years, the country has suffered a number of major air crashes, which took a few hundred lives. While this had the effect of further weakening the economy and impoverishing the people, for the majority of the Javanese, it was also perceived as 'signs' that the 'Heavens' were unhappy with the 'king' and that until he was not removed, these 'disasters' were expected to continue. For the traditional Javanese, these disasters were telltales that the 'king' had lost his 'mandate' to rule the country, and when Suharto fell, there was not much excitement *per se* as this was viewed as the 'will of God'.

EXPLANATION TWO:
POLITICAL CONSPIRACY AND SUHARTO'S FALL

What is equally important is the issue as to how come Suharto lost control of the political situation and as to whether there were groups working to achieve this goal? A number of political observers have argued that Suharto's downfall was contrived by his political opponents, who were the main beneficiaries of the collapse of the New Order. This brings us to the second factor that brought Suharto down, being a fallout of one of Suharto's key creations, namely, ICMI in December 1990.[6] President Suharto realised the important role Islam was playing in Indonesia, in part, due to the fact that 80 percent of the population were of the Islamic faith. Any government in the country had to live in an uneasy partnership with the Muslims and this has been a reality since the time of the Dutch. After managing, and at times, suppressing them, by 1990, Suharto realised that he had no choice but to respond to the pressure to establish ICMI. By doing so, Suharto hoped to engage the Muslim intellectuals and extremists, whom he thought could be placed in a 'golden cage'. For Suharto, ICMI was to serve two key purposes: first, to garner support from the majority of the people for the general elections, first 1993 and later, 1998, and second, to reduce the tension between the Muslims and ABRI, especially since the Muslims were increasingly arguing that they were being 'persecuted' by the Christian-Abangan dominated ABRI leadership, with the Lampung and Tanjung Priok shootings pointed out as evidence of this discrimination. By giving the Muslims a political platform, the President hoped that various issues and grievances could be aired and a direct clash with ABRI averted. At the same time, it was also Suharto's way of managing ABRI, which was believed to have become increasingly restless and unhappy with the President and his policies, especially with regard to the First Family 'business' interests in the country.

ICMI was officially launched by the President in December 1990 with B. J. Habibie, the Minister of State for Research and Technology and concurrently Chairman of the Agency for the Assessment and Application of Technology, appointed as Chairman of the organisation. Habibie's political clout was first demonstrated in 1993, when he was given a relatively free hand to select a large number of ministers to the cabinet. Following this, the role and influence of ICMI have been in the ascendant with Habibie increasingly described as the 'super-minister' mainly due to his access to President Suharto. This continued through to the following election when Habibie was elected as the country's Vice-President in March 1998.

Here, some have argued that Habibie's was chosen as Suharto's running mate mainly due to the growing clout of the Islamic lobby, especially ICMI. However, there was also the view that Suharto chose Habibie mainly to silent and domesticate the increasingly restless, at times hostile, Islamic lobby.

This view argues that Habibie's nomination as the running mate of Suharto was totally the result of Suharto's calculations and that it had nothing to do with the pressure from the Muslims. Habibie may feel good that the Muslims may be behind him but in reality, Habibie owe the Muslims nothing. If anything, Habibie's selection as the Vice-President was a masterly move by Suharto to co-opt the Muslims. If this was true, then the Muslim lobby, especially ICMI, had much to fear and be disheartened with Suharto, including the nomination and election of Habibie as the Vice-President, as ICMI was nothing more than a tool for Suharto to remain predominant in Indonesian politics.

The view that Habibie and ICMI were the objects of Suharto's machinations was confirmed by a number of senior ICMI officials who were privy to most of the politics involving Habibie and ICMI from the pre-MPR period right up to the fall of Suharto in May 1998. According to this thesis, in Indonesian history, only two individuals can claim the status of being 'extraordinary individuals', namely, Sukarno, as the proclamator of national independence and Suharto, as the saviour of the nation following the PKI coup in 1965. This also explained the long rule of both individuals. For Suharto, during his long rule, he made many mistakes but was tolerated by the people as long as he did not threaten the country's unity and development. Unfortunately, however, the cumulative effect of his mistakes was to undermine his legitimacy and when it reached a particular point, there was only one thing on people's mind – they wanted the downfall of Suharto as they no longer feared him and wanted nothing to do with him any more. Due to growing awareness of the people, on the one hand, and the increasingly blatant practices of corruption and nepotism by the First Family, on the other, especially when people's misfortunes were at the height during the economic crisis, people's rage reached a climax and when this 'political anger' was mobilised and exploited by ICMI and its strategists, Suharto had no answer but to step down as he did not know how to deal with the opposition of 'people's power'.

According to this view, Suharto could have been saved if he had been less arrogant of his staying power and had read the political realities that had emerged since the general elections in May 1997 a little more carefully. When Habibie was selected as Suharto's running mate, the President thought that ICMI and their supporters could be acquisced as their leader had been given the second most important political post in the country. However, ICMI leaders, especially Adi Sasono, its Secretary-General, wanted more. Adi's key unhappiness was his realisation that Suharto had appointed Habibie as the Vice-President only to give his daughter and son, Tutut and Bambang respectively, a free hand to choose the key members of the new cabinet. In fact, both the Suharto's siblings were said to have opposed Habibie's nomination as the Vice-President and in exchange, Suharto succumbed to the pressure of both his children as far the cabinet's design was concerned. For Adi, Habibie's elevation to the Vice-Presidency was nothing more than a 'golden cage' to constrain ICMI and its growing role. When this became known, Adi and his supporters were said to have lobbied very strongly, including through Habibie, to have some of ICMI members appointed to the cabinet but to no avail. According to this thesis, if only Suharto had accommodated Adi's demands, then the President could have been saved in a dignified manner and the May Revolution could have been averted. If Suharto had accommodated Adi and his friends with regard to the cabinet appointments and where only some ministries were being requested, Suharto may even have emerged stronger. Instead, not only did Suharto fail to accept a single ICMI candidate into the cabinet, Habibie was 'exiled' abroad by being given a range of duties which dealt with foreign affairs rather than domestic politics. Adi and his friends interpreted this as a Suharto provocation to make ICMI irrelevant and marginalised in Indonesian domestic politics. The consensus in ICMI leadership was the Suharto had 'used' ICMI for his electoral purposes and following this, the President discarded the Muslim organisation by offering nothing except candies. Thus, when Suharto announced his cabinet line-up on 14 March 1998, Adi and his friends, in disgust, were said to have activated their plans to overthrow Suharto by revolutionary means with the battle to be fought on the 'streets' through 'people's power'. This thesis maintains that the 'war against Suharto' was declared immediately after the President had announced his cabinet line up on 14 March 1998. A ranking General close to the then President Suharto told the author that the belief that Suharto was grooming his daughter to take over as the future President and the manner both Tutut and Bambang were given a 'free hand' to appoint the Cabinet were extremely important in bringing about Suharto's fall. In fact, if anything, according to this General, the onset of the Bambang-Tutut cabinet was in reality 'the straw that broke the camel's back'.[7]

Adi and ICMI agitators exploited the massive unhappiness in society, especially the economic crisis and more important, the various demands raised by the students. In the end, it was the students which Adi exploited the most, with the demonstrations and their demands gaining momentum day by day. The students were, however, disunited and radarless, fearful of Suharto's security forces and apparatus as well as of being infiltrated and manipulated by agent provocateurs. The students were also without an economic base to sustain a prolonged struggle and had no real political roadmap as where the demonstrations would lead to. ICMI leaders saw the students as being very idealistic, impressionable and even gullible. The ICMI leadership, especially Adi, argued that the student political constituency should be exploited before it was taken over by other elements disgruntled with the Suharto regime, including the military as was the case in the period 1965-1966. During this period, especially from 14 March until early May 1998, the students were only united by their opposition to Suharto's failure to put the economy right, something which was said to have been worsened by the 'crony-oriented' cabinet.

On the whole, the students were not ideologically driven or united. They only wanted 'political fun' and the mileage and freedom that they had enjoyed thus far was acting as a magnet, drawing more and more students from all over the country to Jakarta. The students had no nation-wide organisation or action plan. It was in these circumstances that Adi and his key lieutenants decided to give the student movement a direction and form, so as to mobilise them against Suharto and his government. One of Suharto's biggest mistakes was to appoint Wiranto Arismunandar, the former Rector of Bandung Institute of Technology, as the new Education Minister. Wiranto Arismunandar was particularly hated by the students in Bandung and was known in the student community as someone who was unsympathetic to the students' cause. This was like pouring fuel into the fire and something which ICMI activists readily exploited.

ICMI activists succeeded in mobilising the students and from then onwards, the students started saying provocative things and became more aggressive, with Suharto and his family becoming the main targets of the demonstrations. In this endeavour, Adi succeeded in garnering the services and support of Amien Rais, the Chairman of Muhammadiyah and a fellow ICMI activist. Adi's instructions to his activists was simple: ICMI's hand in mobilising the students should be unseen with Amien Rais projected as the leader of the movement. This was prompted by two reasons: first, it was in line with Amien Rais' speeches where he had been talking about and calling for a 'people's power' movement to overthrow Suharto and his regime, and in this regard, his leadership and support for the student demonstrations would appear normal and natural; second, being a political scientist from the Uni-

115

versity of Gadjah Mada, Amien's leadership of the students would be regarded as something normal and understandable and would not raise unnecessary questions of political engineering or manoeuvering. Thus, on both scores, Amien was acceptable to all the key political constituencies bent on bringing Suharto down, especially the students. In the main, from April 1998 onwards, most of the students' political demands, statements and demonstrations were co-ordinated by ICMI activists, Adi's primary aim being to maintain the 'anti-Suharto momentum' in an effort to force the President to make concessions as far as reforms were concerned, especially with regard to a cabinet reshuffle. This theme continued right up to 12 May 1998 when the students at Trisakti University were shot. According to this view, until 12 May, the basic slogan of the student movement under control of ICMI was a phrase borrowed from W. S. Rendra, the country's leading poet and this was 'struggle'. The shooting at Trisakti University changed all this with a new slogan, 'victory', replacing the earlier one. However, the eventual 'victory' was not easily achieved as there were many occasions when the 'old fox', Suharto, almost outmanoeuvred the ICMI activists.

The 12–21 May 1998 Conspiracy: 10 Days that Transformed Indonesia

The opportunity to undermine the Suharto regime was best provided by the President's absence from the capital for a week from 9 May onwards as he left for Egypt to attend the Group of 15 Summit followed by a state visit to Egypt. As he was leaving the country, the President spoke to the journalists at the airport in Jakarta as follows:

> I have confidence in the people. I am leaving the country calm, hopeful that political and national sta-

116

bility can be maintained. In my absence, I hope every thing goes well, especially the work on reforms. But we must not let demands for reform destroy everything we have achieved through development. I plead for the people's understanding. I understand their suffering because I come from a poor family...I trust that the people will put the interest of the country and nation ahead of their individual interests. If we forget the importance of political stability and national stability, our efforts to solve the crisis will be undermined.[8]

However, on the ground, the situation had reached a point of no return, especially as far as the student movement was concerned. The stakes were further raised when Amien Rais announced on 11 May that a 'people's leadership team' would be formed on 20 May, the day celebrated in Indonesia as National Awakening Day. Amien told a press conference that they should 'just wait and see sometime around May 20.... There will be about 30 or 40 public figures from various elements of society who will be demanding numerous improvements in the economic and political life of Indonesia'.[9] Amien argued that this was urgently needed as the Suharto regime was like 'stagnant water': 'Just as water stagnates in a sewer, that is how we are now. Being stagnant like that, the water only collects disease. That is why it has to flow'.[10]

What was supposed to be a simple 'flow of water' in a sewer was transformed into a massive *tsunami* that hit the whole of Indonesia, especially Jakarta, and the catalyst for this was provided by the fatal shooting of 4 Trisakti University students by security forces on 12 May. While the identity of the people who shot the students is still being debated, the impact of the killing was to add a totally new dimension to the anti-Suharto movement. The conspiracy theory argues that the shooting was deliberately provoked to fan the student movement and there were hopes that if the students went on a rampage in Jakarta, the President, who was abroad, may panicked and 'exile' himself abroad *a la Marcos*.

The dead students were buried the following day as 'reform heroes' and speech after speech, including by Ali Sadikin, W. S. Rendra, Amien Rais and Megawati Sukarnoputri, exhorted the masses to take revenge and overthrow Suharto. The Rector of Trisakti University, Professor Mudanto Martejo, for instance, stated, when he handed over the four dead bodies to their family members that 'this is a grey day for Trisakti University's Big Family with the death of the students. I am convinced the title of 'Heroes of Reformation' conferred on them will find wide acceptance among all the people who crave reforms [even though] they may not be regarded as heroes in the government's eyes because they were considered to be disturbing national stability'.[11]

The anger and rage of the people against the shooting at Trisakti University triggered a full-scale violent rioting and looting in Jakarta on 13 May. With more than 5,000 buildings torched and more than 1,300 people killed. The main target of the violence was the economically prosperous ethnic Chinese and their properties and businesses. What was somewhat surprising was the 'low level' security presence throughout the capital. Here, two explanations were provided. First, the security forces were withdrawn in order to prevent further clashes with the students for fear of causing further bloodshed. Second, the security forces, on instructions of their superiors, may have connived with the 'conspirators' to exacerbate the insecurity situation by giving the demonstrators a 'free-for all' opportunity to wreck havoc against the ethnic Chinese and their businesses, which to many, was the most obvious symbol of Suharto's cronyism and corruption, and where the victims were the *Pribumi* masses.

According to a senior ICMI official, at about 3.00 p.m. on 13 May, in view of the worsening security situation in the capital, the Commander of the Army Strategic Reserves Command, Lieutenant-General Prabowo Subianto, together with a large escort force, descended on ICMI and CIDES Headquarters and held discussions with Adi Sasono and the ICMI leadership. General Prabowo's main concern was the fast deteriorating security situation in the capital and he asked Adi and his friends to help calm down the situation. When the ICMI leadership asked Prabowo to explain the reasons behind the worsening security situation, the General replied that intelligence reports suggested that anti-government forces, both from the left and right as well as opportunists were behind the violence. General Prabowo was to repeat this three days later when he told a press conference that 'there was a shadowy political motive behind the recent rioting. Some people have been waiting for this to happen. There are groups that want this country to collapse into catastrophe'.[12] General Prabowo opined that the anti-Chinese thrust of the violence, riots and looting was aimed at mobilising the Muslim majority against an easily 'identifiable economic and political enemy' which was also a minority, and to that extent, these riots were highly engineered and organised.

On 14 May, the rioting and violence continued in Jakarta, including the alleged mass rapes of Chinese females. This was almost akin to 'ethnic cleansing' *a la Indonesia* with the object of frightening the ethnic Chinese in the country. According to a senior ICMI officials, a senior police officer in-charge of the capital region told him that he would like to remain neutral in the emerging conflict: 'Don't ask me. I am not involved in this politics and I have no intentions of taking sides with anyone'. This implied that the law and order agencies and its officers must have concluded that what was taking place in Jakarta since the shooting of the four students was a 'political operation' in which the Police had no role and was no longer a simple 'security operation'.

That the worsening situation was being engineered by certain groups became more obvious when a number of ICMI

119

leaders flew to Jogjakarta on 14 May to organise themselves politically so that sustained pressure could be mounted on Suharto. Adi led this group and his main purpose was to confer with Amien Rais on the setting up an umbrella organisation that would lead the 'revolution against Suharto'. The umbrella organisation would establish a 'united front' among all the key Islamic organisations in the country. Earlier, on 11 May, Amien Rais had proposed the establishment of a 'People's Leadership Council' or *Majelis Pemimpin Rakyat*. Adi was, however, opposed to this idea as it was being described as a 'shadow government' and this would be counterproductive to the mobilisational efforts since it could undermine the growing momentum against Suharto and his government. Adi proposed the establishment of the *Majelis Amanah Rakyat* or Council for People's Mandate and which would exclude Abdurrahman Wahid and Megawati. Adi's thrust was to emphasis on the 'people' rather than 'leadership' dimension as this would be a 'winner' in the prevailing circumstances and mood, which demanded the empowerment of the people and not leaders. Amien found this agreeable and Adi flew to Jakarta the same day. MAR was inaugurated the following day in Jakarta by Amien Rais and his friends.

After Adi left for Jakarta, a little while later, Amien did the same, and this was undertaken deliberately so that the 'alliance' between Adi and Amien would not be exposed. On reaching Jakarta, Amien headed for the Muhammadiyah office located at Menteng, Jakarta and throughout the journey in the capital, he was mobbed by the students who saw him as their hero. Later, Amien called on Adi at the ICMI Headquarters and in this meeting, General Prabowo was also invited to attend. Others present were senior ICMI leaders including Ahmad Tirtosudiro. What was important about this particular meeting was the emergence of ICMI's position that for the sake of Indonesia's unity, stability and to prevent further bloodshed, Suharto should be persuaded to step down. While

Prabowo was brought in to 'sensitise' the ABRI leadership about the fast changing developments, the KOSTRAD Commander also pointed out that ABRI was trying to avoid clashes with the demonstrators as this was counterproductive all the more since ABRI was supposed to be from the people.

Later, in the evening of 14 May, MAR held its inaugural meeting and in the words of a senior ICMI official, the gathering was like a 'rainbow coalition' of all those who wanted to bring Suharto down. If anything, the only consensus MAR could reach was with regard to their ultimate target, namely, Suharto's resignation. At the same time, it was agreed that the pressure on Suharto should be sustained as a similar 'historic opportunity' may not come again. That evening, Adi and Amien slept in the Muhammadiyah office in Menteng.

That evening too, Adi and his friends were informed that 'anti-ICMI' elements were planning to launch a counter 'rainbow coalition' and this group was to be led by secular and *Abangan*-oriented leaders. The new 'rainbow coalition', the *Forum Kerja Indonesia* was to be headed by Amien Rais, Megawati and Gus Dur and this was to be launched on 15 May. On hearing this, Adi and his key lieutenants decided to 'sabotage' FKI by making sure that Amien was not part of the group. Even though the FKI people continued to call Amien 'almost non-stop', the messages did not reach him. On 15 May, Amien was scheduled to give a talk at Al Azhar Mosque in Jakarta and there were also other plans for him to talk to students. Adi, however, quickly got his boys to organise an important meeting in Jogjakarta and immediately following Amien's Al Azhar speech, the Muhammadiyah Chairman was whisked to the airport and when FKI was launched, Amien was not part of it even though earlier it had been announced that he was one of the three leaders. Strategically, it was a great success for ICMI and its like-minded groups as Amien Rais, symbolically of great political value, was not shared with the secular-Abangan group. A senior ICMI official thought that this 'cloak and dagger' mission was interesting but very stressful and tense due to the high stakes involved.

If anything, on 15 May, Adi scored another great success and hence, added another nail in Suharto's political coffin when the *Badan Kordinasi Ummat Islam* or the Body for the Co-ordination of Muslim Followers. In essence, this body was formed to co-ordinate the activities of all major Muslim mass organisations and in the words of a senior ICMI official, it brought together, in a formal way, all the Masjumi-oriented organisations in Indonesia under one body. This was organised so that it could be used as a 'show of force' in the near future when necessary.

On the following day, 16 May, Adi spoke at Al Azhar Mosque and where he launched a blistering attack on Suharto. According to a ranking ICMI official, this was the launch of the 'war cry' and it marked an important turning point in the 'War Against Suharto' as the ICMI leaders were now openly calling for the overthrow of Suharto. Following this, Adi telephoned Harmoko and Syarwan Hamid, the Chairman and Deputy Chairman of the MPR and DPR respectively but could not contact them as they were in a meeting with key cabinet ministers. Adi than rushed to the MPR/DPR complex and conferred with both Harmoko and Syarwan. Adi impressed upon both parliamentary leaders that as representatives of the people, their main obligations were to the people and not the leader, Suharto. Adi told the parliamentary leaders that they should start thinking of structuring a political system for the post-Suharto era and to this, both Harmoko and Syarwan responded positively and asked Adi to be part of the post-Suharto power structure. Adi told Harmoko to present a 'reform cabinet' that would be acceptable to the people and the latter was agreeable on condition that Adi was part of it. Then, Harmoko turned the tables against Adi and asked the latter to draw up a cabinet line-up which the former said he would concur. This meant that by 16 May, the parliamentary leaders together with Adi were already hatching plans for Suharto's overthrow and laying the foundations for the post-Suharto order with Adi as the 'kingmaker'.

What is equally interesting was that the ABRI leadership was kept informed of this development. Thus, even though Wiranto and Prabowo were at loggerheads, the fact remained that both were being courted by the Muslim lobby and that both worked hard to keep tap of ICMI's effort to undermine and eventually bring about Suharto's downfall. If ABRI had not co-operated or acquised with Adi's plans, there was the danger of bloodshed and Suharto's downfall may not have been that quick. A ranking General, who was almost privy to the blow-by-blow events taking place in Jakarta then, told the author that when it became clear that Suharto could not hold on to power any longer, ABRI's main concern was to make sure that a 'soft landing' took place for the President. The consensual view was that there should be a graceful exit for Suharto and that a repeat of what happened to President Marcos in the Philippines should be averted. In the end, even though President Suharto was forcibly made aware of his mistakes and compelled to undertake reforms, according to this General, these were 'too little, too late' and the only option left was for Suharto to go.[13] This was all the more so as the only reason the 'street' was united was that they wanted to see Suharto removed and once this was undertaken, the opposition to the government was expected to be less vociferous.

While Adi agreed with Harmoko and Syarwan's suggestion that Adi draw up the new cabinet, Adi also demanded that both the parliamentary leaders accept the fact that the new cabinet must receive the endorsement of Amien Rais. Harmoko and Syarwan were agreeable to this proposal. Adi then left the MPR/DPR complex and contacted Amien and told him of his discussion with Harmoko and Syarwan and the proposed cabinet line-up. Amien was agreeable with the plan. When this was agreed upon, Adi instructed one of his key lieutenants, Mr Jumhur Hidayat, the Executive Secretary of CIDES, to draw up the proposed post-Suharto 35-member cabinet list on grounds that he knew 'whom Adi wanted in and out'. The ICMI/CIDES people were extremely happy with this turn of events as they felt that a potential bloody clash with Suharto's security apparatus would be averted by this move and that it amounted to a bloodless coup, especially since the ABRI leadership had given its explicit support. Thus, what actually happened was that it was the concerted and calculated pressure by Adi Sasono, working through Amien Rais, that tore the Suharto system, apart with Adi as the cornerstone in the 'May revolution'.

On the following morning, 17 May, at 5.00 a.m., a meeting of ICMI leaders took place to concretise the plans that had been agreed upon even though Jumhur was yet to submit the final list of the proposed cabinet. At the meeting, Adi dropped a bombshell, announcing that he will not be part of the new cabinet. He argued that following his consultations with key Muslim leaders, it was agreed that ICMI should not accept the Harmoko-Syarwan plan nor make peace with Suharto that easily as they suspected that the 'old fox', Suharto was up to some tricks and manoeuvre. Instead, the Muslim leaders argued that Suharto should be brought down totally and not given any chance whatsoever to influence developments in the post-Suharto era or make a comeback. To ensure this, the pressure must be sustained so that Suharto surrenders and is defeated, and only then, should Adi and his friends construct and structure a post-Suharto order.

A senior ICMI official argued that this new development meant that Adi and his friends had to challenge and declare a 'total war' against Suharto. In view of the past experience, this also meant that much bloodshed could be expected. Many of the younger ICMI and CIDES leaders were not totally agreeable with the sudden turn of events all the more since there was an opportunity to peacefully resolve the problem.

While many attempts were made to dissuade Adi from his new decision, the ICMI Secretary-General remained adamant arguing that if great things were to be achieved, than risks will have to be taken and if need be, more lives will have to be sacrificed. Adi reasoned that it was the case in 1945 and 1965 and it would also be the case in 1998. Having failed to dissuade Adi and impressed by his determination, the younger ICMI leaders decided to go along with the 'General' and it was 'total war' after that, no matter what and how many lives were lost.

On the afternoon of 17 May, Adi called on Harmoko and Syarwan to inform them that the earlier understanding had to be scrapped. Adi apparently told his ICMI subordinates that they should leave the management of the two 'Suharto loyalists' to him. When Adi met Harmoko and Syarwan, he told them in no uncertain manner that he will not work on a new cabinet until Suharto is down and out. Adi also warned both Harmoko and Syarwan that the mood of the public has been transformed and if both of them did not play along and did what was obviously necessary, meaning, help Adi to bring Suharto down, then 'both of you are also finished'. This somehow frightened both of them and being pragmatic, they began to move accordingly. A ranking ICMI official confided that both Harmoko and Syarwan believed that Adi was the 'dalang', puppeteer, behind the student demonstrations, something which was credible due to Adi's background as a political activist and 'father of NGOs' in Indonesia. Both Harmoko and Syarwan also believed that Adi was in collusion with Amien Rais and that Adi was in a position to unleash 'people's power' through Amien and that ABRI will not do anything to stop it. What this meant in reality was that there was nothing that could save Suharto and since the President's fall was imminent, self-preservation dictated that both Harmoko and Syarwan should play along with Adi and preserve what little power and influence they could by being the 'midwife' of the post-Suharto era since they were in control of the constitutional process through the MPR and DPR, and where Harmoko was still Chairman of GOLKAR. According to an ICMI official, Adi was extremely pleased with the day's achievements and believed that the floodtide was swinging in his favour and the fall of Suharto was only a matter of time.

On the morning of 18 May, a special meeting was held in ICMI between 8.00 and 10.00 a.m. Present in this meeting were B. J. Habibie, Akbar Tanjung, Adi Sasono, Ahmad Tirtosudiro, Parni Hadi, Lieutenant-General Sayidiman, Jumhur Hidayat and a number of other ICMI officials. Adi chaired the meeting and briefed those present of the fast changing political dynamics and situation in Jakarta, and where, despite Suharto's return from Cairo, he was unable to regain control. Adi exhorted the group that what was needed was courage to make the best of the opportunity. Otherwise, the 'revolution' which has already started will consume everyone and the country as a whole and the wrong group will come to power and Indonesia will be back to square one, of being ruled by the wrong man and group. While Adi exhorted everyone to play his part, he directed his main attention to B. J. Habibie, the country's Vice-President. Adi told Habibie that the situation was such that the Vice-President had no choice but to pluck courage and tell the President to step down. Otherwise, the damage to the President, his family and the country as a whole would be much greater. Adi also told Habibie that if he did not play that role well and constructively, then he would also be condemned by history as he was in a unique and strategic position to convey to the President that particular message, probably the most important message in Habibie's 49 years relationship with Suharto. Adi argued that if anyone else carried the message, Suharto's reactions would be very different as the messenger would be viewed as an enemy trying to corner him, and not a friend or son as Habibie was regarded. After listening attentive, Habibie agreed that the political-security was deteriorating very fast in the capital and the country as a whole.However, it would not be easy to tell Suharto that he should step down as it was impossible to do so. However, he would think about it and promised to work on the suggestion.

Following the meeting, Adi called Harmoko and Syarwan, and Adi was told that he expects to chair a 'very difficult' meeting of senior parliamentary leaders. Harmoko said that the basic message he was going to deliver was that the only way for the country to win peace and stability was for Suharto to *lengser keprabon*, to abdicate, something Suharto had stated many times that he was willing to do; otherwise, the President would not only destroy himself but also bring the country down with him. Harmoko argued that as representatives of the people, the parliamentarians would be told to do their job, regardless of the consequences; otherwise, history would condemn them for being weak and irresponsible. Adi was happy with Harmoko and Syarwan, and wished both of them luck. Within a short period, Adi called Harmoko again, and Adi was informed that the parliamentarian meeting was taking place. Adi then told his subordinates that it was time to relax and they ordered '*Soto Maruf*' for tea.

Then at 3.00 p.m., Harmoko called for a press conference and publicly called on Suharto to resign. When Adi heard this, he was elated as both Harmoko and Syarwan had been won over and were technically now part of the 'team' to topple Suharto. As Adi told his 'boys', 'the market, streets and now, the parliament were against Suharto. Let us see how long more can he hold on, especially since even the Vice-President and ABRI leadership were also playing along'. An ICMI official argued that 'Adi's 'orchestra' was playing the right tune with the 'audience' singing and dancing along and every passing minute, the 'conductor' was becoming the star in the centre stage with all the players prepared to move in any direction the conductor wanted it'.

At 5.00 p.m. that day, a special meeting was arranged at Habibie's residence in Kuningan, Jakarta. A number of Habibie's key advisers, mostly from ICMI, including all the people who attended the 8.00–10.00 a.m. meeting at ICMI earlier, minus Sayidiman were present. The key issue discussed was Harmoko's statement two hours earlier and what it would mean for the country's politics. Both Habibie and Adi were relieved with the turn of events, and it was against this backdrop that Habibie told the meeting of his readiness to assume the Presidency if it was undertaken in a legal and constitutional manner with Suharto agreeing to it. This would mean that by this time, the key leaders of ICMI were convinced that Suharto should step down, with Habibie prepared not only to deliver the 'message' but also to take over the mantle of leadership as was provided for by the constitution. Habibie told the meeting that when he conveys the message to Suharto, it will be the first time in 49 years he would be telling Suharto that he disagreed with him and also knows that Suharto would be extremely unhappy with Habibie's action. Habibie is reported to have said that while requesting Suharto to step down is going to be difficult, even hurting, he will do it anyway as it was necessary to avert the emergence of a dangerous situation that could engulf the country.

Following this, Adi and his key advisers called on Madam Rinny Adwani, the person President Suharto had appointed to head the agency involved in rehabilitating the banks. Rinny laid down the bare facts about what was wrong with the economy and the problems that were involved in improving the banking system. Apparently, to Adi and the political activists present, the message appeared rather unintelligible as they were not trained in economics or financial matters. In the meantime, Habibie was planning to visit Suharto at his residence to deliver the 'resignation advice'. Somehow, Habibie panicked and called Adi from his car asking how he should deliver the message. A senior ICMI official thought that this was rather comical as someone, Habibie in this case had been dubbed as an 'adopted son' of Suharto and one who had such long contacts with the President, should have acted in this manner. Adi than dictated to Habibie what and how to deliver the message. Among others, in view of the deteriorating situation in the capital and country at large, the increasing anger of the people against the President and the First Family, the increasingly aggressive demands for accountability, the need to ensure the President and his siblings' security as well as the longevity of Suharto's achievements in the last 32 years, etc, there was no choice but for Suharto to step down. With this, Habibie proceeded to the Vice-President's office, hoping that he would be given an audience by the President.

In the meantime, Adi had earlier arranged a special meeting at 10.00 p.m. that evening to evaluate the day's events and what move or action to take next. However, at 7.00 p.m., Adi was shocked by General Wiranto's statement saying that Harmoko's earlier 3.00 p.m. statement was not legitimate, did not represent the collective view of the MPR and should be discarded as nothing more than a position of an individual. According to an ICMI official, when Adi and his lieutenants heard Wiranto's statement, they panicked. The mood became tense with Adi becoming angry that his plans for Suharto's overthrow had been undermined. Adi interpreted Wiranto's statement as nothing more than a Suharto's manoeuvre, through his loyal Generals to subvert what was seen as a 'people's power' movement. Adi then contacted Habibie but failed. Instead, Habibie's adjutant told Adi that the Vice-President's scheduled meeting with Suharto for the day had been cancelled and that even the one for the following day had been called off. Also, the President was reported to be very angry with his Vice-President for colluding with the President's enemies. Suharto identified ICMI as the main source of his troubles and his anger was all the more intense since it was Suharto who helped the Muslims establish ICMI and gain influence and legitimacy in the country. In Indonesian parlance, ICMI had become the '*anak macan*', a tiger's cub, which after being nursed and nourished from young, devours its master. Habibie is also reported to have become frightened, fearing that Suharto may just act against him.

Adi was expecting the worst that night, fearing that Suharto may invoke his Emergency Powers and declare Martial Law. Adi told his advisers that the best thing left was to pray and hope that God listens. Adi feared that many political activists would be arrested and that there would be bloodshed on the streets. Fearing arrest, on the night of 18 May, Adi and a number of key lieutenants did not go home but spent the night incognito in Hotel Ambara incognito. Adi admitted that he was fearful and that the worst could happen to him. However, to contain his fear, Adi told his 'boys' that one must do two things: have enough food and sleep. Only than will they be in a position to confront the emerging crisis. While Adi went to sleep, by midnight, he was up again as Amien Rais came calling to discuss the recent developments and what steps to take next. It was decided to hold a 'core group' meeting at 7.00 a.m. the following morning. What made the 'core group' meeting all the more important was the fact that Amien and Adi were informed that Suharto had invited a number of leading Muslim scholars and religious leaders to his residence for a 'special emergency meeting'.

Adi met his 'core group' at No. 14, Jalan Indramayu, the residence of Malik Fajar, one of Adi's staunchest supporters and one of the persons invited by Suharto for the 'special emergency meeting' that morning. According to an ICMI official, the house of Malik Fajar holds a special historic significance as it was here that all the key decisions were taken in the last 72 hours prior to the fall of Suharto. This also became Adi's 'Command Post' to direct all the activities of the 'May Revolution' until 21 May. In addition to Malik Fajar, Adi and Amien, the other present at the meeting were Jumhur Hidayat,

Nurcholish Majid, Yuzril Mahendra and Cholil Badawi. Even not all the invitees to the Suharto's 'special emergency meeting' could be mobilised for the meeting that morning, Adi and Amien thought that it absolutely necessary to reach out to as many as possible so that these people could be 'penetrated and influenced' before they met Suharto. The basic idea was to prepare them so that Suharto would not 'hijack' the 'special meeting' for his own purpose. The Jalan Indarmayu meeting that morning concluded that no matter what, Suharto must be persuaded to step down, for Habibie to be appointed as the next President and agreement sought that Habibie would be given the mandate to appoint the next cabinet. Adi told those present that Suharto may pressure the invitees to sign a proclamation, etc and as long as these key points were contained in it, it was alright to do so. Anything less would be unacceptable.

For Adi and his key lieutenants, 19 May was also the day when CIDES had organised an important workshop on 'the Reform Agenda' and where the country's leading poet, Rendra, had been invited to address the meeting. Thus, following the meeting at Malik Fajar's residence, Adi and his key lieutenants, rushed to CIDES to attend the seminar as if nothing unusual had transpired. At the same time, thousands of students had occupied the MPR complex and the number was increasing fast with many fearing that ABRI may storm the country's citadel of democracy. In view of the worsening situation on the streets, Adi told the seminar participants that it was best that the meeting be postponed so that instead of 'talking about reforms', it would be better 'to do something on the streets about it'. As this was being organised, both Adi and Amien were shocked when the national television televised 'live' at 9.00 a.m., announcing that Suharto was holding a special meeting with leading Muslim leaders with regard to the crisis facing the country. Both Adi and Amien concluded that 'the old fox' had laid a trap for the nine Muslim leaders present and that the President would most likely be able to cajole or pressure them to make a statement or say things that would only help to prolong the Suharto regime and hence, continue cheating the people and country.

As was feared by both Adi and Amien, the nine '*Walis*' did not hold a uniform position and Suharto was able to exploit this. An ICMI official argued that Adi was most disappointed with Nurcholish Majid and Yuzril Mahendra, as they appeared rather weak and compromised with Suharto, thereby helping Suharto to buy additional time through his time-honoured strategy of 'divide and rule'. Following a two-hour meeting with the nine '*Walis*', Suharto read a statement live on national television, announcing that as a result of the meeting, he was prepared to undertake wide-ranging reforms, reshuffle the cabinet and appoint a new Reform Cabinet, appoint a Reform Committee and call for a general elections 'as soon as possible' and where he would not be a candidate for President. In other words, Suharto 'stole' the 'reform agenda' and where he now promised to lead the country's reform movement. To Adi, this was unacceptable.

He immediately called Nurcholish Majid and Fahri, a Muslim student leader, to find out the meaning of Suharto's statement and what possible action to take next. What also came out of this meeting was decision that Suharto had 'surrendered' partially due to the pressure that had been mounted so far and the only way to make the President surrender totally was to raise the stakes and intensify the pressure. Adi argued that Suharto's reference to his willingness to step down, that he was not hungry for power and his decision not to contest the next election were all the result of 'street politics' and now the key question was how to break him down so that his only option would be to resign and hand over power to Habibie.

At the same time, the government appeared to be tightening control of information dissemination with a television pool being established. This meant that all news would be censored and released by a single government-controlled agency, which Adi interpreted as a prelude to the establishment of some kind of a martial law or the exercise of emergency powers. That the government was playing games was best evident in a press conference given by Adi, Amien and Nurcholish Majid, and where the television cameras only reported and zeroed on the last while ignoring the first two, suggesting as it were, that both Adi and Amien were in agreement with Nurcholish Majid. It was times like this that Adi felt that he was losing the battle and that all the efforts and sacrifices made thus far would come to nought.

On 19 May, between 2.00 p.m. and 3.00 p.m., Habibie met Suharto at the latter's residence, and in many ways, it was a historic meeting. Habibie was particularly upset with the President for suggesting to the *Walisongos* and later publicly, that his Vice-President was incapable of taking over the Presidency. Suharto's gameplan was to convince the Muslim leaders that they had no choice but to work with Suharto as the Vice-President, who was incapable of managing the country, would automatically take over, if he resigned, as was demanded by them. As Adi was to describe it later, '*Bugisnya Habibie keluar*' or 'the Bugisness of Habibie was exposed' as Habibie argued that he was not only capable but was also liked by the public. Then, the 'new Habibie' showed himself up when he accused the Suharto of bringing the country to a crisis-point and argued that 'unlike you, I am not involved in corruption, collusion or nepotism'. Habibie also maintained that 'today, the people of this country trust me more than you'. Habibie then walked out of Suharto's house. Adi was later to argue that Habibie's outburst against his former mentor must have made a great impression on the President, realising that now, even his hand-picked deputy was not with him. The noose was getting tighter! Suharto's worst fears that ICMI was behind his downfall were also confirmed.

In the evening of 19 May, at about 7.00 p.m., after the evening prayers, Adi met Amien at the Muhammadiyah office in Menteng. It was sometimes then that Yuzril contacted Adi, telling him that he may have some good news. Adi then instructed Yuzril to meet him at the house of Malik Fajar. Yuzril, who had spent the last few days at the President's house and knew almost the blow by blow developments taking place, told Adi that there was a great possibility that the President may resign. Yuzril wanted some advice on how to proceed so that Suharto's resignation is well-managed. Adi informed Yuzril that Suharto's resignation should be in line with the earlier agreement the day earlier, namely, that Suharto should resign, Habibie be appointed as the next President and following which the new President would announce his new cabinet. On these instructions, Yuzril rushed back to Cendana to await the next move of Suharto and his opponents. Adi then told Amien that once Suharto resigns, Amien must give his blessings to Habibie and publicly endorse the new cabinet as this would help to reduce the pressure on the new President. This was viewed as important as Amien was being viewed by the public, especially the students as the single most important voice opposed to the Suharto order. Adi argued that Habibie must start off on the right food and galvanise all the anti-Suharto forces behind Habibie. Amien was agreeable to Adi's proposal.

In the evening of 19 May, both Adi and Amien were back in the Muhammadiyah office in Menteng. By this time, Jakarta was a 'ghost city'. Tension was, however, high as Amien had threatened to unleash a one-million strong 'people's power' on the street the following day, 20 May, which also coincided with the National Awakening Day, commemorating the birth of the nationalist organisation, Budi Utomo exactly 80 years earlier, to which Indonesians trace the birth of their nationalist movement against the Dutch. Suharto, however, to circumvent the 'people's power movement' ordered a countermove, with General Wiranto ordering ABRI, especially the Jakarta

Garrison Commander, to prevent this from actualising. By late night, Jakarta was a garrisoned city with all the strategic points guarded by soldiers armed with live ammunition, barbwire barriers and tanks.

Late on 20 May, Adi, from his 'command post' in Malik Fajar's house, instructed his key lieutenants, including Jumhur Hidayat and Eggi Sudjana, to assist Amien Rais in the launch of the 'people's power movement' the following day. Amien and the various officials from ICMI were, however, fearful that their 'peaceful' revolution was likely to turn bloody as this was more in the Indonesian character, in the light of past experience, the violence in Jakarta since 12 May and in view of the 'offensive' Suharto seemed to have launched to snub all opposition to his regime. Amien was fearful that his actions could lead to the death of many innocent students and this waste of lives troubled him the whole night. Many of the ICMI officials helping Amien in the 'people's power movement' thought that they had already signed a 'death contract' since it had been decided that it would take place the next morning. While the ICMI officials slept in the Muhammadiyah office, in the early hours of 20 May, at about 1.00 a.m., Amien, in his 'sarong' went on an 'inspection tour' of the city, especially near the National Monument, where bulk of the demonstrators were supposed to assembled. To his chagrin, he found thousands of armed soldiers and tanks, and this frightened him, especially as he learned that General Wiranto had ordered live ammunition to be issued to all soldiers and that they have been issued with orders to shoot the demonstrators. Later, Amien also told the press that he had been warned by a Major-General (believed to Muchdi) that ABRI was prepared to undertake a 'second Tiananmen Massacre' if it was necessary to maintain peace. In view of this, at 3.00 a.m., Amien called for a press conference and announced that the 'people's power' show of force has been cancelled in order to prevent a possible bloodshed. Amien's 'orders' were relayed through the nation's television and radio networks for the next few hours. Thus, when the demonstrators and others who wanted to join the 'people's power movement' woke up on 20 May, they discovered that the event had been cancelled, with most of them feeling disappointed and angry that Suharto had again succeeded in circumventing them.

In the morning of 20 May, Adi and his key lieutenants, including Amien, held another meeting at the residence of Malik Fadjar and took the decision that since the 'people's power show of force' could not be implemented, all resources and manpower would be concentrated at the MPR/DPR complex. By some estimates, nearly one million people may have gathered by the afternoon with bus loads coming from every directions with the security forces making no effort to stop the in-flow. Adi, Amien and almost all the key ICMI leaders were also at the MPR/DPR complex. Adi was to confide to his key lieutenants that they were safe in the 'ocean of people', all the more, as the anti-government situation there was very tense, with security forces fearing that this could spill into the streets. In the evening, Adi and his key officials left the MPR/DPR complex and decided to spend the night in the hotel. At around 10.00 p.m. Adi got a call and he left, telling his key lieutenants that they were to wait for his fall as they may be some good news. Shortly after 11.00 p.m., Adi called to say that there may indeed be good news as Suharto may have decided to resign. He also said that if he did not call, it was confirmed that Suharto has, indeed, decided to resign If he called, it meant that a new game and scenario was being played out. However, after 15 minutes, Adi called to say that it was final that Suharto would be announcing his resignation the next morning at 9.00 a.m. and that Habibie would be sworn in as the country's next President in front of the country's Chief Justices as circumstances do not allow the ceremony to take place at the MPR complex. Adi said that Suharto had calculated that the cost of staying in power any further was simply too great and in order to preserve his key interests, he has decided to quit gracefully, with his 'interests and dignity' being guaranteed by the Armed Forces, especially after fourteen of his key ministers indicated in a letter to him that evening that they were not prepared to serve in Suharto's new 'reform cabinet'. The fourteen ministers were Ginandjar Kartasasmita, A. M. Hendropriyono, Akbar Tanjung, Sumahadi, Rachmad Bambagn Sumadhijo, Tanri Abeng, Kuntro Mangkusubroto, Theo Sambuaga, Subiakto Tjakrawardaya, Justika Baharsjah, Giri Suseno, Haryanto Dhanutirto,Rahardi Ramelan and Sanyoto Sastrowardoyo. Sri Bintang Pamungkas, the leader of the Democratic Union Party argued in November 1998 that these fourteen ministers resigned *en masse* on the instructions of 'ICMI's strategists'.[14]

EXPLANATION THREE:
THE EMERGENCE OF SUHARTO AS THE
'COMMON ENEMY' OF THE KEY POLITICAL
FORCES IN THE COUNTRY

In addition to the weaknesses related to the Suharto's power structure and the political conspiracy perspective, there is a third perspective which argued that by mid-May 1998, especially following the Trisakti shooting, Suharto had emerged, for all the main political forces operating in the country, as the 'common enemy' and the main question was not one of Suharto staying on as the President but rather how to persuade or force him to step down from that position.[15] Here, a number of factors and developments led to the emergence of this phenomenon. First, an important key to the understanding of Suharto's fall was the need to understand political-cultural factors that greatly influenced Suharto and his style of government, and where he saw himself as the *Semar*[16] of Indonesian politics. In some ways, Indonesian political-culture is largely pseudo in nature. Thus, when people say 'yes' to the leader, it does not mean that they are 100 per cent loyal to him and this was, in part, due to the influence of Javanese culture, something which Suharto cultivated all these years. In the same vein, if someone disagreed with a particular policy, one will never so say but rather say that "it is better to adopt this or that policy". Thus, Suharto's fall also need to be understood from the cultural perspective and where the Javanese culture played an important role in this regard. When widespread riots took place in most major towns and streets, and people were vocally expressing this, it was manifestly clear to Suharto that he had lost the support of the people, who were no longer loyal to him *per se*.

In traditional Javanese terms, this meant that Suharto had lost the *Wahyu* or Mandate from God to rule the country and this was a very critical cultural factor, especially for the Javanese, whose daily lives are very intimately laced with mystical practices of all kinds. When demonstrations became rampant in Jakarta and the Parliamentary complex was occupied, these were viewed as being politically significant. However, when the city of Jogjakarta, Suharto's birth place, was also engulfed by these demonstrations, ironically led by the Sultan, calling among others for total reforms and Suharto's resignation, it was the most powerful signal indicating that culturally and spiritually, the Javanese had rejected Suharto and there was no choice but to leave. For Javanese in general, mystically this had great significance as it meant that the place from where Suharto originated had rejected him. This cultural rejection was in some ways even more significant that the political rejection that was being expressed in all the major cities of the country and this meant that Suharto had no choice but to plan his exit quickly. When similar demonstrations hit Solo, the birth place of Madam Suharto, it merely confirmed the point that Suharto had reached a point of no return, and that culturally and spiritually, the Presidency was over and what was left to implement was the transfer of power in a manner which would cause the least damage to all concerned.

Second, with the spread of demonstrations, especially in Jakarta and the major cities, and when various symbolically important buildings and monuments were occupied, Suharto being very Javanese knew that he had lost the Presidency and could only stay in power at the cost of great bloodshed. Yet, while the reform movement was spearheaded by various Muslim groups, best symbolised by Amien Rais and his friends in ICMI, in reality various non-Muslims groups, activists and individuals, also joined in, especially various people of Catholic origins, including those sponsored by the Centre for Strategic and International Studies (CSIS). This was all the more so as the media became blisteringly anti-Suharto, especially the Catholic-controlled media such as *Kompas* and *The Jakarta Post*. For this group, their motivation was not just their opposition to Suharto but due to more deeper reaons, namely, their concern for the rise of Political Islam in the country in the post-Suharto era.

Hence, their opposition to the Muslims, in general, and Habibie in particular, as the latter was seen as a person who had been 'engineered' as the leader of the Islamic 'flying geese' movement. These non-Muslims, especially the Catholics, felt betrayed by Suharto, who in the late 1980s not only 'dumped' the CSIS but in its place, established ICMI in December 1990. Ironically, Suharto came to be seen as the new bastion of Islam, of which Habibie was the nominal leader, being Chairman of ICMI. Thus, for the non-Muslims, especially the Catholics, Suharto had to be toppled at all cost as he represented a new source of danger to the non-Muslims and their interests. Hence, Suharto and his regime emerged as the 'common enemy'. The Muslim reformers such as Amien Rais, together with the non-Muslims, who were mainly secular, joined forces to topple Suharto, even though for different reasons. This was not just because they abhored Suharto but the latter was also strongly against the rise of Islam to power. The politically active and conscious Catholics, in particular, felt that Suharto had given Islam a legal chance and opportunity to flourish since December 1990 and this was against their interest, an interest which Suharto supported since the establishment of the new order in 1966. The non-Muslim groups felt that between 1993 and 1998, the Muslim intellectuals had gained dominance in various governmental and non-governmental positions, with Parliament allegedly undergoing a 'green revolution' or being increasingly Islamised. The non-Muslims calculated that they had no choice but to assist in the overthrow of the Suharto government which was seen to be promoting and protecting Islamic interest at their own expense.

Thus, while the various Islamic reformist groups wanted to rid Suharto to end KKN and other abuses, the non-Muslims also wanted to end Suharto's rule on grounds that not only had their lost Suharto's favour but more important, President Suharto was seen to be promoting the interest of Islam, which the Catholics interpreted as being inimical to their interests. This thinking led to the convergence of interest between the Islamic and non-Islamic groups, with both being in one mind in ridding Suharto even though their motivations were different and often at cross-purpose with each other. Thus, when Amien Rais established MAR in mid-May 1998, it was strongly supported by many non-Muslims and Christian activists such as chairman of *Suara Pembaruan* daily, Dr Albart Hasibuan and Goenawan Mohamad, the Editor-in-Chief of *Tempo*, as well as activists such as Pius Lustrilanang. Thus, the 'common enemy' thesis was important in garnering forces in bringing about Suharto's fall, especially with the CSIS playing a role in galvanising the non-Muslim forces. An ICMI official argued that the CSIS and its followers adopted the strategy of attempting to exploit and manipulate Amien Rais and Gus Dur, using both as 'predators' to 'finish off' Suharto while trying to undermine the power of Islam at the same time by keeping it divided and weak [*untuk makan Islam sendiri*].[17] Later, the Ciganjur Declaration can also be seen from this perspective.

Historically, both the Muhammadiyah and Nahdatul Ulama have failed to work together and even if they have worked together, this was driven more by tactical considerations. Both Amien and Gus Dur have irreconcilable differences and have been unable to work together. Gus Dur has openly and stronlgy opposed the establishment of ICMI, which is viewed as nothing more than an organisation which represents the views of modern and urban Muslims found in the Muhammadiyah. ICMI has also tended to represent the views of the now defunct Masjumi, which was Nahdatul Ulama's main rival politically, especially in the 1950s. The Nahdatul Ulama, on the other hand, represents the traditional Muslims, who are largely rural in character and which for the last 15 years or so, never had a representative in cabinet. For Gus Dur, this must be very embarrassing, especially since the Muhammadiyah and its followers in ICMI have become very influential since March 1993.

Third, at the same time, the daughter of former President Sukarno, Megawati Sukarnoputri, had been increasingly projected as a Nationalist leader, in part, as the PDI had the former Indonesian Nationalist Party or PNI as one of the most important components of the PDI. Megawati, was, however, noteworthy for maintaining an image of silence and this is mainly due to her weak intellectual capacity. Thus, during the May 1998 revolution, there was hardly any thing heard from her. Like Gus Dur, she was viewed by many as nothing more than a vehicle being used by various groups, especially CSIS. While intellectually both Amien Rais and Gus Dur are smart and sensitive, by contrast, Megawati is perceived to be much weaker and thus, easily manipulated. In view of this, if there is a growing popularity of the PDI of a sort, it is not so much due to the dynamism or charisma of Megawati as much as due more to the image, charisma and goodwill towards her father, Sukarno. While selected media within Indonesia and without have undertaken a policy of projecting and amplifying her, especially the non-Muslim media, as a 'hero' and a 'victim' of Suharto's New Order, in reality, as far as substance is concerned, there is much to be desired, especially in the light of the post-Suharto political dynamics confronting the country. The Western liberal media had also joined in the fray in supporting Megawati as it also constituted part of the players in the 'common enemy' orchestra that wanted to pre-empt the rise of Islam in the country and this could only be done by first ensuring that Suharto was removed from power.

Fourth, there was also an important player that people have not given much credit in the transfer of power from Suharto to Habibie and in the collapse of the New Order, and that person is Professor Yusril Mahendra, now chairman of Partai Bulan Bintang. Yusril remains one of the few historic witnesses to Suharto's fall, especially in the last three days from 18 to 20 May 1998. Yusril was also in constant contact with ICMI leaders, especially Adi Sasono, Amien Rais and, Parni Hadi, and regularly met them at Malik Fajar's house, especially between 19 and 20 May. Yusril was Assistant to the then State Secretary, Saadilah Murshid, in charge of law, and one of Suharto's key speech writers, whom the former President greatly trusted. Yusril played a critical role on 20 May in persuading Suharto to stand down. Following Suharto's meeting with nine Islamic leaders on 19 May, which also included Yusril, the President promised to establish a Reform Committee as well as to reshuffle his cabinet. On the following day at 7.00 p.m., Yusril visited Adi Sasono, Amien Rais, Parni Hadi and Jumhur Hidayat at Malik Fajar's house. Originally, Yusril was scheduled to call upon President Suharto at that time but the Vice-President, Habibie in turn turned up and met the President. With some time in his hands, Yusril hurried to Jalan

Indramayu and conferred with the 'ICMI' group. At the important meeting, Yusril proposed that he would like to persuade the President to transfer power to Habibie, arguing that such a transfer was both legal and constitutional, in accordance with Chapter 8 of the Constitution. The Indramaju group agreed and Yusril was tasked with the job of persuading Suharto to legally step down.

Yusril then left for Suharto's residence and there, once the President received the letter which indicated the unwillingness of 14 ministers to serve under Suharto and where the Reform Committee could not be formed as people were unwilling to serve in it, Yusril's task of convincing the President became that much easier. Whether the resignation of the 14 ministers was part of the ploy to 'soften' Suharto is difficult to ascertain but what is important was the ability of Yusril to convince Suharto that it was in the best interest of the country for him to step down and that the transfer of power to Habibie would be both legal and constitutional, something Suharto had stated must be the precondition for his stepping down. Once Suharto agreed, Yusril and others began drafting Suharto's resignation speech for the next day, 21 May. Yusril later, became somewhat disenchanted when many critics argued that the transfer of power was illegal and unconstitutional. This stance was mainly taken up by lawyers close to the PDI and Megawati. This was mainly because while Megawati and the PDI, like others in the 'common enemy' alliance, were happy that Suharto had been forced out of office, they, however, did not bargain for the fact that Habibie would become the new President, something considered an anathema by many non-Muslims, especially the Catholic-oriented opposition based in the PDI. Regardless of this issue, Yusril can be considered one of the architects of the Refrom Order who played a historic role in 'toppling' the Suharto's New Order.

Thus, unlike the first two explanations, the third argues that there was an unstructured alignment between the non-

Muslims, Nationalists, Secular-oriented activists, Socialists, Javanese *Abangan* and *Santri*-oriented Muslims who joined forces in overcoming a common enemy, Suharto and following the success of this 'operation', the 'ad hoc alliance' continued to work together in their attempt to dislodge a new 'common enemy', namely, the rise of Political Islam of which Habibie was perceived to be its leader. In this connection, there have also been various efforts to widen the 'alignment', including the co-option of the Sultan of Jogjakarta. A senior ICMI official told the author that the Sultan, who in the past hardly made any major political speech or took a stance, had of late, become very politically active. This was because certain groups from Jakarta approached him and decided to use him as a vehicle.[18] Now he is projected as a hero even though his capability as a political leader is suspect. Many Javanese of *Abangan*-persuasion, however, view him as the best symbol of unity and hence, have tried to project him as the next possible leader of the country. The ICMI leader described the Sultan like an appendix in the human body – it was there but it will not make much of a difference if it was removed. Thus, in explaining Suharto's resignation, the 'combined force' of modern and traditional Islam, nationalists, secular groups, socialists, students and the media played the most dominant role even though these groups were not necessarily united as a whole and had different goals and objectives. This is most clearly borne out by examining the orientations of the key groups below.

Modern Islam

The symbol of this movement was Amien Rais with Adi adopting, publicly, a much lower profile. Amien started talking about succession and the need for Suharto to step down long before most people did. In 1993, at the Muhammadiyah meeting in Surabaya, he was among the first to call for succession in the country and for the people to think about it. He was heavily criticised and confronted for his stance but he continued unabated. Following this, he put forward a number of criteria and called for a discussion by which the next president should be elected. Amien's criteria clearly pointed towards Habibie as the potential candidate, mainly by his inclusion of the need to be internationally known and accepted as well as being knowledgeable in Science and Technology. For various reasons, many were opposed to Amien's proposal? This was because Suharto attempted to project himself as an Islamic leader and the protector and promoter of Islam in the country. It was Suharto who gave birth to ICMI, in a matter of speaking , and it was again Suharto who did all he could to help modern Islam flourish in Indonesia, especially since 1990. Many critics also felt that Amien's proposal was premature and that he should desist from discussing the issue as it could be counterproductive for himself and Islam *per se.* Also, it could be dangerous for Habibie as his enemies could start undermining and character assassinating him.

Despite this, Amien continued his critique of Suharto and his regime, best evident in his articles in *Republika.* One of the first attacked Suharto for selling the country's resources to foreigners, especially with regard to the Freeport mining company in Irian Jaya. The second was with regard to the Busang Affair in Kalimantan. Following this, Amien was sacked from ICMI's Board of Experts on instructions of Suharto. The President ordered Habibie to carry out the 'killing'. Amien was sacked in a typically Indonesian way when he wrote a letter of resignation to Habibie on grounds that he could not cope with his responsibilities as he was too preoccupied with Muhammadiyah activities. Yet, interestingly, Suharto actually backed Amien's Chairmanship of Muhammadiyah in the congress held in Aceh in 1995 and where, to the applause of the audience, Suharto stated he was "a seed of the Muhammadiyah".[19]

145

Despite Suharto's reservations about Amien, this statement can be construed more an attempt to woo the modern Islamic voters and thus, it was more for practical and tactical reasons that such an olive brach approach was observable. Oservers have argued that Suharto deliberately chose to be close to Islam because he wanted to make use of it politcally. Hence, for instance, he went on a Haj in 1991. Many Indonesians, however, felt that there were also personal reasons for going to Haj and being close to the Muslims as culturally and spiritually, being a Javanese, especially once a person becomes old, he tends to become more religious and would want to get closer to God. Thus, Suharto may have wanted to make use of the 'Islamic card' as well as have personal reasons for being close to the Islamic forces. By this time too, Suharto was also intensely disappointed with the non-Muslims, Catholics, especially the CSIS, as well as a number of senior officers in ABRI, making Suharto's tilt towards Islam appearing more Machiavellian than anything else.

Nationalists

This group was headed by Megawati Sukarnopuri. She gathered old and young nationalists around her, who appeared Sukarnoists in orientation. Their main agenda, however, was not to reform the country but more to overthrow and topple the Suharto regime, mainly in revenge for what Suharto did to Sukarno. With the emergence of what appeared to be Suharto-sponsored ICMI, this group became worried that Indonesian Islam would be given an additional boost and this brought together the Non-Muslims and Traditional Muslims into one alignment. Both the Non-Muslims and Traditional Muslims, as in the past, could work together with the Nationalists as they could accommodate various religious grouping and affiliations.

146

Socialists

This group has been playing around for sometime. In the past, it was organised under the PSI or Indonesian Socialist Party. Though small in number, it was largely made up of intellectuals. Adopting a policy of 'flexible penetration', they joined various groups and parties wherever they could gain influence or achieve their political goals Traditionally, the socialists have never been close to the Muslims, especially the Masjumi. In many ways, the socialist intellectuals have been successful in attracting many younger people to their cause due to their higher capacity for analysis and their generally more global and secular outlook. Also, the media has been largely controlled by people associated with this group and it has also played a major role in projecting this group even though organisationally a successor to the PSI has not been established. Some analysts have argued that since 1990, there was an attempt by the 'new socialists' to work together wih the 'new Masjumi' and this alignment may have been successful to some extent, in applying serious pressure on Suharto and his regime, especially in the between 1993 and 1998. Some have alluded that General Prabowo Subianto's close ties with various Islamic group represented this vintage.[20]

Retired Armed Forces' Generals

This refers largely to the *Petisi 50* group, a group of retired officers, including Nasution and Ali Sadikin, who had been known to have become strong opponents of Suharto and his regime. These are largely old and disgruntled generals who have for one reason or another fallen out with Suharto and his regime, and more often than not, where the motivations have been personal than anything else. In the main, this is a loose group, which sometimes support the students or various Muslim groups, especially Gus Dur. Since the fall of Suharto, many retired generals, such as Major-General Theo Syafei, have joined the PDI, which some analysts view as an attempt by the ex-generals to make a comback of some kind, as they would be largely ineffective without the backing of a political party.

Students

Historically, this group has always spearheaded political movement in the country, as was the case in 1966, 1974, 1978 and the latest in 1998. In the past, various groups have also used the students for their own purposes, as the Army did in 1966 in overthrowing Sukarno. In 1998, the students were largely motivated by the reform movement, viewing Amien Rais and the modern Muslims such as Adi Sasono as their main source of inspiration. A particular source of ammunition for the students to change the existing 'New Order' was ongoing economic crisis and the fast widening social-economic gap between the Chinese minority and the *Pribumi* majority, as the students correctly faced a bleak future for next few years and hence, became increasingly alienated and disenchanted with the way the society was organised at large.

Media

This was also a critical agency, which played a major role in creating the environment and mood for change. Day in and day out, the media lambasted at the Suharto regime and posted article after article of what was wrong and how the Suharto regime, including the First Family, was largely responsible for it. Thus, when the regime was brought down or Suharto was under attack, there was hardly any sympathy left for him as the people were already 'socialised' with the 'wrongs'

148

of Suharto and his regime. Here, the non-Muslim, Catholic and Protestant-controlled media played a particularly important role in undermining the Suharto regime, especially in the last six months prior to Suharto's fall.

Thus, in general, there were many players that were involved in Suharto's overthrow – Catholics, Nationalists, Modern and Traditional Islamic forces, Sukarnoists, Socialists, ex-generals, the media as well as various Non-Governmental Organisations, especially which were non-Muslim in character. At the same time same, there were various groups jealous of the growing power of the Islamic forces and this raised the Islamic non-Islamic divide in the country to a new height, including the divide between Modern and Traditional Muslims. ICMI, representing the *Santri*, Muhammadiyah and Masjumi followers, at the same time tried to restraint itself as they had benefited a great deal from Suharto's rule, especially in the last few years. They were happy with Suharto's protection of the Modern Muslims and Islam as a whole. This feeling existed even among Muslim hardliners such as KISDI, who were prepared to defend Suharto up to the present period. Thus, in general, a combination of forces brought Suharto down and all, with almost different motivations. While they were quite united in bringing Suharto down, they were wide differences in viewing his successor, as Habibie was percieved as nothing more than a Trojan Horse of Modern Muslims. In general, to understand Suharto's fall, there is a need to explain the cultural and spiritual factors, the critical role played by Yusril Mahendra in convincing Suharto to step down, Suharto's failure to form the Reform Committee and Reform Cabinet as well as the 'Brutus' role of Ginandjar, where he played a key role in persuading 14 ministers to quit the government. The ongoing economic crisis, Suharto's presumed loss of W*ahyu* and the various internal and external pressures combined to bring Suharto down. Here, the various external pressures, especially from the US, IMF and World Bank were important but not critical. Indonesian leaders, by definition, are stubborn nationalists and they have not budged when pressured from outside. This was true of Sukarno and Suharto and one suspects, it will also be true of his successor, Habibie.

An Analysis

What the foregoing indicates is that intense pressure was placed on Suharto to step down and none of his interim measures, especially those announced on 19 May, were given any chance of success as the elite group in control of the 'streets', mainly ICMI-dominated, concluded that Suharto had to step down, the Vice-President, Habibie had to be installed as the President and a new government established. What the 'conspiracy' thesis would tend to imply is that even though Suharto and his government had been placed under pressure for sometime, particularly from 12 March 1998 onwards, once the situation was considered ripe, especially in the period from 12–20 May 1998, the risky decision of forcing the President was taken and all efforts made to achieve this goal. Success, however, only came when the President decided that the cost of staying in power was simply too great and not worth the while. Only then did he decide to surrender political power which he had held effectively since March 1966.

However, the fall of Suharto cannot be explained or understood simply as being caused by 'street politics'. What cannot be ignored is the constructive and rational role of Suharto, who in adversity, decided that it was best that he stepped down even though technically he could have declared martial law and called on the Armed Forces to clear the streets of the demonstrators. That Suharto's 'fall' was also, in part, caused by his enlightened realisation that it was best to go to reduce further suffering and bloodshed is best captured by a number of considerations that were taken into account in making that critical decision.

Yusril Mahendra, who stayed with President Suharto in the last 72 hours and eventually drafted the resignation statement, had argued that once the President failed to establish the Reform Committee and the Reform Cabinet on 20 May, he concluded that the best option was to step down. From about 9.00 p.m. onwards that day, the President and his advisers were only concerned with the mechanics of resignation rather than staying any further. For this, the 1945 Constitution was used as a guide. It was agreed that the President would announce *fait accompli* that he was resigning and that was the end of the matter. If he had merely declared an intention to resign, then there would be a need for a Special Session to endorse the President's resignation. However, by a *fait accompli* resignation, a power vacuum would have been created and Article 8 of the Constitution stated that in such a situation, the Vice-President would automatically assume the Presidency. However, Law Number 7, 1973 stated that the swearing in of the Vice-President must take place in the DPR; if that was not possible, then it would be undertaken before the Chief Justice. As the DPR was occupied by demonstrators, the latter course was adopted, and to that extent, it was argued by Yusril and others that, that the transfer of power was a constitutional and legal.[21]

However, more critical was the decision taken to implement the resignation decision the following day. Why was it managed the way it was? Was it because the ICMI and its 'street orchestra' were too powerful? Or were there other pressing concerns? It would appear that President Suharto, realising that he had failed to deliver the Reform Committee and the Reform Cabinet, as he had promised, feared that the parliamentarians, especially under Harmoko's leadership, may be forced to institute a Special MPR Session, as Harmoko had threatened earlier. Considering the severity of the political-security situation, the President felt by 20 May night that such a move would be dangerous. According to Yusril, the Presi-

151

dent argued that 'these people [referring to those calling for the impeachment of the President] do not understand that their politics could lead to massive bloodshed and instability. And if there is a Special MPR Session and this ends up in a deadlock, the military was likely to take over'.[22] The President repeatedly argued he was against a military government. Hence, the decision to prevent a vacuum of power in the country while finding an acceptable exit from power for Suharto, something which was given a further boost following General Wiranto's declaration that the Armed Forces would support developments along constitutional lines. According to Yusril, the top military leadership, especially General Wiranto, General Subagyo, the KSAD, as well as Lieutenant-General Prabowo, the KOSTRAD Commander and Major-General Muchdi, the KOPASSUS Chief, were kept informed of the developments so that they were prepared for any eventualities.[23]

To that extent, while the authors of the 'conspiracy theory' may believe that the ICMI-led 'street orchestra' may have forced Suharto to resign, it is also possible to argue that President Suharto may have decided to step down as part of his pre-emptive strategy to avoid being compelled to undertake certain moves that were against his wishes. In this regard, his resignation can be seen more as a self-imposed coup to avoid being 'shot' by his political opponents and where it was better to transfer power to his trusted and loyal ally rather than to someone who could unravel everything that Suharto had stood for and more important, launch the 'politics of revenge' so that the new incumbent could gain public legitimacy. That there were also intensifying external pressures on Suharto to step down, especially from the United States and other Western economic powers, may have only convinced Suharto that this was the best, probably only course of option left to him.

152

NOTES

1   See John McBeth, 'Indonesia: Shadow Play', *Far Eastern Economic Review*, 23 July 1998, p. 23.

2   *The Straits Times*, 22 July 1998.

3   See 'Suharto's downfall was engineered', *The Indonesian Observer*, 27 June 1998.

4   Author's interview with President B. J. Habibie at Istana Merdeka on 3 October 1998, Jakarta, Indonesia.

5   Author's interview with Minister of Co-operatives and Small Business at the Department of Co-operatives on 22 December 1998, Jakarta, Indonesia.

6   This theory has been put forward publicly by many analysts, including Sri Bintang Pamungkas. *See Megapos*, Vol. 1, No. 4, 29 November – 5 December 1998, pp. 3-4.

7   Author's interview with a ranking general in Jakarta in September 1998.

8   Cited in *The Jakarta Post*, 10 May 1998.

9   See *Ibid*, 12 May 1998.

10   *Ibid*.

11   *Ibid*, 14 May 1998.

12   Cited in *The Sunday Times*, 17 May 1998.

13   Author's interview with a ranking general in Jakarta in September 1998.

14   See "Sri Bintang Pamungkas Buka 'Rahsia Negara': 14 Menteri Gulingkan Soeharto", *Megapos*, Vol. 1, No. 4, 29 November-5 December 1998, pp. 2-3.

15   The 'common enemy thesis' has not been widely discussed in the Indonesian media even though a number of informed scholars and policy makers, in their discussions with the author, have preferred this explanation while remaining anonymous.

16 In the Javanese Wayang or Shadow Play, the *Semar* refers to the servant of the good heroes and where despite the *Semar*'s 'low position' is reputed to be blessed with magical powers from God. In short, the *Semar* is the representative of God in the King's palace.

17 Interview with a senior ICMI official in Jakarta on 24 December 1998 who wants to remain anonymous.

18 Interview with a senior ICMI official in Jakarta on 24 December 1998 who wants to remain anonymous.

19 Interview with Mr Parni Hadi, Chairman of *Republika* and General Manager of *Antara News Agency* in Jakarta on 23 December 1998.

20 Interview with a senior officer from ABRI Intelligence Agency (BIA) in Jakarta in December 1998.

21 *See Gatra*, 30 May 1998, pp. 42-43.

22 See *Forum Keadilan*, Vol. 7, No. 5, 15 June 1998, p. 64.

23 *Ibid*, p. 65.

6

Post-Suharto Indonesia: The Potential and Limits of Habibie's Reforms

INTRODUCTION

After only 72 days as the country's Vice-President, Professor B. J. Habibie was sworn in as the country's third President since independence in 1945, and he was expected to undertake 'corrective reforms' where Suharto had failed and was forced to resign. What made things worst for Habibie was that he brought with him many negative images, including his penchant for 'wasteful mega-projects', his poor or lack of understanding about the workings of the economy, his lack of acceptance by ABRI, of being a front or tool for Islamic fundamentalism and probably worst of all, of being nothing more than a 'pawn' and 'puppet' of Suharto. This image was not helped by the fact that many viewed Habibie as being installed by his long-time friend and patron Suharto and where he was expected to serve out the remainder of Suharto's five year

155

term until 2003. In view of this, Habibie was viewed as nothing more than a transitional or interim figure, who became President by default of the constitution and whose role was to oversee peaceful change through 'corrective reforms' of the political and economic system.

Thus, Habibie was not given any chance at all. As was blatantly argued by *Asiaweek*:

> Habibie is the President, but he is also a pawn. He has little power of his own, he will be buffeted by economic and political forces he cannot control. Military leaders and most technocrats tolerate him, but don't respect him. There is the Armed Forces head Gen. Wiranto, the most powerful person in the country's (now) most powerful institution, and there is Ginandjar Kartasasmita, the senior economic minister and chief IMF negotiator. Each have political aims. For now, Habibie will stay in power as long as he does what he is supposed to. Which is clean up the economy, open up politics, oversee elections and most, important, keep the military happy. Habibie is in the awkward position of having to ease himself out, as soon as possible but certainly before his terms officially ends in 2003.[1]

In contrast, a number of local observers were a little more sympathetic towards the new President. *The Indonesian Observer*, for instance, argued that the Habibie government should be given a chance to undertake the difficult task ahead. In this connection, it was argued that 'President Habibie assumed office with two heavy burdens that could put an end to his Presidency. His main problem is to try to solve Indonesia's months-old economic crisis. The Rupiah is worth a quarter of its 1997 value, many of the factories have stopped working and unemployment is on the rise. Secondly, recent demonstrations against the government and foreign embassies point to a

156

lack of political stability which may lead to mixed feelings among investors'. In view of this, the editorial cautioned that 'those seeking to take over in Indonesia will have to be far more responsive to the sentiments of the people'.[2]

Realising that he was being confronted with a serious credibility problem, Habibie the 'engineer' and known as 'Mr Crack', quickly started work to prove his critics wrong. In his inaugural address to the nation as President on 21 May, he outlined the need to undertake 'gradual and constitutional reforms'. Calling on the people to rally behind him, he promised to 'remain open to all inputs and criticisms from the people to hasten the reform process'. He described the widespread student protests as a 'breath of fresh air' and stated that he 'grasped' their aspirations. For the sake of national unity he called for the 'end of these divisions between us so that the limited time we have can be used effectively to resolve the crisis we face'. The new President also specified three areas that would be given priority. In the political arena, he stated that a new cabinet, professional in outlook and characterised by dedication and integrity, would be announced. Their immediate task would be to revise laws in order to upgrade the country's political vitality with particular attention paid to electoral laws. Legal reforms will take the shape of revising the Subversion Law. On the economic front, he argued that reforms would be undertaken to expedite the elimination of monopolies and unhealthy competition. With an eye to the international financial community, especially the IMF, President Habibie promised that his government 'will implement all commitments agreed with foreign parties, specifically in implementing the economic reform programmes agreed upon with the IMF'. Concluding his inaugural address, the President also reminded the people that as an Asian and cultured nation, they should not forget the contributions and leadership of former President Suharto, in times of crisis and in bringing about development 'which has brought parts of the country to

157

a higher standard of living compared to three decades ago, before it was hit by the crisis sweeping Asia'.[3]

While it is true that the international, mainly Western media, was painting and reinforcing a negative view of President Habibie, yet in reality, through the due process of the law and Constitution, Indonesia was bequeathed with a new President, who by almost every measures, was the most educated, exposed to Western ideas, especially of Science and Technology and probably too, the most intelligent. Yet, ironically, a systematic campaign of character assassination was launched with the object of undermining the new political leadership both internally and externally. Why was this so? One school of thought has argued that this was necessitated by the fact that Habibie was seen as a 'Trojan Horse' of the fundamentalist Islamic lobby, especially the ICMI group and he had to be undermined so that political Islam did not gain dominance in the country. A second view has argued that there was the fear that Habibie would be able to apply his intellectual brilliance and transform Indonesia into a major power, and this was something feared by a number of countries in Southeast Asia as well as their benefactors in the West. Here, there was the need to undermine Habibie so that Indonesia was successfully maintained as a weak and backward state as the prospects of a strong Indonesia was something that many countries did not welcome or cherish, in the same manner, a strong China and India were viewed as an anathema by many countries in their respective regions and beyond. Habibie's single-minded crusade to undertake a 'great leap forward' for his country in Science and Technology, best evident in his successful establishment of a viable aerospace industry, were tell-tales of what could be expected from this well-connected German-trained engineer. In this connection, it can be argued that the concerted negative campaign against Habibie and his Presidency was largely motivated, not so much, due to the incumbent's weaknesses and shortcomings as much as a fear that he could

158

turn the country around and transform Indonesia into a power that could be unsettling for many states in the region and beyond.

Habibie's Cabinet

A day after taking office, Habibie unveiled his 'national unity Reformation-Development Cabinet' at the Merdeka Palace. The 36-member team was made up of the following individuals:

CO-ORDINATING MINISTERS

1. **Political and Security**
    Feisal Tanjung

2. **Economy, Finance and Industry**
    Ginandjar Kartasasmita

3. **People's Welfare/Poverty Eradication**
    Haryono Suyono

4. **Development Supervision/State Administrative Reform**
    Hartarto Sastosoenarto

MINISTERS HEADING DEPARTMENTS

5. **Home Affairs**
    Lieutenant-General Syarwan Hamid

6. **Foreign Affairs**
    Ali Alatas

7. **Defence and Security/Chief of Armed Forces**
Gen. Wiranto

8. **Justice**
Muladi

9. **Information**
Lieutenant-General Yunus Yosfiah

10. **Finance**
Bambang Subianto

11. **Industry and Trade**
Rahardi Ramelan

12. **Agriculture**
Soleh Salahuddin

13. **Mines and Energy**
Kuntoro Mangkusubroto

14. **Forestry**
Muslimin Nasution

15. **Public Works**
Rachmadi B. Sumadhijo

16. **Communications**
Giri Suseno Hadiharjono

17. **Tourism, Arts and Culture**
Marzuki Usman

18. **Co-operatives, Small and Medium Enterprises**
Adi Sasono

19. **Manpower**
Fahmi Idris

20. **Transmigration, and Resettlement of Forest Squatters**
A. M Hendropriyono

21. **Health**
Farid Anfasa Moeloek

22. **Education and Culture**
Juwono Sudarsono

23. **Religious Affairs**
Malik Fajar

24. **Social Services**
Yustika S. Baharsyah

STATE MINISTERS

25. **State Secretary**
Akbar Tanjung

26. **National Development Planning/Chairman of National Development Planning Board**
Boediono

27. **Research and Technology, Chief of Agency for Assessment and Application of Technology**
Zuhal

28. **Promotion of State Enterprises/Chief of State Enter-prises Management Agency**
Tanri Abeng

29. **Food and Horticulture**
   A. M. Saefuddin

30. **Population/Chief of National Family Planning Board**
   Ida Bagus Oka

31. **Land Affairs/Chief of National Land Agency**
   Hasan Basri Durin

32. **Investment/Chief of Investment Co-ordinating Agency**
   Hamzah Haz

33. **Housing and Settlement**
   Theo L. Sambuaga

34. **Environment/Chief of Environmental Impact Management Agency**
   Panangian Siregar

35. **Women Affairs**
   Tutty Alawiyah

36. **Youth Affairs and Sports**
   R. Agung Laksono

Of the 36 ministers, 20 were from the last cabinet of Suharto, with 16 new faces added. This opened Habibie to charges of being a continuity rather than a change from the previous regime. In an apparent bid to widen his political support, Habibie, for the first time in more than 30 years, included three ministers from the two leading minority parties, the PPP and PDI. Habibie's cabinet had a strong 'professional touch' with many holding doctorate qualifications recruited from the academia.[4] Left out were those individuals who had been tainted as symbols of corruption, collusion and nepo-

162

tism. When announcing his cabinet line-up, Habibie proclaimed that 'we will build a clean and independent government free from inefficiency, corruption, collusion and nepotism'.[5] In this connection, markedly absent from Habibie's cabinet was Suharto's eldest daughter, Siti Hardiyanti Rukmana, her close political ally, General R. Hartono and timber tycoon, Bob Hassan. Despite this, Habibie's team only got a cautious welcome from various quarters, including the local business community. Amien Rais, the vocal anti-Suharto critic and Chairman of the Muhammadiyah stated that he was 'neither endorsing nor opposing the cabinet'. However, in his view, 'this cabinet is not aimed to last until the year 2003, but only to function as a transition team until fully democratic elections are held'.[6] Marzuki Darusman, the deputy Chairman of the National Commission on Human Rights also argued that he did not 'see the cabinet making any significant political changes. The challenge for the cabinet now is to give solid evidence through pro-reform policies'.[7]

HABIBIE'S REFORMS AND THE 'DESUHARTOISATION' OF INDONESIAN POLITICS

Undeterred by the negative judgements about his leadership ability and commitment to see through Indonesia's problems, on 25 May, Habibie outlined his government's reform programmes. He announced that the chief priority was to root out corruption, collusion and nepotism, and to create a clean government. On the political front, Habibie announced that the government would be reviewing five political laws of the existing political system, namely, those deal with mass organisations, the House of Representatives (DPR), the People's Consultative Assembly (MPR), political parties, regional administrations and elections. The President also announced that the law on subversion would be revised immediately. He also called on his ministers to draw up a national reform agenda and proposed seeking a national consensus on limiting the number of five-year terms of the President to a maximum of two. With regard to questions about the legitimacy of his government, he stated that he would 'accept all those opinions gracefully' especially in the light of the fact that 'some members of the public are still questioning the legality and legitimacy of the government'.[8] He also promised to hold a Special Session of the MPR and general elections as soon as these were feasible.

The President, however, cautioned the public that reforms should not be rushed as this could prove counter-productive. In a speech to students and academics at Pajajaran University in Bandung, President Habibie compared the reforms taking place in the country to that of a foetus' growth in a mother's womb:

> A baby in a womb cannot be forced to come out... God willing, the baby in the womb of its mother is total reform, and we, the entire nation, will bring this baby to birth, hand in hand. Therefore, so that the baby is not aborted or born crippled, we should all concentrate on this. Even a baby who nears perfection will not instantly mature, will not instantly become superior – it still has to be nurtured and allowed to grow.[9]

Hence, he called for the people's understanding and patience so that the reforms he embarking on would be successful even though his critics continued to argue that the timetable was too long and that the reform process should be accelerated.

At the same time, the President announced that his cabinet would begin working on solving the two key economic problems facing the country, ensuring a sufficient supply of food and basic needs are kept at an affordable price, and get the economy moving again. In this endeavour, the government would be looking into ways to stabilise the rupiah exchange rate, control inflation and implement the IMF reform agreement in order to restore local and foreign investors' confidence. Other measures which were promised included: boosting output from agriculture, agri-business, export-oriented industry and tourism sectors, safeguarding the implementation of the 1998/1999 state budget, accelerating the bank restructuring programme and resolving the problem of corporate foreign debts. The President also ordered ministers to dismantle the special facilities and privileges that were granted by the previous administration to certain people and business groups. In order to demonstrate his leadership and commitment to the reform process, the President announced that unlike his predecessor who only led the monthly cabinet meeting on the economy, he would be leading three cabinet meetings per month, dealing with the economy, politics and welfare respectively.

More important, within hours of taking over the Presidency from Suharto, Habibie promised wide-ranging political and economic reforms, signalling a break from his predecessor and former patron. This was made more explicit when Habibie, in unveiling his new cabinet, stated that he hoped to build a 'clean and independent government free from inefficiency, corruption, collusion and nepotism', sins which the former President and his government were accused of indulging in, which in the process, exacerbated the country's economic crisis. Habibie's 'deSuhartoisation' policies could be seen immediately when he excluded from his cabinet Suharto's eldest daughter, who was a Minister of Social Services and Suharto's golfing partner, Bob Hassan, the Minister of Trade and Industry, the two individuals who were regarded as symbols of Suharto's nepotism and cronyism. President Habibie also, in stages, began purging the MPR of Suharto's appointees.

Signalling a marked break from the past, Habibie also included Hamzah Haz and A. M. Saefuddin from the PPP, and

Panagian Siregar from the PDI into the cabinet, in the hope of creating a cabinet of national unity. Instead of viewing the student demonstrators as 'enemies', Habibie described them as a 'breath of fresh air'. As promised earlier, Habibie very quickly also announced moves to end 'monopolies and unhealthy competition' in the economy. In this regard, among the first to be axed were two co-operative agreements signed by the Jakarta Administration with two private companies involved in water management, respectively with companies owned by Suharto's eldest son, Sigit Hardjojudanto and Liem Sioe Liong.[10] In the same vein, the Tangerang Regency government (just outside Jakarta) also cancelled a co-operative water supply agreement on drinking water with a company owned by Siti Hardijanti Rukmana, Suharto's eldest daughter.[11] Habibie also ordered the relevant ministers to review a highly questionable contract the state oil company, Pertamina, entered into with firms related to the sons of former President Suharto.[12]

President Habibie also issue a decree to abolish a two percent levy imposed on individual and corporate taxpayers to finance the Suharto-established *Dana Sajahtera Mandiri* Foundation set up to undertake poverty-alleviation projects. Also, the management and finances of all the other foundations under Suharto and his family, whose worth had been estimated at more than US$16 billion, were to be reviewed and made accountable to the government.[13] In this regard, in addition to *Dana Sajahtera Mandiri* Foundation, the other four to be queried were *Amal Bakti Muslim Pancasila*, *Supersemar*, *Dharmais* and *Dakab* Foundations even though Sudharmono, the former Vice-President argued that these foundations were established by Suharto in his private capacity and donations to them were given on a voluntary basis, and thus could not be subject to government regulations.[14] On 3 July, President Habibie revoked all presidential decrees and instructions issued by Suharto which mandated financial contributions to government-linked foundations.[15] Another major break in policy undertaken by Habibie was the government's decision to release political prisoners. Within five days of Suharto's resignation, the first to benefit from the policy were the country's two most prominent political prisoners, former legislator, Sri Bintang Pamungkas and labour leader, Muchtar Pakpahan, who were released under the full glare of local and international media. In many ways, this single act was one of Habibie's first political reforms since taking office on 21 May. Sri Bintang, who met the Justice Minister, Muladi called on the government to undertake three main measures as follows: 'to study the case of each political prisoner and the operationalisation of selective and gradual release; that the jailing of the political prisoners was due to the mistakes of he previous government and their release was thus a human rights issue; and that the government should apologise to the political prisoners in a bid to restore their reputation'.[16] Muladi, however, stated that certain categories of political prisoners would not be released, including those jailed for their involvement in the 1965 communist coup attempt and those linked to the outlawed Indonesian Communist Party.[17] With regard to the 'high profile political prisoner', East Timorese Jose Alexandra Xanana Gusmao, Muladi argued that he was one not eligible for release. Notwithstanding these qualifications, Muladi promised to release some 200 political prisoners in the near future.

The Habibie government also revoked various laws of the Suharto era which placed restrictions on the press. Announcing this, the Minister of Information, Muhammad Yunus issued a series of new regulations on press and radio broadcasting which were described as part of the reformation of the information sector. For instance, the Minister of Information Regulation 1/1998 cancelled a 1984 ruling signed by Harmoko, the former Minister of Information and currently Chairman of the MPR, with the object of giving certainty 'to the press so that they can carry out their tasks, functions and obligations to the best of their ability'.[18] At the same time, President Habibie appointed Parni Hadi, a long-time friend as the General Manager of *Antara* News Agency, the state-run news agency, charged with dissemination of information in the country.

President Habibie also began a policy of 'cleaning up' and 'loading' the MPR with his supporters, in a clear effort to 'deSuhartoise' the most important political-legal body in the country. On 30 June, he named 41 new members to the MPR in place of those who had resigned, retired or passed away. Conspicuous among the list of those replaced were Moch. Yogie S. M., R. Hartono, Fuad Bawazier and Muhammad Hassan, all known to be Suharto loyalists. Conspicuous among the incoming members were Habibie's cabinet ministers Farid Moeloek, Soleh Salahuddin, Boediono and Bambang Soebinato, as well as close aides such as Parni Hadi, Lieutenant-General Sintong Panjaitan, Dewi Fortuna Anwar, Afan Gaffar, Fachri Ali and Sayidiman Soerjohadiprojo. Habibie's supporters, however, denied that 'cronyism' was a consideration in the appointments. Akbar Tanjung, Minister/State Secretary argued that 'the President considers them as having the capacity to play a positive role in the Assembly' and that the new members were not meant to 'cleanse' the Assembly of Suharto's loyalists.[19]

At the same time, President Habibie also instituted reforms that would change the structures of the political system, with the key object of making them more accountable to the public. In addition to new electoral laws and practices, one of the reform introduced pertained to making the President more accountable to the legislature. The new laws stipulated, among others, that the President must seek Parliamentary approval for all executive appointments, including ministers and ambassadors. This would make the President subordinate to the MPR, the country's supreme legislative body. Under President Suharto, the MPR met once every five years and the body was dismissed by most as nothing more than a rubber-stamp. The new law required the MPR to meet annually to evaluate the President's performance as well as to address key issues raised by the people. At the same time, the size of the MPR is to be trimmed from 1,000 to 750 members, including 500 Parliamentary representatives, 135 regional representatives and 115 nominees from functional groups. Even though the President will have the prerogative to appoint, he can only choose from among those who had been nominated by various groups.[20]

Proliferation of Political Parties

As part of the substantive break from the 'Suharto's Order', within a short period, Indonesia witnessed, in the Habibie era, the blossoming of political parties, thereby breaking the stranglehold that the three 'umbrella' parties, GOLKAR, PPP and PDI had over Indonesian politics since 1971. By mid October 1998, more than 80 new political parties had been registered, many of them along religious lines. Within a few days of becoming President, Habibie announced that his government would permit the establishment of any political parties as long as their political platform was not tainted by SARA, an Indonesian acronym for polarising society through differences in tribal affiliations, religion, race and societal groups.

Habibie's announcement was welcomed with mixed reactions. Leading Muslim scholars such as Amien Rais and Nurcholish Madjid objected to the birth of religious-affiliated political parties due to their fears that such parties may be tempted to play up religious differences and tear the country asunder. Others, such as Yusril Mahendra, Hartono Mardjono, Ahmad Sumargono, Abdul Qadir Djaelani and Kholil Ridwan argued that since the majority of the country's population was of the Islamic faith, the establishment of an Islamic Party was both just and legitimate. Sumargono, in a speech at Al Azhar Grand Mosque stated on 31 May that he would support the slogan of 'Islam, yes. Islamic party, yes'. However, he warned that they should not 'repeat the mistakes of the old regime'. He argued that 'we welcome those who want to establish Catholic parties, Christian parties, Secular parties or whatever, but don't prevent Muslims from forming an Islamic party because of fear that it would endanger the nation. The fear is a sign of Islamophobia'. He argued that 'this line of thought is a remnant of Suharto's regime formulated by thinkers at the CSIS'.[21]

Some thought that the sprouting of a myriad of small parties with divisive tendencies, especially those concerned with particular issues such as gender, ethnicity, environment or religion may even out as they will either perish due to the lack of support or be forced to coalesce with other bigger parties in order to remain relevant. Thus, the proliferation of the various political parties should not be viewed as a threat as it was only a harmless reaction to the past repression which prevented political parties from being formed. Thus, the myriad of political parties were a testimony of the new era of reform under President Habibie and while the dangerous tendencies to harm the unity of the country were to be monitored, on the whole, they were to be viewed as a positive sign and development. Also, these parties were a reaction to the people's unhappiness with the monopoly and practices of the three existing parties. As was pointed out by Jusuf Syakir, a member of the Supreme Advisory Concil and a former leading member of the PPP, 'these people's break from the existing parties is not due to principles such as *Pancasila* or religion or race, but more out of discontent with the political practices of the three parties and government. This is what we need to reform', he argued, while endorsing the blanketing of the country with new political parties.[22]

In many ways, the burgeoning of many new political parties, despite existing law that only recognised the legitimacy of GOLKAR, PPP and PDI was due to the failure of the existing parties to accommodate the aspirations of the public. The spurt in political party formation was also due to the proposed electoral reforms that would allow people to vote directly for their district representatives in Parliament. The new provisions would also provide for non-constituency seats so that smaller parties will have a chance to join the legislature. Under the new electoral reform, any political party with one million registered supporters, branches in at least 14 provinces and 50 percent of the districts and not exclusive to any race, religion, ethnic group or gender would be permitted to contest in the general elections. While retaining the current method of choosing the President through an electoral college comprising Parliamentarians and appointees rather than direct elections, the college would however see more representatives from minority communities while ABRI presence would be reduced from 75 to 38 seats. Under this system, 'multi-party politics will be a reality' and 'an independent, strong Parliament with limited authority for the President', ushering in 'a new era of democratic life'.[23]

In view of this, the following were some of the new parties established since Suharto's fall:

Political Parties Established Since the Fall of Suharto

1   *Partai Adil Makmur* (PAM)
    (Just and Prosperous Party)

2   *Partai Ahlus Sunnah Waljama'ah* (PAS)

3   *Partai Aksi Keadilan Sosial Indonesia* (PAKSI)
    (Indonesian Social Justice Action Party)

4   *Partai Aliansi Demokrat* (PADI)
    (Indonesian Democrats Alliance Party)

171

5   *Partai Aliansi Kebangkitan Muslim Sunni Indonesia* (AKAMSI)
(The Alliance for Indonesian Muslim Sunni Awakening Party)

6   *Partai Aliansi Rakyat Miskin Indonesia* (PARMI)
(The Alliance of Indonesian Poor People's Party)

7   *Partai Amanat Penderita Rakyat* (AMPERA)
(People's Aspiration Party)

8   *Partai Amal Bhakti Muslimin Indonesia*
(Indonesian Muslims Charity Party)

9   *Partai Api Pancasila*
(Pancasila Fire Party)

10 *Partai Barisan Abdi Rakyat Indonesia*
(Indonesian Front for Slaves Party)

11 *Partai Bhinneka Tunggal Ika* (PBI)
(Indonesian Unity in Diversity Party)

12 *Partai Budaya Bangsa Nusantara* (PBB.NUSANTARA)
(The Indonesian National Culture Party)

13 *Partai Budaya Bangsa Pembangunan Desa Indonesia*
(Indonesian Rural Development National Culture Party)

14 *Partai Buruh Nasional*
(National Labour Party)

15 *Partai Cinta Damai*
(Peace Loving Party)

16 *Partai Demokrasi Islam Republik Indonesia* (PADRI)
(Indonesian Republic Islamic Democracy Party)

17 *Partai Demokrasi Kasih Bangsa* (PDKB)
(Love the National Democratic Party)

18 *Partai Demokrat Katolik* (PDK)
(Catholic Democratic Party)

19 *Partai Demokrasi Liberal*
(Liberal Democratic Party)

20 *Partai Dua Syahadat*
(Two Syahadat Party)

21 *Partai Gema Masyarakat Indonesia*
(Indonesian Society Echo Party)

22 *Partai Gema Masyarakat* (PGM)
(Society Echo Party)

23 *Partai Gerakan Insan Muttaqin Indonesia* (GIMI)
(Indonesian God Fearing Poople's Party)

24 *Partai Hijau Rakyat*
(People's Green Party)

25 *Partai Ikatan Pendukung Kemerdekaan Indonesia* (IPKI)
(Independence Vanguard Party)

26 *Partai Indonesia Bersatu* (PIB)
(Indonesian United Party)

27 *Partai Islam Demokrat* (PID)
(Islamic Democratic Party)

28 *Partai Islam Indonesia* (PII)
(Indonesian Islamic Party)

29 *Partai Islam Persatuan Indonesia* (PIPI)
(Indonesian Islamic United Party)

30 *Partai Keadilan*
(Justice Party)

31 *Partai Keadilan Sosial/Marata Saruksuk*
(Social Justice for All Party)

32 *Partai Keadilan Sosial* (PAS)
(Social Justice Party)

33 *Partai Kebangkitan Bangsa* (PKB)
(People's Awakening Party)

34 *Partai Kebangkitan Kaum Ahlussunnah Waljama'ah*
(PAKKAM)
(The Ahlusunnah Waljama'ah Peoples' Awareness
Party)

35 *Partai Kebangkitan Muslim Indonesia* (KAMMI)
(Indonesian Muslims Awakening Party)

36 *Partai Kebangkitan Ummat*
(Followers Awakening Party)

37 *Partai Kebangsaan (1)*
(National Party)

38 *Partai Kebangsaan (2)*
(National Party)

39 *Partai Kedaulatan Rakyat (PILAR)*
(People's Sovereignty Party)
40 *Partai Kedaulatan Rakyat* (PKR)
(People's Sovereignty Party)

41 *Partai Kedaulatan Rakyat Indonesia* (PKRI)
(Indonesian People's Sovereignty Party)

42 *Partai Kedaulatan WNI* (2)
(Indonesian People's Sovereignty Party)

43 *Partai Kemakmuran Tani dan Nelayan* (PKTN)
(Prosperous Farmers and Fishers Party)

44 *Partai Kemandirian Rakyat* (PKR)
    (People's Self-Reliance Party)

45 *Partai Kemanusian/Partai Hijau*
    (People's Party/Green Party)

46 *Partai Kerukunan Beragama dan Berbangsa* (PKBB)
    (National Religious Harmony Party)

47 *Partai Kesatuan Umat Indonesia*
    (Indonesian United Believers Party)

48 *Partai Kesatuan Wahdatul Ummah*
    (United Wahdatul Followers Party)

49 *Partai Kesejahteraan*
    (Prosperity Party)

50 *Partai Kristen Nasional Indonesia* (PKNI)
    (Indonesian Christian Party)

51 *Partai Lansia Indonesia*
    (Indonesian Lansia Party)

52 *Partai Mega Banteng* (PMB)
    (Mega Buffalo Party)

53 *Partai Mencerdaskan Bangsa*
    (National Intelligence Party)

54 *Partai Merah Putih* (PMP)
    (Red White Party)

55 *Partai Musyawarah Kerja Gotong Royong* (MKGR)
    (Mutual Co-operation Conference Party)

56 *Partai Muda Pembangunan Indonesia* (PMPI)
    (Indonesian Youth Development Party)

57 *Partai Murba*
    (Proletariat Party)

58 *Partai Mutiara Indonesia*
    (Indonesia Pearl Party)

59 Partai Nahdatul Ummat (PNU)
    (Nahdatul Followers Party)

60 *Partai Nasional Bangsa Indonesia* (PNBI)
    (Indonesian Nation National Party)

61 *Partai Nasional Demokrat*
    (Democrats National Party)

62 *Partai Nasional Indonesia* (PNI)
    (Indonesian National Party)

63 *Partai Nasional Indonesia* (PNI)
    (Indonesian National Party)

64 *Partai Nasional Indonesia* (PNI)
    (Indonesian National Party)

65 *Partai Orde Asli Indonesia* (PORAS)
    (Indonesian Aboriginal Order Party)

66 *Partai Patriot Bangsa* (PBB)
    (National Patriotic Party)

67 *Partai Patriot Indonesia*
    (Indonesia Patriotic Party)

68 *Partai Pekerja Indonesia* (PPI)
    (Indonesian Workers' Party)

69 *Partai Pelopor Pembangunan*
    (Development Pioneer Party)

70 *Partai Pelopor Reformasi* (PPR)
(Reform Leader's Party)

71 *Partai Pemangku Adat Republik Indonesia*
(Indonesian Customs Promotions Party)

72 *Partai Pembaharuan Indonesia*
(Indonesian Restoration Party)

73 *Partai Pembaharuan Indonesia*
(Indonesian Renewal Party)

74 *Partai Pembela Rakyat Jelata*
(Common People's Defenders Party)

75 *Partai Pendukung Reformasi* (PPR)
(Reform Supporters' Party)

76 *Partai Penerus Proklamasi Indonesia* (PARPINDO)
(Indonesian Continuation of Proclamation Party)

77 *Partai Perempuan Indonesia* (PPI)
(Indonesian Women Party)

78 *Partai Perjuangan Amanat Rakyat* (PPAR)
(People's Mandate Struggle Party)

79 *Partai Perjuangan Pelajar dan Pekerja*
(Students and Workers Struggle Party)

80 *Partai Perjuangan Rakyat Indonesia* (PPRI)
(Indonesian People's Struggle Party)

81 *Partai Persatuan Islam Indonesia* (PPII)
(Indonesian Islamic Unity Party)

82 *Partai Persatuan Perjuangan Rakyat Republik Indonesia*
(PARRI)
(The Republic of Indonesia United Struggle Party)

83 *Partai Persatuan Warga Negara Indonesia*
(United Indonesian Citizens Party)

84 *Partai Rakyat Bersatu*
(People's United Party)

85 *Partai Rakyat Indonesia* (PARI)
(Indonesian People Party)

86 *Partai Rakyat Indonesia* (PRI) (1)
(Indonesian People's Party)

87 *Partai Rakyat Indonesia* (PRI) (2)
(Indonesian Peoples' Party)

88 *Partai Rakyat Marhaen*
(Marhaen People's Party)

89 *Partai Rakyat Miskin Indonesia* (PRMI)
(Poor People's Party)

90 *Partai Rakyat Persaudaraan Rakyat Indonesia Merdeka*
(PRIMA)
(Free Indonesian United People's Party)

91 *Partai Rakyat Tani Usaha Informal dan Pemuda Putus Sekolah Indonesia* (PARTISIPASI)
(Farmers, Informal Traders and Dropouts Party)

92 *Partai Reformasi Cinta Kasih Kristus Kebangsaan Indonesia*
(Love Jesus Christ National Reform Indonesia Party)

93 *Partai Reformasi Indonesia*
(Indonesian Reform Party)

94 *Partai Reformasi Nasional Indonesia* (PRNI)
(Indonesian National Reform Party)

95 *Partai Reformasi Perjuangan Bangsa Indonesia*
(National Indonesian Struggle for Reform Party)

96 *Partai Reformasi Sopir Sejahtera Indonesia*
    (PARESSINDO)
    (Indonesian Drivers for Progressive Reforms Party)

97 *Partai Reformasi Tionghoa Indonesia* (PARTI)
    (Chinese-Indonesian Reform Party)

98 *Partai Remaja dan Pemuda Progressive Indonesia*
    (Progressive Youth and Teenagers Party)

99 *Partai Republik* (PR)
    (Republic Party)

100 *Partai Republik Indonesia*
     (Indonesian Republic Party)

101 *Partai Rukun Tetangga dan Warga Indonesia*
     (PERTIWI)
     (Indonesian National and Neighbourly Party)

102 *Partai Satu Bangsa*
     (One Nation Party)

103 *Partai Satu Keadilan Teknologi dan Ekonomi*
     (One Just Technology and Economic Party)

104 *Partai Satu Nusa Satu Bangsa*
     (A Single Nation, Single People Party)

105 *Partai Sejahtera Indonesia*
     (Indonesian Success Party)

106 *Partai Siliwangi Indonesia*
     (Indonesian Siliwangi Party)

107 *Partai Solidaritas Pekerja Seluruh Indonesia* (SPSI)
     (All-Indonesian Workers Solidarity Party)

108 *Partai Solidaritas Uni Indonesia* (SUNI)
     (Indonesian Solidarity Party)

109 *Partai Sosial Demokrat*
(Social Democratic Party)

110 *Partai Syarikat Islam Indonesia* (PSII) (1)
(Indonesian Syarikat Islam Party)

111 *Partai Syarikat Islam Indonesia* (PSII) (2)
(Indonesian Syarikat Islam Party)

112 *Partai Tahrikat Islam*
(Islamic Tahrikat Party)

113 *Partai Umat Islam* (PUI)
(Islamic Followers Party)

114 *Partai Umat Muslimin Indonesia* (PUMI)
(Indonesian Muslim Party)

115 *Partai Unggul Indonesia* (PUI)
(Indonesian Supremacy Party)

116 *Partai Universal Rakyat Mahasiswa Indonesia Seutuhnya*
(Indonesian Universal Students Party)

117 *Partai Uni Sosial Kemasyarakatan* 45 (PUSAKA)
(45 Social Union Party)

118 *Partai Warga Bangsa Indonesia*
(Indonesian Citizens Party)

119 *Partai Pelopor Pendidikan Indonesia*
(Indonesian Pioneer Development Party)

120 *Partai Dinamika Ummat* (PDU)
(Dynamic Followers Party)

121 *Partai Amanat Nasional* (PAN)
National Mandate Party

122 *Partai Bulan Bintang* (PBB)
Crescent Star Party

123 *Golongan Karya* (GOLKAR)

124 *Partai Persatuan Pembangunan* (PPP)
United Development Party

125 *Partai Demokrasi Indonesia* (PDI)
Indonesian Democratic Party

126 *PDI-Perjuangan* (PDI-P)
Indonesian Democratic Party – Struggle

Source: Compiled by the Author. Also see *Adil: Tabloid Berita Mingguan*, Vol. 13, No. 67, 30 December 1998 –5 January 1999, p. 8

In many ways, the country watched with amusement the proliferation of so many political parties within such a short span of time, and more important, what it would mean for the country's political landscape. As a number of parties were born by splitting from the three existing parties, GOLKAR, PPP and PDI, one of the biggest questions facing the three existing parties of the Suharto era was the spectre of disintegration. Another issue which concerned many political observers was whether the country would be experiencing a 'back to the future' experience of the 1950s when the 'free fight' parliamentary democracy resulted in a period of endless political bickering, continuous instability, national disunity and polarisation which gravely undermined economic growth and investments.

THE CONTEST AND REVAMP OF
GOLKAR'S LEADERSHIP

As GOLKAR was synonymous with Suharto's rule and where the former President used it as his key political machine to

181

win every elections and hence, legitimise his rule, the fall of the former President also meant that the party was in crisis. In the face of growing dissension and calls for reforms, the country's leading and ruling party announced on 3 June that it would be holding an extraordinary congress from 9-11 July instead of the originally scheduled five-yearly congress and election of the Chairman in October 1998. GOLKAR, whose supervisory board was still chaired by former President Suharto, was established in October 1964 as an amalgamate of several organisations, including the Armed Forces, labour groups and co-operatives. The party which won every elections since 1971 had faced the threat of disintegration since Mr Suharto resigned. In addition to calls for Mr Harmoko, the Chairman, to resign, due to the lack of confidence in his leadership, an important factor leading to the early GOLKAR congress was the decision of one of GOLKAR's traditional allies, *Musyawarah Kekeluargaan Gotong Royong*, (Conference for Family Values and Mutual Self-Help) to break ranks and establish itself as an independent political party. Another ally, the KOSGORO, GOLKAR's business wing, was also considering a similar move.

Mr Harmoko, in announcing the extraordinary congress, stated that he did not wish to be re-nominated in the next chairmanship election. He also stated that the July congress would be deciding on various matters, including the next GOLKAR leadership and whether it was still necessary to maintain the board of patrons and board of advisors. The GOLKAR leadership was also expected to discuss its position on future laws on political parties as well as the government's plan to hold an extraordinary session of the MPR and general elections.

Preceding the extraordinary meeting, the GOLKAR leadership was split into two main groups on how and what criteria to utilise in choosing its new leader. Abdul Gafur, the GOLKAR Supreme Council member, wanted someone younger than

Harmoko for the post while Moestahiad Astari disagreed, arguing that Mr Gafur's statement was a personal view.[24] At the same time, ABRI, which had formed the backbone of the party since its formation, called on GOLKAR to become more self-reliant. For instance, Brigadier-General Wahab Mokodongan, ABRI's spokesman argued that 'a more independent GOLKAR should be sought in such an era of reform'. However, what ABRI's exact relations with GOLKAR would be in the near future was left unclear. Brigadier-General Wahab argued that 'I think the people should wait until GOLKAR's extraordinary congress is held. And ABRI still hasn't come up with a firm position as yet, not until the new law on political parties is introduced'.[25] In the same vein, ABRI Chief of Socio-political Affairs, Lieutenant-General Bambang Yudhoyono argued that despite ABRI's historical relationship with GOLKAR, 'ABRI wants GOLKAR to be independent and to fight its own political battles in the future. I believe GOLKAR's future is bright if it can truly represent the people's aspirations, offer the nation the best alternatives and take an active role in national development'.[26] He also denied that ABRI was involved in setting up various mechanisms and the agenda of GOLKAR for its July Congress.[27]

Despite the statements by Brigadier-General Wahab and Lieutenant-General Bambang, on 28 June 1998, the PPP leadership criticised ABRI's commitment to political reforms in the country as it was accused of allegedly holding a 'co-ordination meeting' with GOLKAR on 27 June at the Armed Forces Headquarters in Cilingkap, Jakarta. According to Mr Tosari Wijaya, the PPP Secretary-General, 'that meeting is diametrical to ABRI's own concept of reform which says that it stands above all the political parties'. Mr Tosari expressed the PPP Executive Board's 'strong regret and objection' as ABRI had failed to maintained its self-proclaimed equal distance from al the political parties in the country.[28]

The PPP statement jolted ABRI somewhat, forcing General Wiranto to comment on 29 June, that ABRI would not be taking sides with GOLKAR in the general election nor give it any 'special treatment'. He reasserted that 'ABRI will stand above all the political parties and not take sides'. He argued that 'we still maintain a historical link with GOLKAR but that is it. GOLKAR is no different from the other political parties'. Unlike the position taken rather unwisely, by General Hartono in 1996 when he argued that every ABRI personnel was a GOLKAR cadre, General Wiranto argued that the military would remain neutral and 'keep an equal distance between all parties'.[29]

Against this backdrop, as the timing for the Special GOL-KAR Congress neared, the infighting and struggle within the dominant party intensified. Importantly, on 29 June, a planned meeting of GOLKAR was cancelled by Suharto, the former President and still Chief patron of the GOLKAR. In the words of Try Sutrisono, the deputy chairman of the GOLKAR's board of patrons as 'the meeting arranged by Habibie, who is the acting chairman of GOLKAR's board of patron and the secretary of the board, Akbar Tanjung, was not in line with GOLKAR's proper procedures' the meeting could not be convened. According to Try, 'as acting Chairman, Pak Habibie should have consulted with Pak Harto before calling the meeting'. Speaking at the Armed Forces Pensioners Association, PEPABRI, of which Try is the Chairman, he said that the meeting was cancelled following Habibie's discussion with the GOLKAR board.[30] This event clearly sign-posted that GOLKAR was bipolarised into two main camps, those for and against Habibie, with alleged 'Suhartoists', on the one side, and supporters of Habibie, on the other.

With a week to go to the Extraordinary GOLKAR Congress, the two 'camps' exposed their respective candidates for the GOLKAR Chair, namely, Akbar Tanjung and Edi Sudradjat. The former was backed by supporters of Habibie and strangely, the Armed Forces Headquarters, while the latter

184

was closely aligned with PEPABRI, led by former Vice-President Try Sutrisno as well as a faction within GOLKAR under the leadership of Sudharmono, another former Vice-President. For many, the Akbar-Edi contest was a simple proxy battle between the supporters of Habibie and those who wanted to promote 'Suhartoism', even though a closer analysis of Edi's supporters would indicate that their allegiance to Suharto was not clear as many of them had suffered or were disadvantaged by the former President in one way or another.[31] Many also viewed Akbar as representing 'pro-reform' with Edi being perceived as a 'gradualist' as far as reforms were concerned.

At the GOLKAR board of patrons meeting, technically chaired by Suharto, on 3 July 1998, the Executive Board, chaired by Harmoko, was heavily criticised for failing to anticipate and respond appropriately to the calls for reforms. The meeting chaired by President Habibie, also reproached the Executive Board for failing to respond positively and imbue a sense of calm on the people following the May 1998 riots. For instance, Try Sutrisono argued that 'GOLKAR leaders have been slow to anticipate developments in the progress of reforms and late in taking necessary action to comply with the spirit of the movement'. In view of this, Try argued that 'the board of patrons, advisors and councillors as well as the three major GOLKAR groupings – the Armed Forces, the bureaucracy and the Representatives of Social and Religious Groups – must be reviewed and adjusted in a bid to comply with the aspirations of the people and the coming future'.[32] In this connection too, Sarwono Kusummatmadja, the former Environment Minister, argued that 'it was GOLKAR's executive board which re-nominated Pak Harto for the Presidency. So why then was it them who also asked him to step down?'.[33] This point was also taken up by Indra Bambang Utoyo, a GOLKAR legislator who stated that 'GOLKAR executives should examine themselves' in view of their past be-

185

haviour, in particular, with regard to Suharto's re-election. He cited the decision by Harmoko in October 1997 to renominate Suharto even though the President had asked GOLKAR to reconfirm with its cadres and members nationwide whether they really wanted Suharto to serve another term. However, 'Harmoko immediately said that the GOLKAR Executive Board would renominate Pak Harto without even checking with GOLKAR cadres and members'.[34]

Members of the GOLKAR Executive Board rejected the accusations of their 'patrons', arguing that the board did do what was possible within the constraints of the circumstances. Agung Laksono, a GOLKAR Deputy Chairman and Minister of Youth Affairs in the Habibie cabinet argued that 'it is baseless for the patron board to accuse us of failing to react positively and imbue a sense of calm among the people following the May riots'. He argued that the Executive Board did instruct its cadres to establish 'crisis centres' to provide shelter for victims of the unrest. Agung, in dismissing Try's accusations as 'unfounded' also lambasted the patrons for failing to coordinate with the executive board in finding solutions to the problems of the country.[35] What the exchange between the Board of Patrons and Executive Board highlighted was the deep split in the GOLKAR leadership, with, allegedly, the 'Suhartoists', on one side and supporters of Habibie and Harmoko, on the other. It was the latter which also called for the abolition of the Board of Patron and it be replaced by an Advisory Board.

Following the opening of the extraordinary GOLKAR Congress by President Habibie on 9 July and where all the key leaders called on the party and its members to be 'reform-minded', the divisions between the 'two camps' emerged very quickly when there was a need to appoint a representative from the board of patron to the seven-member Executive Committee. While Try Sutrisono nominated Siswono Yudohusodo, the Habibie camp put up an unknown, Soelasikin Moerpratomo with Try's choice prevailing following his meeting with Habibie.[36] However, the real fight was for the Chair of GOLKAR and it was here that the future of GOLAKAR, Habibie, ABRI and possibly, Indonesia was to be decided. Initially, Edi Sudradjat was believed to be in the lead with 21 out of the 27 provincial branches supporting him, mainly due to the fact that most of the GOLKAR branches were under the leadership of retired ABRI officers. However, by the time the results were, the outcome was reversed with Akbar Tanjung, Habibie's man, winning the race by garnering support from 17 branches compared to only 10 for Edi, thus becoming the first ever elected Chairman of GOLKAR.

This victory was largely due to the direct intervention of the ABRI Headquarters, in particular, General Wiranto. Not only did Akbar Tanjung win due to the belief that he was Habibie's candidate, represented the forces of reform and was a much younger candidate in age, the image of Edi as representing the 'Suhartoists' and thus the 'old and defeated forces' sounded the death knell for the latter. ABRI Headquarters' support for Akbar was also, in part, motivated by the need to prevent a paralysis in national political leadership, which was most likely the outcome if Edi had won the GOLKAR Chair. A victory for Edi would have allowed the former Armed Forces Chief and Minister of Defence and Security, and his supporters to mount a bid to force President Habibie out of office at the 10 November 1998 Extraordinary MPR Session. At the same time, the ABRI Headquarters was believed to have made a 'deal' with the Habibie camp with some important GOLKAR posts being given to the people from the 'Wiranto camp' even though Akbar's victory was also due to strong sentiments that GOLKAR should be more like other political parties and where its links with the military should be terminated, requiring thus, a civilian rather than a retired military general at its helm. Akbar later announced that GOLKAR's Secretary General would be Major-General (Rtd) Tuswandi, a former instructor at the National Resilience Institute. The

187

'Suhartoists' defeat was even more profound as the provincial delegates voted to abolish all the three of GOLKAR's patronage bodies, namely, the board of patrons, board of councillors and board of advisers, the first which was headed by Suharto and which had veto powers over all party decisions.

Following the electoral victory of Akbar Tanjung, the major controversy that erupted involved General Wiranto's role in ensuring the defeat of Edi Sudradjat. Thus, despite General Wiranto's earlier statements that ABRI would stay neutral in the contest, in the end, in the name of stability and continuity, many believed that the Armed Forces Chief intervened on the side of Akbar and Habibie. Many believe that General Wiranto and his Chief of Socio-political Affairs, Lieutenant-General Bambang Yudhoyono instructed Major-General Mardiyano, Bambang Yudhoyono's assistant, to telephone regional military commanders to influence GOLKAR's chapters nationwide to vote for Akbar. Also, General Wiranto is believed to have met with chairmen of 17 GOLKAR regional chapters at Hotel Shangri-la in the morning of 11 July, the day of the voting, to 'impress' upon them to vote for Akbar, something which angered Edi, Wiranto's former mentor.[37] The Director-General of Socio-political Affairs in the Ministry of Home Affairs, Dunidja, was reported to have made similar calls on the various GOLKAR chapters on the instructions of Syarwan Hamid, the Minister of Home Affairs.

Thus, essentially, even though it was a GOLKAR election with civilians being gradually empowered, the post-Congress ramifications were to widen the divide within ABRI body politic, especially between serving and non-serving officers. For one, Wiranto succeeded in upsetting his former mentor, Edi Sudradjat when he effectively succeeded in ensuring Akbar's victory even though on paper, Edi was expected to win without much difficulty. It also led to many retired ABRI, especially Army officers, to express their unhappiness with ABRI Headquarters and the role it was playing in national politics, accusing Wiranto, to some extent, of betraying the Army and its interest. In this connection, a group of 13 retired Generals from the 1945 and post-1945 Generation, for instance, lashed out at ABRI Headquarters, especially Wiranto, for interfering in the GOLKAR Congress.[38] Indirectly, however, ABRI Headquarters and Wiranto's actions were beneficial for the longer term interests of the Armed Forces as it guaranteed its continued influence while at the same time succeeded in creating an image that that key ABRI leaders were pro-reformist and distant from Suharto. For the believers in the 'conspiracy theory' all this was viewed as part of the Indonesian 'Wayang Kulit' with former President Suharto and others wanting Edi and Try to 'appear' to challenge Akbar Tanjung, when, indeed, this was the outcome that was being desired anyway, being the best course and option for the time being as Habibie and his government were viewed as the safest option for the country and corporate interests of all the key players in the country.

The retired ABRI, especially Army senior officers' unhappiness with Wiranto's actions led to the establishment of *Barisan Nasional* or the National Front immediately following the GOLKAR's Congress, which also became one of the most critical forum against the Habibie government. A More serious outcome was the decision of these senior officers to withdraw from GOLKAR and to establish a political party, the Justice and Unity Party under the leadership of Edi Sudrajat. A serving senior officer told the author that this was not just because the retired generals were unhappy with General Wiranto's close co-operation with GOLKAR but even more important, these generals were disturbed in the manner GOLKAR was being managed and instead of being reformed, it was rather being 'Islamised'.[39]

ABRI'S REFORM AND SOUL-SEARCHING

An important consequence of Suharto's fall was the lightning 'adjustments' that took place within the ABRI High Command, best represented by the removal of officers deemed loyal to Lieutenant-General Prabowo Subianto, Suharto's son-in-law, and who was regarded as the key rival to Wiranto. Within thirty-six hours of Suharto's resignation, two key officers commanding elite troops and based in the capital, and who had only been appointed two months earlier, were relieved of their commands. Lieutenant-General Prabowo Subianto was relieved as Chief of the Army Strategic Reserves Command or KOSTRAD and replaced for 18 hours by Major-General Jhony Lumintang, a Wiranto loyalist, who subsequently handed the command to Major-General Djamari Chaniago, the former commander of the *Siliwangi* Division. The Commander-General of the Army Special Force or KOPASSUS, Major-General Muchdi Purwopranjono was replaced by Major-General Syahrir M. S., who was then Chief of the *Udayana* Command, overseeing Bali, East and West Nusa Tenggara and East Timor. Both Prabowo and Muchdi were close allies.

Wiranto denied that the removal of both Prabowo and Muchdi, especially the former, was untimely or unusual. General Wiranto argued that 'the Prabowo transfer has long been planned but the national situation prevented us from carrying it out. Now that things are calmer, we can replace the chiefs of KOSTRAD and KOPASSUS. We adopt the principle of transfer of area and transfer of duty'. General Wiranto also tried to dismiss rumours that Prabowo's removal was due to any personal rivalries but rather due to the fact that 'General Prabowo to date has never held any commanding post in education. He has always been in combat and operational units. We feel that any senior officer must have a complete overall experience'.[40] With regard to the unprecedented 18 hours command of the

190

KOSTRAD by Major-General Lumintang, General Wiranto argued that the appointment was only a 'caretaker' one to consolidate the KOSTRAD troops which were deployed in various parts of the capital as a result of the student demonstrations and rioting. Once this had been undertaken, the command was transferred to his successor, Major-General Djamari. As to why General Prabowo was not tasked with the 'consolidation' of the KOSTRAD soldiers was never explained by General Wiranto, fuelling further that the removal of both Prabowo and Muchdi was nothing more than a 'cleanup' of Wiranto's rivals and his attempt to consolidate ABRI under his command. There were also strong rumours that the removal of Prabowo and Muchdi was also related to their alleged involvement in various kidnapping and torturing of political dissidents, especially prior and during the 'May Revolution' as well as alleged attempts by Prabowo to force President Habibie to remove Wiranto as PANGAB and replace him either with Lieutenant-General Hendropriyono or even Prabowo himself.[41]

Additionally, Wiranto also relieved Major-General Kivlan Zen, the Chief-of-Staff of KOSTRAD and the Commander of the Jakarta Garrison, Major-General Syafrie Sjamsoeddin, of their commands and posted them to ABRI Headquarters. Both officers were known to be close associates of Prabowo. They were replaced by Major-General Ryamizard Racucu and Major-General Djaja Suparman respectively, both of whom are known to be close to Wiranto. General Wiranto was also instrumental in removing the Air Force Chief, Air Marshal Sutria Tabagus, the Navy Chief, Admiral Arif Kusharyadi and the Police Chief, General Dibyo Widodo, all of whom were Suharto appointees. In their place, Wiranto appointed Vice Admiral Widodo, Vice-Marshal Hanafie Asnan and Lieutenant-General Roesmanhadi as the new chiefs of the Navy, Air Force and Police respectively, thereby consolidating his control of the Armed Forces. At the same time, on 8 June, in or-

191

der to spruce ABRI's public image, General Wiranto restructured the Armed Forces' information centre by combining it with that of the Ministry of Defence and Security. The former Armed Forces' spokesman, Brigadier-General Wahad Mokodongan was replaced by a two-star general, Major-General Syamsul Ma'arif and the new replacement immediately announced that he would not censor the media as 'it is extremely outdated to apply a censorship approach against the mass media. I think it is more important to strike a common perception between the mass media and the Armed Forces Headquarters'.[42]

In addition to the changes in ABRI's top leadership, another important development that occurred was the investigation and trial of a number of ABRI personnel who were believed to be involved in various wrongful activities, including the shooting of the students at Trisakti University and the kidnapping of political activists opposed to the Suharto regime. In late May 1998, General Wiranto announced that 19 members of ABRI would face a court-martial for their alleged involvement in the 12 May shooting at Trisakti University which left four student protesters dead. On 30 June, General Wiranto admitted that some members of the military were involved in the abduction of political activists. The Commission for Missing Persons and Victims of Violence (KONTRAS) had earlier identified the involvement of various ABRI units, including 'the Duren Sawit military subdistrict, the East Java military district, the Jakarta Military Command, the Jakarta Police, the National Police and members of the Military Police'. Additionally, the KOPASSUS and ABRI's Intelligence Wing (BIA) were also alleged to be involved.[43] As a result, General Wiranto instituted investigations into the role of a number of ABRI's officers in the kidnapping of political activists.

On 14 July, the Military Police Chief, Major-General Syamsu Djalal announced that a number of KOPASSUS personnel were arrested for their role in the abduction of political activists as they 'exceeded their orders' and committed 'procedural errors'.[44] Increasingly, pressure build-up with Suharto's son-in-law, Lieutenant-General Prabowo Subianto, being perceived as a major player in the kidnappings. Prabowo, who was the Commandant-General of the Army's crack forces, KOPASSUS, until late March 1998, stated on 17 July that in the light of the ongoing investigations, he was 'ready to take responsibility' for what happened.[45] Commenting on Prabowo's remarks, President Habibie announced that 'I believe and am sure that ABRI will systematically, wisely and tactfully handle the problem, specifically in handing over the results of their investigations to the existing legal authorities so that those in the wrong receive proper punishment'. He also stated that ABRI 'have their Military Honorary Board and they also have military judges and we will leave the problem to that mechanism. We have to be prudent and careful and we must also trust the fact that ABRI are one with the people and when the people are at a disadvantage, ABRI feels the pain. So let us leave it to ABRI'.[46]

On 3 August, General Wiranto instituted the Military Honorary Council to investigate the actions of three senior officers with regard to the kidnapping of political activists. The officers were Lieutenant-General Prabowo, Major-General Muchi Purwopranjono, Prabowo's successor of the KOPASSUS and Colonel Chairawan, Commander of KOPASSUS Group IV, which covered intelligence operations. On 24 August, Lieutenant-General Prabowo was retired from the military for misinterpreting an order that had come from his unnamed superior. Both Major-General Muchi and Colonel Chairawan were also stood down.

In December 1998, the long-awaited trial of 11 Army officers from KOPASSUS, charged with kidnapping nine political activists, opened in Jakarta, with the main defendant, the Commander of the 'Rose' kidnapping team, a young Major, arguing that he made the decision to kidnap the activists "on the basis of his own conscience". He argued that the activists

193

were radicals whose actions threatened national stability as they were organising anti-government demonstrations. Critics, however, continued to express dismay with the trial by arguing that a 'cover-up' was in the offing and expressed surprise that such blatant disregard of the military chain of command and the law could have taken place. *The Jakarta Post* editorial maintained that the trial was nothing more than a 'kangaroo court'.[47] There were also moves by other groups to have the trial halted, especially by the National Commission on Human Rights, which argued that "as a measure to restore faith in ABRI's sincerity, the trial proceedings should be stopped for justice, truth and the respect for human rights". The Commission saw the trial as nothing more than an "effort to cover-up the case".[48]

Another related aspect of ABRI's 'clean-up' was with regard to its future role in the country's politics. Suharto's regime and political order since 1967 was very much associated with the heightened role of the Armed Forces in the country's politics. Following Suharto's resignation and the assumed role of 'people's power' in it, one of the key demands associated with 'political reforms' has been the demand that ABRI's political role should be reduced so that the country's fledgling democracy can take off. ABRI's concept of dual function has justified and rationalised its active social-political role alongside its traditional role in security and defence. With the resignation of Suharto, a former military General, many political analysts argued that it was timely and necessary for ABRI to relinquish its socio-political role before any successful democratic reforms can take place. Dr Yahya Muhaimin, the Head of the Centre for Security Peace, Gadjah Mada University in Jogjakarta argued that ABRI must abandoned its security approach through which it justify using stern measures to maintain national stability or risk losing popular support. He, however, commended ABRI for supporting the democratisation process and accepting the reduction of its seats in the DPR from 100 to 75.[49] In this connection, other scholars such as Dr Ryaas

Rasyid, the Rector of the Institute for Public Administration, argued that ABRI's political role should be further reduced and among the first steps in the direction would be to reduce further seats allocated to it to only 50 in the DPR. Dr Ryaas, who headed a seven-member team which worked on drafts for three political laws covering general elections, political parties and function of the DPR and MPR, stated that such a proposal had been included in the draft proposal that was being submitted to the government.[50] Eventually, ABRI was given no seats in the DPR, indicating clearly that ABRI's role in politics was still valued by the national political mainstream. The 40 seats were a compromise between ABRI's opponents asking for the presence to be reduced to 5 percent while ABRI continued to demand 10 percent of the seats. In the end, a compromise of 7 percent was reached, which amounted to 40 seats instead of the 55 originally allotted to the Armed Forces.

Responding to popular calls on ABRI to ease out of its political role, on 21 June 1998, Lieutenant-General Bambang Yudhoyono, ABRI Chief of Socio-political Affairs, announced that 'the idea of ABRI now is to readjust its role, to build a new political role-sharing [sic]'. He argued that 'ABRI must participate in developing the nation. We have to continuously readjust and reposition'. The catalyst for this readjustment was the unexpected resignation of Suharto which in turn elevated Habibie to the Presidency, led to the formation of many new political parties, the release of some political prisoners and the flowering of the kind of open debate that in the pre-21 May era would have been cruelly suppressed. Lieutenant-General Bambang compared these changes to the shock of an atomic bomb explosion. He argued that such shocks 'happened in the past in the Soviet Union and Eastern Europe. It happened now in our country. I think this is a shock that exist in our country. We have to adjust rapidly'. In this connection, an important aspect of ABRI's 'new thinking' would be the need to pull back from its traditional 'dual function' involvement in politics.

The ABRI Socio-political Chief argued that 'in some cases, is some regions, ABRI may still influence society directly. But in other cases and other regions, in may be better to influence indirectly. It is an open chapter'. In this connection, while ABRI agreed that there was a need 'to adopt a universal principle of democracy', Lieutenant-General Bambang also cautioned that 'the precise method should be adapted to local history, local values and local culture'.[51]

Related to the call for a review of ABRI's role was the growing pressure to have the Police Force separated from the Armed Forces. On 10 June 1998, the National Commission on Human Rights recommended that the police force be separated from the Armed Forces so that it could become independent and be in a better position to serve the public. The National Commission told the House of Representatives Commission for Defence and Security, Foreign Affairs and Legal Affairs that the Police Force should no longer be the 'political tool' of the government or ABRI. It should professionally serve and protect the public rather than become a 'security tool of the power holders'. The National Commission also argued that the police should be separated from the Armed Forces due to the inherent conflict in their professional doctrines: 'The military's doctrine is to crush enemies while that of the police should be to protect and serve the public. The Police will never become professional unless it follows its own doctrine'.[52] Following from this, different groups, including members from the national police force itself, started arguing that the best way to strengthen the Police force was 'for the police to leave ABRI'.[53] In this connection, when Dr T. B. Ronny Nitikasbara, a lecturer at the Police Institute delivered a speech on the subject at the graduation ceremony of 150 cadets from the Indonesian Police Institute on 18 June, the National Police Chief, General Dibyo Widodo commented that 'you can see for yourselves how the long clapping expresses their wish to leave ABRI'.[54]

Another aspect of the 'new thinking' in ABRI under the

new political paradigm was the withdrawal of the Armed Forces from various theatres of military operation in the country. First, President Habibie announced that 1,000 combat troops would be withdrawn from East Timor. Following this, General Wiranto announced on 7 August that ABRI would withdraw all combat troops from Aceh while apologising for the 'conduct of the troops while they were assigned in Aceh'.[55] In June 1998, the National Commission on Human Rights reported that more than 39,000 Acehnese had died in military operations over the past decade with more than 1,000 believed to be in military detention.[56] General Wiranto also lifted the province status as a 'military operation region' thereby allowing normalcy to the Aceh after more than a decade.

Additionally, ABRI was involved with two other initiatives, which had a direct bearing on its role in the country's politics. First, it involved the establishment of new body called the Council for Enforcement of Security and Law. Though chaired by the President, the day to day running was in the hands of General Wiranto, who chaired a smaller Executive Committee. Even though the President had established the Council, by decree on 9 November, it was only made public a month later, on 8 December 1998. Consisting of 34 member, including 23 cabinet ministers, the body was tasked 'to ensure the success of the reform agenda and to overcome various crises in society, in the realms of social affairs, the economy, politics, law and defence and security'.[57] President Habibie promised that the Council would not operate like the oppressive KOPKAMTIB or the Operational Command for the Restoration of Security and Order, which operated from the mid-1960s through to the late 1990s.[58] However, what the establishment of the Council did signal was that the security situation in the country was worsening and that there was a need to give ABRI a stronger clout to the deal with the situation.

The second development related to the proposed establishment of armed civilian militia or *Rakyat Terlatih* (RATIH).

197

RATIH was later renamed KAMRA or *Keamanan Rakyat* (People's Security). Following the experience of using vigilantes during the Special MPR Session in November, the idea that a more professional and well-trained civilian militia should be established gained support. Even though there were many critics, in principle, there was widespread support for the idea, as similar organisations existed in other countries, such as the National Guards in the United States.[59] Opponents of KAMRA, however, maintained that the national security situation did not warrant such a force and if anything, it would only worsened the conflict among the people.[60] In his budget statement on 6 January 1999, President Habibie defended the idea of raising a 40,000-strong civilian militia on grounds that it was urgently needed to uphold law and security and to bolster the over-stretched Police Force. Finance Minister, Bambang Subianto had earlier announced that the government was setting aside 300 billion rupiah or about $US38 million to establish the militia. President Habibie argued that "considering the urgency of the need to uphold the law and create a feeling of security in society, there is a need to involve the concrete participation of the people in efforts to defend the nation". Also, "the setting up of KAMRA,...will also provide temporary employment for job-seekers whose numbers have been on the rise because of layoffs". The Indonesian President also stated that a 70,000-strong militia would be raised within two years bringing the ratio of Police to citizens from 1:11,000 to 1:750 even though ideal ratio would be 1:300.[61]

CHALLENGES FACING HABIBIE AND HIS GOVERNMENT

The Credibility Gap

This challenge was most glaringly highlighted by an editorial in *The Jakarta Post* on 23 May 1998 as follows:

The greatest hurdle yet facing President Habibie is his own public image; he is perceived as too closely associated with the failings and notorious landmarks of the departing President. Habibie, known for quirky economic theories and profligate spending in his years as Research and Technology Minister, should have realised that right now he is not only short of political legitimacy, but is perceived as an anti-market personality who favours nepotism and crony capitalism. His family and close relatives reportedly control or partly own more than 80 enterprises. One of the first measures he took upon his election to the Vice-Presidency in the middle of March was to appoint his own brother, J. E. Habibie, as the head of the Batam Development Authority.

All these are not the characteristics befitting a leader whose primary task is to establish integrity and credibility of his own and regain public confidence in the government. Public confidence is crucial for soliciting full co-operation and understanding on the part of the people, who will have to endure many hardships within the next two to three years at least before the nation's economy, already paralysed, stabilises and recovers.[62]

That Habibie had many detractors, from within and without the country, was known long before his became President. The country's prominent labour leader, Muchtar Pakpahan, who had been jailed by the former President similarly dismissed Habibie as his 'own man' arguing that Habibie was only a 'stalking horse for Suharto'. Muchtar, while in Geneva to address the International Labour Organisation stated in an interview with the press that Habibie 'has always been Suharto's puppet and Suharto is still pulling the strings behind the scenes. The people do not trust the present government because it carries the imprint of the former regime'.[63]

In all fairness, President Habibie, in his own way, tried to regain and win public confidence, by making various state-ments and more important, through various measures, to dem-onstrate that the perceived image about him and his policies were faulty. For instance, within a few days of becoming President, his brother, Junus Effendy, quit his post as Head of the Batam Industrial Development Authority and his son, Il-ham Habibie, stepped down from his post as special assistant to the Head of the High Technology Division of the Agency for the Assessment and Application of Technology. This was to make good the new President's promise that he would crack down on corruption, collusion and nepotism. This move was later followed by other public officials such as General Wiranto, whose wife and daughter resigned their posts as members of the People's Consultative Assembly from the GOLKAR faction.[64] It was in view of these moves that in contrast to *The Jakarta Post* editorial that a editorial in *The Indonesian Observer* argued that 'the present government is off to a good start by making the right decisions in a timely manner and this will endear parties such as multilateral finan-cial bodies and pro-democracy forces'.[65]

President Habibie also had to contend with many critics who argued that his assumption of the Presidency was illegal. Many argued that former President Suharto resignation and the subsequent assumption of power and the post of the Presi-dency by Habibie was not constitutional. For instance, the for-mer speaker of the House of Representative, Wahono, stated in early June that Habibie was not a legitimate President as he lacked a mandate from the MPR.[66] An important basis of this argument was due to the fact that the MPR had not been con-vened to revoke the mandate it gave Suharto in March 1998. In view of this, Political Scientist, Arbi Sanit argued that 'if the extraordinary session of the Assembly does not revoke the mandate of Suharto, the debate on Habibie's legitimacy will never end'.[67] At the same time, a group of 33 Indonesian law-yers filed a suit against former President Suharto for violating civil law by installing Habibie on 21 May. They argued that 'it is clear that this act disregarded the Constitution and breached Article 6M of the constitutional law of 1945, which states that a President and Vice-President must be elected by a majority in the People's Consultative Assembly. Owing to that we demand that Suharto immediately cancel the appointment of Habibie as President'.[68] Habibie's supporters have, however, tried to deflect such criticisms. One group that has come forward strongly to defend Habibie has been ICMI. On 19 June, ICMI's acting Chairman, Achmad Tirtosudiro told the press that attacks on Habibie should cease and the President given a chance to govern and implement reforms. He accused Habibie's critics of being unfair as the economic turmoil was essentially a legacy of the Suharto government. He argued that 'Habibie's Presidency is legitimate' and there was a 'need to convey this because there are people who are still disputing Habibie's legitimacy'. He argued that there were certain groups which were trying to overthrow the President 'because they do not like Habibie personally' and may be because 'they think they could do better'.[69]

CONVENTION OF THE EXTRAORDINARY
MPR SESSION

For many political and legal analysts, the need for the Special Session of the MPR was considered important due to the 'legitimacy crisis' and legality of the Habibie government. The new President's opponents argued that the Habibie government was invalid due to the various procedural defects inherited from the transfer of power from former President Suharto. However, Habibie's supporters argued that the transfer of power fulfilled all aspects of the law and this gave Habibie the right to remain in office until 2003. It was mainly the debate around this question that led many to dub the Habibie

201

government as being 'transitional' in nature, with the crisis of confidence continuing unabated.

While most political analysts agreed about the need for an extraordinary MPR Session, the debate essentially has been how soon it should be held and more important, what the meeting was expected to accomplish. For some, the MPR meeting should only have one agenda, namely, to set the date for the next general election. However, others have argued that the MPR should appoint a new Chairman for itself as well as a new President and Vice-President for the country. On 3 July, Harmoko, the MPR Chairman announced that the extraordinary Session of the MPR would be held on 10 November 1998, coinciding with the country's celebration of National Heroes Day. According to Harmoko, 'we decided to take advantage of the momentum of Heroes Day. It will give a certain nuance to the extraordinary meeting, to strengthen the unity and cohesion of the nation'.[70] A day before the Extraordinary GOLKAR Congress started, President Habibie argued that the November Extraordinary MPR Session should not debate the election of a new President as this would further create instability in the country. Rather, the Session should debate and endorse new laws with regard to the elections, on political parties and the structure of the MPR and DPR.[71]

Eventually, the Special Session of the MPR was held from 10-13 November 1998 and twelve draft decrees were passed. These included:

1. The decree on the amendment of Assembly's internal rules;

2. The decree to revoke the 1983 Assembly decree on referendum;

3. The decree to revoke the March 1998 decree on the State Policy Guidelines (GBHN);

4. The decree to revoke the 1998 decree granting the President extraordinary powers;

5. The decree to revoke the 1978 Assembly decree on the Propagation and Implementation of *Pancasila*;

6. The decree on general elections;

7. The decree limiting the Presidential and Vice-Presidential terms of office;

8. The decree on the principles of developmental reform in the light of safeguarding and normalising life in the nation;

9. The decree on the administration of regional autonomy, management, distribution and harnessing of natural resources in a just manner to strike a fiscal balance between provincial administration and the central govern-ment within the unitary state of the Republic of Indonesia;

10. The decree of human rights;

11. The decree on good governance free from corruption, collusion and nepotism; and

12. The decree on political economy within economic democracy.[72]

Holding of General Elections

Following Suharto's resignation, various political groups argued that general elections should be held as soon as possible to legitimise the political leadership in power through popular mandate. However, once the Habibie government began examining the various options that were opened, it became obvious that practically this was not possible. As was argued by Dr Afan Gafar, 'even if the government passes the new election laws in December [1998], it will still take a lot of time to complete the administrative requirements and to earn campaign funds. I think the end of 1999 would be the soonest an election could be held'. Elaborating his position following a hearing at the House of Representatives Commission II on 8 June 1998, he argued that 'we have to prepare political laws that cover the general elections, political parties and status of parliament. Even more important is gathering funds for the election. Where are we going to find funds at a time of economic crisis?'[73] In addition to the long-drawn and complicated process involved in organising the election as well as the dearth of funds and the drain on the economy such an even would have, Dr Afan also argued that many people in the regional areas disagreed with plans to hold an early election, fearing that such an election may produce 'unexpected and undesired consequences'.[74]

In the light of the ongoing debates and discussion the political leadership concluded that general elections could be held by May 1999 even though the ABRI leadership had proposed an earlier date of March 1999. The ABRI Chief of Socio-political Affairs, Lieutenant-General Bambang Yudhoyono argued that 'after discussing the schedule with the Ministry of Home Affairs and the team responsible for drafting the new political laws, ABRI understands that preparations for the general election will take time'.[75]

Critics of the government's timetable for general election showed no let-up and continued to criticise the government for prolonging the country's political and economic sufferings. Critics such as Emil Salim, argued that by delaying the general election, the government was inadvertently also delaying the country's political and economic recovery. They argued that until a 'legitimate government' brought about by popular mandate was not in power, domestic and international confidence will not be forthcoming, something which was viewed as vital to revive the ailing economy.[76] On 3 December 1998, the Speaker of the House of Representatives, Harmoko, announced that the country's next general election would be held on 7 June 1999.

The Presidential Elections

One of the key questions bedevilling post-Suharto Indonesia and the Habibie Presidency has been with regard to the next presidential elections. Even though following Suharto's resignation and the swearing-in of the then Vice-President Habibie, the new incumbent was to constitutionally serve out the term of Suharto, that is, until March 2003, massive pressure was placed on the new President to hold fresh presidential elections following the general elections. To this, President Habibie was largely agreeable. However, what was not clear was whether President Habibie would run for the Presidency himself. In an interview with Reuters on 9 June, he indicated that he had no plans to become the country's President after the general elections which were scheduled for 1999. However, in his discussion with a Japanese newspaper, *Nihon Keizai Shimbun* in mid-June 1998, President Habibie announced that he would neither declare his candidacy for the Presidency voluntarily nor join parliamentary elections by setting up a new party. However, he would do so if urged by his supporters as 'I am not a coward'.[77]

At the same time, the names of other potential candidates were being proposed. One of this was General Wiranto, the Minister of Defence and Security and Armed Forces Commander. For instance, during General Wiranto's visit to the Bahrul Ulum Islamic Boarding School in Jombang, East Java, its Chairman, Hasib Abdul Wahad argued that 'I think he [General Wiranto] fits well as to what we need to become the nation's future leader'. Another religious teacher, Badli Masduqi argued that 'if the nation does not have other candidates, Wiranto is the one'. In the same vein, another religious teacher from Surabaya argued that 'the Armed Forces commander should become the number one person for legal and political reform in the country'.[78] General Wiranto, however, side-stepped the issue by arguing that he was 'one of the leaders of the nation already'.[79]

Just as with the general elections, there were many debates as to when the General Session of the MPR would be held and when would the accompanying Presidential elections take place. On 3 December, Harmoko announced that the MPR would convene on 28 August, when the new members of the House would be sworn in. Three days later, it was announced that the MPR Session would convene on 28 October 1999, which is also Youth Pledge Day and on 10 November 1999, which is National Heroes' Day, the country's President and Vice-President would be installed.[80]

Remedying the Ailing Economy

One of the most critical challenges facing Habibie and his government has been to improve the economy, which faced its worst crisis in more than thirty years. On becoming President, even though Habibie promised to stabilise the rupiah exchange rate, control inflation and implement the IMF reform agreement with the object of restoring foreign and domestic investor confidence, the response of the international finance agencies had been lukewarm at best. For instance, during a meeting of APEC Finance Ministers in Kananaskis, Canada, both Michel Camdessus, the Director of the IMF and Robert Rubin, the US Treasury Secretary argued that Indonesia would have to establish political stability first before any aid can be dispensed. Mr Rubin asserted that it would be premature for the IMF to resume aid to Indonesia, which was earlier delayed amid the political upheaval that led to Mr Suharto's resignation, on grounds that it was necessary 'to have the kind of economic and political circumstances in Indonesia that will make a programme effective'.[81] Mr Camdessus, endorsing Mr Rubin's stance, argued that it would take some time before the IMF would resume aid to Indonesia, merely helped to fuel speculations that the West, through the IMF, was in part responsible for Suharto's downfall. The IMF Chief, however, dismissed the charge arguing that 'the political turmoil and all the development have not been caused at all by our efforts to restore a solid basis for economic development'.[82]

Despite this, Habibie economic team led by the Co-ordinating Minister for Finance, Trade and Industry, Ginandjar Kartasasmita, announced in late May 1998 that the government was taking steps to rehabilitate the ruined economy and that it would meet its sovereign debt obligations. By May 1998, Indonesia's private foreign debt stood at US$64 billion, involving some 1,800 companies.[83] On 10 June, the IMF Asia-Pacific Director Hubert Neiss arrived in Jakarta to assess the economic situation in post-Suharto Indonesia while holding no quick hope of a quicker disbursement of the promised funds. He argued that there was a need to review the economic programme of the country, mainly to 'redo the macroeconomic framework and to set budget and monetary policy within that framework. The other focuses are to continue the financial and structural reforms'. Until these were not undertaken, the disbursement of the next US$1 billion of the US$43 billion rescue package for Indonesia would not resume.[84]

However, slowly and steadily, and partly, fearing a backlash which could plunge Indonesia into further crisis, the

Western nations began to trickle financial assistance into Indonesia. This began with the Japan Exim Bank granting a US $1 billion loan which was to be used for guaranteeing letters of credits issued by Indonesian banks. Even though several other donors had pledged to provide multi-billion dollars letters of credits guarantee to Indonesia, including US$1 billion from United States Exim Bank, A$400 million from Australia, US$3 billion from Singapore and DM300 million from Germany, all of these commitments had not been realised as their terms were difficult to implement, said Rahardi Ramelan, the Minister of Trade and Industry.[85]

Of particular importance was the role of the United States in this regard. The United States Agency for International Development announced on 18 June that it would give US$50 million in aid in the form of food and loan guarantees. The United States Secretary of State Madeleine Albright also announced on 17 June that Washington would resume support for international lending to Indonesia. She argued that 'we will support proposals for new World Bank and Asian Development Bank lending to Indonesia', something the US withheld during the political and economic turmoil that hit Indonesia and brought about Suharto's resignation. Ms Madeleine argued that she hoped that the IMF team visiting Jakarta would be able to make some headway so that the suspended funds could be released. In her assessment, it was too early to know whether the Habibie government would pursue and succeed in making political reforms based on democratic principles. However, in her view, 'it is not too early to reaffirm America's commitment to do all we can to help the Indonesian people. This is the right thing. It is also the smart thing because prospects for a stable transition to democracy will increase if humanitarian needs are addressed'.[86]

By mid-June 1998, the IMF had disbursed US$4 billion to Indonesia since the crisis, more than any other international donor. Despite this, Indonesian political and community lead-

208

ers continued to criticise the IMF and its 'hidden agenda'. For instance, in early June 1998, the Indonesian Parliament wrote to the IMF Managing Director, Mr Camdessus, expressing its concern over delays in IMF's funding to Indonesia. In response, the IMF Chief argued that he was aware of the parliament's 'concern about the country's economic situation and the toll it is imposing on the people'. However, he added that 'before any funds can be provided, the IMF and the government must first agree on an economic strategy for overcoming the deep economic crisis'.[87] Mr Camdessus' assurances were however dismissed by community leaders such as Dr Amien Rais. The Muhammadiyah leader argued that 'if we observe closely, it will not be wrong if we become suspiciou of the IMF's intentions to help Indonesia because it is always postponing, as though to interfere in our internal affairs'.[88]

Despite the handout, the economic situation of the Indonesians has been worsening, with the future appearing bleak rather than otherwise. This was best evident from the statistics released by the Central Bureau of Statistics on 2 July 1998. According to the bureau, the number of Indonesians living below the poverty line had soared to nearly 80 million, about 40 percent of the population. What was worst, the figure was likely to increase to 96 million or 48 percent of the total population by the end of the year as there was no sight of economic recovery.[89]

The Jakarta Riots and the Ethnic Chinese Enigma

One of the major issues to emerge in the immediacy of Suharto's resignation involved the causes of the Jakarta riots, especially between 12–15 May. Following Suharto's resignation, many alleged that an 'organised group or groups' were behind these riots. For instance, Dr Amien Rais, while addressing a gathering of 2,000 Chinese-Indonesians in Surakarta, Central Java in late May 1998 argued that the Jakarta and Surakarta riots were not spontaneous. Rather, 'there were people who masterminded the riots in Jakarta and Solo (Surakarta)'.[90] It was in this context that President Habibie ordered the ABRI leadership to investigate the matter. In a statement made public on 11 June, he said that 'I particularly ask the Armed Forces leadership to reveal the truth over allegations that an organised group was seen inciting people to burn and loot buildings in several areas where disturbances occurred'.[91]

Part of the reason for the government's reaction was the growing pressure from various public interest groups on the government to investigate and punish the culprits. Two such groups were the Co-ordinating Body for National Unity (BAKOM-PKB) and the Indonesian New Brotherhood Association (PERSABI). A BAKOM spokesperson for instance argued on 11 June that 'the government must conduct an investigation into the mid-May riots, find the provocateurs and announce the results of the investigation. If the government fails to clarify what happened, BAKOM-PKB will invite an international human rights organisation to conduct the investigation'.[92]

In the same vein, leaders of all the country's major religions condemned the 'racial riots' in Jakarta that left more than 1,000 people dead and call for an independent team to investigate was described as 'despicable and barbaric acts'. The religious leaders, meeting in the residence of the *Nahdatul Ulama* Chairman, Abdurrahman Wahid, argued that the riots were incited in an 'organised and systematic' manner by people who exploited existing racial and socio-economic differences. In a petition to the government, the religious leaders urged the government 'to take concrete steps to show its remorse toward this barbaric affair. We also call on the government, the authorities and anyone who feel compelled to uphold justice, to use all their power to terminate immediately all forms of

210

behaviour that try to divide the nation by exploiting differences. Today, it is happening to people of Chinese descent. Unless we eliminate this, it will happen to other ethnic groups'.[93]

Indonesia's ethnic Chinese were believed to have suffered the most during the riots preceding Suharto's resignation. Within days of Habibie taking over as the new President, pressure mounted on the new government to conduct an inquiry into the litany of reports that were coming in with regard to rape, abuse and public humiliation of women during the Jakarta riots, especially of Chinese descent even though the police did not register any reports during this period. Increasingly, it became clear that widespread gang rapes took place during this period and that 'these brutal acts were done by an organised group'.[94] As was reported by *The Straits Times*, 'the consensus among human-rights workers and rape counsellors is that the attacks were mostly organised by unknown groups, in the same way that increasing evidence suggests that organised groups were involved in instigating attacks of arson and vandalism aimed largely at ethnic Chinese neighbourhoods during the rioting. This evidence is based on reports that groups of men arrived simultaneously at various targets in the city with petrol bombs and other weapons and initiated the violence'.[95]

While internal and external pressure mounted on the Habibie government to investigate the alleged rapes, especially of Chinese women, the task of the government was not made easy by the lack of evidence. While many allegations were made of the crime, yet there was little to go by beyond that. As was alluded to by Women Affairs Minister Tuti Al-lawiyah, 'it seems that the rape victims are keeping their cases secret and that we have difficulties unveiling them'. While the government described the alleged rapes as 'very inhuman', most of the victims remained silent either due to shame or fear of retaliation.[96] In mid-July, Marzuki Darusman, the

211

Vice-Chairman of the National Commission on Human Rights argued that 'there is no doubt that mass rapes happened during the riots in Jakarta from May 12 to 14. We have concluded from the reports we received that there was a pattern of sexual violence against ethnic Chinese'.[97]

On 15 July, President Habibie, in a meeting with a delegation from the Women's Anti-Violence Society expressed his 'deep regret for what happened' and promised to be 'proactive in giving protection and security to the whole society to avoid repetition of the most inhuman event in the history of the nation'.[98] He also announced that an independent commission would be established to investigate the alleged rapes.

Additionally, most of the shopping centres, shops, shophouses, private homes and vehicles attacked, looted and burned during the riots belonged to ethnic Chinese. According to one initial report, nearly 1,200 people were killed during the riots along with 40 shopping centres, 2,479 shop/houses and 1,604 shops attacked, looted and burned, along with 1,119 vehicles, 1,026 private homes and 383 offices.[99] Ariel Heryanto was even more graphic in describing the tragedy. He argued that no racial or ethnic groups in Indonesia, no matter how agitated, could possibly inflict the systematic violence in which 1,198 lives (of which 27 died from gunfire) were lost, 150 females were raped, 40 shopping malls and 4,000 shops were burned down, and thousands of vehicles and houses were set afire simultaneously in 27 areas in a capital city of 10 million inhabitants in less than 50 hours'.[100]

Partly in recognition of the special problem of the ethnic Chinese in Indonesia, the Habibie government drafted new laws to erase the distinction between its indigenous and non-indigenous people and to give all citizens equal rights. As was stated by Mr Tanri Abeng, the Minister for State Enterprises, 'President Habibie is making a special effort to eliminate this-called distinction between *pribumis* and non-*pribumis*'. One of the ways was to remove the special codes in identity cards that enforced the distinction. According to Tanri Abeng, President Habibie stated categorically that his 'priority now is to convince the ethnic Chinese that they are Indonesians and they should be coming and doing their usual businesses'.[101]

At the same time, the Habibie government realised the dilemma it was in as the ethnic Chinese in Indonesia controlled a disproportionate portion of the nation's economy and if this was not corrected structurally, the problem would continue unresolved, with the native Indonesians being unhappy and the ethnic Chinese being targeted for attacks. In view of this problem, many Indonesian leaders, including some in the Habibie cabinet saw the exodus of Chinese businessmen and their wealth from the country as a golden opportunity to undertake structural reforms that would lead, eventually to the '*pribumiputraisation*' of the country's economy. Not only did the departure of the ethnic Chinese from Indonesia provided new opportunities for other Indonesians to move into businesses that had in the past been dominated by the former, it also created the setting whereby various political, economic and legal measures could be undertaken to effect this. While the Habibie government realised that the ethnic Chinese were an important key to the recovery of the Indonesian economy, the government was, however, frustrated with the slowness with which many Chinese businessmen were returning home with their capital. It was in this connection that in an interview with *The Washington Post* that the Indonesian President remarked that 'if the Chinese community doesn't come back because they don't trust their own country and society, I cannot force, nobody can force them. But do you really think that we will then die?....Their place will be taken over by others'.[102]

It was against this backdrop that one must appreciate and understand the rise of what has come to be known as the people's economy, spearheaded by Adi Sasono, the Minister for Co-operatives and Small Businesses. Under the slogan of *Ekonomi Kerakyatan* or People's Economy, Adi has attempted to solve various economic and social problems confronted by the ordinary people, especially in the villages and small towns as a result of the exodus of the ethnic Chinese overseas. This problem was further aggravated by the existence of various monopolies in the country. As Adi told the author, even though the government increased the subsidies for the various basic commodities in the country, in the first three months following the resignation of Suharto, that is, from May to July 1998, the prices of basic commodities continue to spiral and this was due to the monopolistic practices prevalent in the country, especially in various businesses that affected the basic livelihood of the ordinary citizen.[103] Adi argued that one of the negative legacies of the Suharto's economic system was that a few individuals were given awesome power, especially in the national economy, that could have detrimental consequences for the polity as a whole. Thus, one company controlled 50 percent of cement supplies, two companies controlled all aspects of paper supplies, from production to transportation, three companies controlled the cooking oil monopoly, one company controlled eighty percent of wheat flour production and the property market was largely in the hands of Suharto's children and his cronies. What this 'early dirty primitive capitalism' meant was that as far as the distribution network was concerned, it was not driven by the market but rather by an imperfect market controlled by a few individuals.[104] It was to break this economic stranglehold that Adi, from July 1998 onwards, started using the more than 780 cooperatives and 600 small businesses to supplement the existing 'monopolistic distribution network'. If nothing was done, the spiraling prices would have caused a crisis of confidence in the government of B. J. Habibie and as well as created a near-revolutionary situation, as people would have revolted, as they were not receiving their basic essential commodities. It was to salvage the serious political and economic situation that Adi was compelled to undertake various measures to promote the People's Economy so that it will be immune from various monopolistic practices in the country. By July 1998, three percent of the distribution system was in Adi's hands. By December 1998, the figure reached 22 percent and according to Adi this 'deterrent figure is sufficient to ensure that the 'monopolists behave themselves' as what he had actually done was to make the market a little more competitive for the benefit of the consumers.

On 3 November 1998, the Chairman of the Joint Fact-Finding Team, investigating the May 1998 riots, released its report titled '*Laporan Akhir Tim Gabungan Pencari Fakta (TGPF) Peristiwa Tanggal 13-15 Mei 1998, Jakarta, Solo, Palembang, Lampung, Surabaya dan Medan: Ringkasan Eksekutif*' [Final Report of the Joint Fact-Finding Team Investigationg the 13-15 May 1998 Incident, Jakarta, Solo, Palembang, Lampung, Surabaya and Medan: an executive summary]. The report concluded that 'the root cause of the May 13 to May 15 riots was the interaction of two key processes, namely the process of struggle on the part of the political elite in connection with the problem of maintaining the power of the national political leadership and the process of rapid economic and monetary deterioration'. The report concluded that 'the May 13 to May 15 riots were the culmination of a series of violent events, such as kidnappings (which in reality had been committed as far back as 1974, in the form of intelligence operations which could not be effectively supervised) and the Trisakti incident'. The report stated that 'the TGPF is convinced that the Trisakti incident was the trigger of the riot'.[105] The report also noted that 'within the struggle between the political elites there were key agents in the field who played an important part in the riots. In connection with this, the meeting at the KOSTRAD headquarters on May 14, 1998 should be seen as competent to disclose the roles of the actors within the struggle that led into the riots'.[106]

The report was, however, received with mixed reactions.

While some argued that the report further undermined the credibility of the government and Army, others were disappointed with the manner the whole inquiry was conducted. While Mochtar Buchori argued that it was a 'good report' even though he quickly admitted that 'it was not as complete as it should be'.[107] In actuality, the report was released amidst great divisions and rifts even among the team member. A number of the members staged a walk-out when the report was released, including the team's secretary Rosita Noer, who also funded the inquiry to the figure of Rp100 million. As the Singapore *Straits Times* reported, there were a number of important dissenting voices within the team, 'with some members becoming increasingly embittered by disagreements over parts of its contents, in particular, whether the gang-rapes of women during the unrest were organised'.[108]

Compared to the massive 'disinformation campaign' launched regionally and internationally by various groups, the team could only agree to the some 52 rape cases during the riots and could not conclude that these were undertaken in an organised fashion. In fact, the author was told by an important member of the investigation team that only 12 confirmed cases of rapes were recorded and he was startled when he read the figure of 52. He wondered where the additional 40 came from. In the end, the report and its framers did discredit themselves to some extent, as they were seen to be using the inquiry for various personal or group political purposes. According to a key member of the investigation team, it became obvious that a number of the members wanted to use the report to 'demolish the Habibie Government, to discredit ABRI, in particular the Army and KOPASSUS as well as to highlight gross human rights violations, especially against the ethnic Chinese even though there was inadequate evidence to prove these allegations'. Additionally, some members of the investigation team wanted to use the report 'to destroy two individuals, namely, Lieutenant-General Prabowo Subianto and Major-

216

General Syafrie Syamsuddin and as such, the report was framed accordingly'. Thus, 'even though the investigation team knew very well that nothing 'conspiratorial' transpired at the 14 May meeting at the KOSTRAD headquarters, yet it was included, notwithstanding the fact that an important member of the Habibie cabinet, Fahmi Idris, was also present'. Additionally, despite being informed of the 'possibly more important meetings of different elite groups that were taking place in Jakarta', the report opted for silence, demonstrating very clearly the biased and prejudical nature of the so-called 'final report' and which in the final analysis, did not prove useful to anyone, except possibly to some of its framers.[109]

Management of Political and Security Abuses of the Previous Regime

A unique challenge confronting the Habibie government has been the need to manage political and security abuses undertaken by the Suharto regime, most of which has also involved ABRI in one way or another. In addition to the cases involving detainees involved in the abortive PKI coup in 1965, the most important cases in this regard have been those involving the Tanjung Priok riot (September 1984), Lampung, Aceh, East Timor, Irian Jaya and the attack on the PDI Headquarters on 27 July 1996.

With regard to Tanjung Priok, the National Commission on Human Rights called on the government to establish a 'truth and reconcilation commission' to look into the riot and the hundreds of people who have been missing ever since. ABRI had maintained that only 18 people were killed when soldiers opened fire on anti-government protesters on 12 September 1984.[110] The Suharto government also declared the matter to be closed. However, relatives of the victims formed an action group, National Solidarity for the 1984 Tanjung Priok Affair

(SONTAK), together with support from other quarters have been pressuring the government to reopen the case, especially in accounting for the more than 400 people who are still missing. Calls have also been made for ABRI officers involved in the affair to be tried, namely, General Try Sutrisono, then Jakarta Military Commander and General Benny Moerdani, then Armed Forces Commander.

The Issue of Suharto's 'Comeback', 'Crimes' and Wealth

Due to Suharto's long rule and the assumption that he continues to have influence on the Habibie political leadership as well as ABRI, whose top leaders were essentially Suharto appointees, many continued to believe that Suharto would either directly or indirectly try to make a comeback. The fact that both Habibie and Wiranto owed their careers to Suharto did not help the matter. Habibie, for instance, was on record of having referred to the former President as the 'Super Genius Suharto'.[111] Hence, without much surprise, in mid-June 1998, various stories began to surface that the 'Suhartoists' were trying to make a comeback. Even an innocuous banner was enough to spark a debate about 'Suharto's comeback' as happened in mid-June 1998. A banner at a major road junction in central Jakarta, with the following words, 'Stop All Criticisms of Former President Suharto So As To Prevent Bloodshed From Occurring' was interpreted in certain quarters as the attempts by the 'Suhartoists' to make a comeback.[112] The article, for instance, argued that the dismissal of the Attorney General Soedjono and GOLKAR's continued control by the Suharto family, where the former President remained as the patron of the Supervisory Board and his two children, Bambang Trihatmodjo and Siti Hardiyanti Rukmana, continued to hold key positions, were attempts by the 'Suhartoists' to make

218

a comeback and dislodge Habibie. The 15 June GOLKAR meeting which elected Waskito Reksosoedirdjo, Ary Mardjono and Aulia Rahman to head the committee to organise the extraordinary GOLKAR Congress were obvious results due to the interventions of Bambang and Siti Hardiyanti, as they wanted to gain control of GOLKAR so that the Special MPR Session could be used to dismiss Habibie, who was viewed to have become increasingly hostile towards the interests of the former President. According to this view, the 'Suhartoists' wanted to make a comeback by putting into key positions individuals such as Try Sutrisono and Edi Sudradjat, who were believed to be more sympathetic towards the former President.[113]

The ABRI leadership, however, dismissed allegations that former President Suharto or his proxies were making a comeback in any way as it was 'anachronistic' to do so. On 19 June, Lieutenant-General Bambang Yudhoyono argued that ABRI has vowed to prevent any attempt by the 'old political forces' to make a comeback. He argued that it was 'illogical, unrealistic and antagonistic if old political forces want to return and run the state's affairs'. And if that happens, 'ABRI, together with all elements in society, will prevent them from making a return' as the time for the old political forces had long since passed.[114]

The ABRI leadership, however, maintained that there was nothing wrong in maintaining personal ties with the former President. General Wiranto, for instance, argued that it was not a secret that there were close ties between him and the former President. However, this did not mean that ABRI remained loyal to him and was taking orders from him. General Wiranto argued that 'I cannot just refuse or be scared to see him after what has happened to him. Our culture does not permit that'. He also said that it was not just the ABRI leaders who were maintaining ties with the former President. In Wiranto's view, 'every official who had served and known

him was also close', including cabinet ministers, ABRI officers and even President Habibie. Wiranto argued that organisationally, 'ABRI has no more links with Pak Harto. When he
was Supreme Commander, he could give his views and orders. But now that type of relationship does not exist anymore. And Pak Harto is a good Indonesian. He understands
that he is not in a position to do such things'.[115]

The issue of probing into Suharto and his family's wealth
began immediately following his resignation on 21 May 1998.
In addition to being part of the anti-corruption drive, the object of this move was, in part, to uncover the abuse of power
by the former President during his more than 30 years of
power. This is because Suharto and his family were alleged to
have amassed a massive personal fortune and this was believed to have been undertaken through unfair means. In this
connection, when President Habibie suddenly replaced the
Attorney-General, Soedjono Atmonegoro in mid-June 1998
with Major-General Muhammad Ghalib, the country's top
military prosecutor, many feared that it was aimed at sabotag-
ing an investigation into Suharto's wealth, something the government denied. The new Attorney-General promised to continue the probe into Suharto's wealth even though critics continued to believe that Soedjono was removed due to his preparedness to investigate the Suhartos.[116] The former President,
through his lawyer, Yohanes Yacob, however, denied any
wrongdoing in this matter. Suharto is reported to have argued
that 'I have money and this money I keep in Indonesian banks
and the money comes from my salary as a former member of
the Armed Forces and as President for 32 years'. The former
President was also quoted as saying that 'if there are people
who are not satisfied, saying that Suharto has abundant savings in
foreign banks and wealth everywhere, if they can find it, people
can take it for the interest of the nation'.[117]

The issue of Suharto's alleged wealth took on a particular
importance in view of the pathetic state of country's economy.

Most of Suharto's children headed large business empires which they built over the last decade or so. The largest of them is Citra Lamtoro Gung headed by Siti Hardiyanti Rukmana, followed by the Bimantara Group headed by Bambang Trihatmodjo, the Humpus Group headed by Hutomo Mandala Putra and the Arseto Group headed by Sigit Hardjojudanto. Suharto also controls many businesses through foundations he built and heads in an individual capacity.

Various groups had been formed since 21 May to look into the issue. One such group was the Movement of Concerned Citizens on State Assets (GEMPITA). Its leader, lawyer Frank Taira Supit had proposed using the state laws to investigate Suharto and his family's excesses. Another group, Indonesian Corruption Watch, headed by leading Human Rights lawyer Todung Mulya Lubis, also endorsed using the legal system to investigate Suharto's wealth. However, Mohammad Sadli, a former Minister of Mines and Energy in the Suharto government called on the Habibie government to nationalise all the assets and corporate stocks belong to the former President and his family and to use its proceeds to ease the country's economic crisis. He argued that 'the legal procedures were too complex and time consuming'. Instead, a 'short-cut method would be to nationalise their assets, just like when we nationalise the assets of Dutch companies in 1957'.[118]

Probing and confiscating Suharto's ill-gotten wealth took on a new direction when a respected senior General endorsed such a move as being constitutional in line with the various decrees passed by the Special Session of the MPR. On 24 November 1998, Lieutenant-General Bambang Yudhoyono, ABRI's Territorial Chief, for the first time, on behalf of ABRI, joined the growing public clamour for investigations into the wealth of former President Suharto, thereby providing moral support for those who have pressed for such a course all these time. The call by General Bambang, known for his pro-reformist views within ABRI, also contained the potential for splitting the

221

Armed Forces as some senior General, such as General Wiranto, were believed to be opposed to such a course, primarily due to their loyalty to the former Supreme Commander.

Islam and the 'ICMIisation' of Indonesian Politics

One of the major concerns and negative images associated with the Habibie Presidency and government has been charge that it is either a front or a sophisticated attempt to conceal what is nothing more than the beginning of the birth of an 'Islamic-oriented Indonesia', best evident from the 'ICMIisation' of the country's politics. Other than the fact that the country went through the 'May Revolution' which was not only anti-Suharto but also anti-Chinese in character as seen from the physical attacks on Chinese businesses, properties and the alleged 'ethnic cleansing' of the Indonesian Chinese from Jakarta and the other major cities, best evident from the rapes of Chinese women that were purported to have taken place, since then, the country's politics is also said to be dominated by groups that are largely Islamic rather than secular in character.

For some, the coming to power of B. J. Habibie, the founder-Chairman of ICMI since December 1990 and where he handed over executive power to Tirtosudiro only in March 1998 when he became the Vice-President and later became its Chief Patron in May 1998, was nothing more than the actualisation of a political scenario that had been long planned by the ICMI strategists. According to this game plan, the establishment of ICMI itself in December 1990, and later, its ability to position its key members in different sectors of the government, especially in the cabinet, the Armed Forces and the bureaucracy, were nothing more than manoeuvres to eventually takeover political power in the country. This was to be implemented gradually but constitutionally and the first order of things was to ensure that in the March 1998 elections, the 76 years-old Suharto was 'selected' as the President with B. J. Habibie as the Vice-President. Then, within two years, by 2000, President Suharto, if he was still alive, would be 'persuaded' to step down and in line with the constitution, B. J. Habibie, the Vice-President would become the President. With it, the political paradigm would automatically shift toward 'political Islam', with ICMI directing the country's affairs, having taken over through the due process of the law and constitution.[119]

While this was not the way B. J. Habibie came to power, the fact that this game plan may have been given a 'historical push' by ICMI's role in the 'May Revolution', with the desired outcome becoming a reality, have led many to conclude that in power today in Indonesia is 'political Islam' with ICMI as the key power broker. Among the first political observer to warn of this possibility was the Australian Max Walsh. Writing in *The Sydney Morning Herald* a day after B. J. Habibie was sworn in as Indonesia's President, Max Walsh warned that 'Islamisation' was likely to be 'the new axis'. According to him:

> In Malaysia, Dr Mahathir has demonstrated how to retain popular support by emphasising his Islamic credentials and by running an anti-Western line of rhetoric....With Habibie in Indonesia and Mahathir in Malaysia, it is quite possible we will see a joint strategy which stresses the Islamisation of the region. This would not mean Iranian-style fundamentalism but it would certainly be a shift from the secular style of government that has had in the past....Even if this is not formally done, it is most unlikely that Dr Habibie will maintain the same relationship with the Chinese entrepreneurial community as his predecessor.[120]

Max concluded that there would be literally no choice but

'to establish fresh links with the Islamic power base which Habibie will see as his survival strategy'. Habibie's appeal to ICMI leadership in March 1998, when he handed over executive leaderhip to Achmad Tirtosudiro that 'ICMI must not leave me alone in the golden cage' would continue to ring in the ears of many Islam-phobes for a long time to come of Habibie's dependency on this political group for his support, even survival.

This thinking was given a further boost by a number of developments that followed Habibie's assumption of the Presidency. First, there was the placement of a number of 'ICMI heavywieghts' in Habibie's cabinet announced on 23 May. Among others, these included Adi Sasono, Akbar Tanjung, Fahmi Idris, Rahardi Ramelan, Soleh Salehuddin, Malik Fadjar, A. M. Saefuddin, as well as two ranking Generals who had close ties with ICMI, namely, Feisal Tanjung and Syarwan Hamid, the former ABRI Chief and the Chief of Social-Political Affairs respectively. Next, there was the concerted effort by the new President to 'load' the MPR with his appointees, many of whom were also affiliated with ICMI such as Adi Sasono, Parni Hadi. Dewi Fortuna, Sayidiman Soerjohadiprojo, Fachri Ali, and Afan Gaffar. Third, following the Special GOLKAR Congress, again there was the trend to place people associated with ICMI in that key political party. Under the leadership of Akbar Tanjung, who was once a leader of the HMI, the politically powerful Muslim-oriented student body, a number ICMI-oriented people, including Adi Sasono, were appointed to the Executive Board. Fourth, the Presidential and Vice-Presidential Advisory Team is almost wholly dominated by people associated with ICMI such as Dewi Fortuna and Jimly Asshidiqie.

In this connection too, there was also a concerted effort for ICMI-linked personalities to gain control of the key political and economic sectors of society and more important, where these can be easily transformed into a powerful political base of ICMI. Following the next MPR Session, November 1999, ICMI's Executive Chairman, Achmad Tirtosudiro, has been tipped as the new MPR Chairman, replacing Harmoko. A new and powerful labour union has also been created, the Federation of Indonesian Free Trade Union with a close associate of Adi Sasono, Jumhur Hidayat, currently the Executive Director of CIDES, named as its Chairman. A Muslim-oriented trade union, *Persaudaran Buruh Muslimin Indonesia*, has also been created with Eggi Sudjana, a close Adi associate, made its Chairman. Parni Hadi, the general manager of ICMI's daily *Republika* was named as General Manager of the Government's news agency, *Antara*. A close confidant of President Habibie and an active member of ICMI, Lieutenant-General Zen Maulani, who was appointed Secretary to the Vice-President in March 1998, was later appointed as the Chief of the National Intelligence Agency, BAKIN in September 1998.

At the same time, Adi Sasono, as the Minister for Cooperatives and Small and Medium Enterprises, also launched a series of populist-oriented economic policies. One of the most high-profile policy in this regard was the efforts undertaken by Adi's ministry to provide subsidies to various cooperatives as well as to subsidise the cost of basic commodities. Adi came under strong criticism for this policy, with his opponents deriding the measures as being driven by political calculations to win popular support, especially among the rural folks. Adi's policies were also said to be economically unsound and helping only to undermine the near-bankrupt national economy. Adi, however, dismissed these allegations, arguing that the subsidies were necessary to contain the further outbreaks of social unrest, especially the growing phenomenon of looting and pillaging. He argued that 'people are hungry. The key word for social unrest, riots and looting is poverty. People loot because they are in dire straits'. He also countered by arguing that 'I am a bit sad that this is still cricitised as wasting money while less criticism is directed toward the government for having to cover the private sector's debts'.[121] Another major initiative by Adi in the economic arena is to gain control of the economic distribution network, which in the past was dominated by the ethnic Chinese. The distribution network broke down following the May 1998 riots, especially when many of the Chinese-owned businesses were burnt or when the Indonesian Chinese fled overseas. While in the short run, the breakdown of the distribution network enhanced the misery of the Indonesians, with shortages of basic commodities being experienced countrywide, yet it was also an opportunity for Adi and his supporters, once and for all, to destroy the ethnic-Chinese economic stranglehold over most of Indonesia, and more important, to replace it with one dominated by ICMI, under Adi's direction.

At the same time, ICMI and its leadership have made no bones about their support for Habibie and the programme of reforms that he personifies. At the end of a three-day ICMI National Co-ordinating Meeting in July 1998, its Executive Chairman, Achmad Tirtosudiro announced that 'ICMI considers Habibie as President now until 1999. ICMI will support Habibie if the people nominate him during the General Session of the MPR in 1999'.[122] Earlier, Adi Sasono was even more transparent in this commitment. The ICMI Secretary-General and one of the key ministers, some say, the most powerful minister, in Habibie's cabinet, stated that ICMI fully supports President Habibie efforts to bring about political and economic reforms and is against any moves to have him replaced. He said that 'the present government's drive is to promote clean government by getting rid of all the projects involving corruption, collusion and nepotism'. In his view, these measures have not found favour with many in the establishment and they were seeking ways to undermine President Habibie. However, Adi argued that 'the primary concern of many people is economic survival. They support the present government's efforts in respect of the reform process. By con-

226

trast, those opposed to Dr Habibie only came from small elites whose interests are threatened by the reform process'.[123] He was, however, emphatic that ICMI did not want to see Dr Habibie replaced as President, arguing that these anti-Habibie people were the 'old stock' who wanted to install a leader more in tune with the former Suharto regime.

What the above events have demonstrated is that the balance of power in Indonesian politics has definitely shifted in favour of ICMI since May 1998. Since then, all efforts have been made to sustain this power position so as to ensure that the political paradigm shift in favour of 'political Islam' is almost permanent. In this endeavour, ICMI will only be successful in sustaining its political power if it can ensure that the infighting within the organisation is kept to a manageable level, that the economic power of the ethnic Chinese is somehow managed and most important of all, the power of ABRI and its propensity to involve in national politics is reduced and eventually, totally eliminated. If this can be assured, then the chances are that Indonesia would become more Islamised, partly in view of the fact that 87 percent of its population are of Islamic faith but more important, due to the coming to power of a political elite that believe in 'Islamising' the country's politics, economy and social order. Thus, even though President Habibie declared on 25 June 1998 that Indonesia 'will never adopt a single official religion because it regards all religions as equal' and that Indonesia would not declare itself as an 'Islamic state',[124] the political, economic and social trends, however, would tend to indicate that 'political Islam' is on the rise, primarily due to the emerging phenomenon of 'ICMIisation' of the country's politics, economy and social structure.

It was partly in view of this factor that in early January 1999, two important religiously-oriented incidents that had some bearing to the issue of Islamisation and ICMIisation took place. On 5 January 1999, a new group, calling itself the

Islamic Defender Association, which is made up of seven Islamic organisations, lodged a report with the Police, alleging that Major-General Theo Syafei was guilty of spreading 'groundless rumours' and of 'incting hatred against Islam'.[125] Prior to this, the organ of the Partai Bulan Bintang published a number of articles on the issue. Theo alleged to have made these disparaging remarks in his address to Christian activists in Kupang, West Timor, which among others argued that the Muslims were ambitiously pursuing the goal to establish an Islamic state by 2005 and where they would do anything to achieve their goal.[126] What this incident signals is that politics and conflict in Indonesia in the near future is likely to be along religious lines and this could have dire consequences for the country and its future. That this is not a speculation but a reality was best made manifest following General Wiranto's announcement of changes in the ABRI line-up on 5 January January 1999. While the changes affected 100 officers from the entire Armed Forces, some analysts immediately concluded that what Wiranto did was to "weed out the Muslim elements from ABRI".[127] This conclusion was reached as a result of the alleged 'demotion' and 'loss of power' of Lieutenant-General Fachrul Razi as ABRI's General Affairs Chief and of Major-General Zacky Anwar Makarim, the Head of ABRI Military Agency. Lieutenant-General Soegiono replaced Fachrul Razi while Major-General Tyasno Sudarto replaced Zacky. Both Soegiono and Tyasno were alleged to be 'red-white nationalists' and closer to Suharto in terms of loyalty than the people whom they succeeded. At the same time, a Christian, Lieutenant-General Jhony Lumintang, the former Commandant of ABRI Staff and Command College, was appointed as the Deputy Chief of Staff of the Army. To many Muslim analysts, this represented a 'de-greening' process in ABRI and hence, their unhappiness with it, confirming clearly how political and military appointments have become heavily politicised and where they are increasingly viewed from 'ethnic and religious lenses'.[128] Presently, some eight purely Islamic parties can be identified as follows: *Partai Umat Muslimin Indonesia, Partai Syarikat Islam Indonesia, Partai Islam Indonesia, Partai Bulan Bintang, Partai Masyumi Baru, Partai Gerakan Insan Mustakin Indonesia, Partai Nahdatul Ulama* and *Partai Sunni.* At the same time, the United Development Party or PPP, which represented Islamic interest during the New Order era decided to revert to its Islamic identity in November 1998, by using the *Kaaba*, the black holy shrine in Mecca as its symbol. At the same time, political observers believe that since May 1998, the polarisation between the Islamic and Secular forces in Indonesia has intensified and this divide can have dire consequences for the country's future, especially for its outlook towards the *Pancasila* ideology and even for its unity and unitary character.[129] Some observers argued that the ICMI-initiated Congress of all Islamic parties or *Kongres Umat Islam Indonesia*, which was held from 3 to 7 November 1998, was meant to consolidate Islamic political power and to preempt any attempt by the secular forces to divide the fast emerging Islamic political power.

NOTES

1   See Susan Berfield and Jose Manuel Tesoro, 'A Nation Asserts Itself', *Asiaweek*, 5 June 1998, p. 23.

2   *The Indonesian Observer*, 8 June 1998.

3   See *The Jakarta Post*, 22 May 1998.

4   *Ibid*, 23 May 1998.

5   *Ibid.*

6   *Ibid.*

7   *Ibid.*

8   *Ibid*, 26 May 1998.

9   *The Straits Times*, 19 June 1998.

10   *Ibid*, 25 May 1998.

11   *Ibid*, 28 May 1998.

12   *The Indonesian Observer*, 26 May 1998.

13   *The Jakarta Post*, 4 June 1998.

14   *Ibid*, 6 June 1998.

15   *Ibid*, 4 July 1998.

16   *The Jakarta Post*, 26 May 1998.

17   *Ibid*, 26 May 1998.

18   *Ibid*, 6 June 1998.

19   *Ibid*, 2 July 1998.

20   See 'New Bill Reduces Habibie's Powers', *The Straits Times*, 9 July 1998.

21   *Ibid*, 1 June 1998.

22   *Ibid*, 26 June 1998.

23   *The Straits Times*, 22 June 1998.

24   Cited in *The Straits Times*, 15 June 1998.

25   *Ibid*.

26   *The Jakarta Post*, 20 June 1998.

27   *The Straits Times*, 30 June 1998.

28   *The Jakarta Post*, 29 June 1998.

29   *The Straits Times*, 30 June 1998.

30   *The Jakarta Post*, 1 July 1998.

31   The 'misfortunes' of Harsudiono Hartas and Edi Sudradjat were good examples of this. The former was summarily removed from his post as ABRI Chief of Socio-Political Affairs following ABRI's proactivism in supporting Try for the Vice-Presidency while Edi was passed over by Suharto for the post of Co-ordinating Minister for Politics and Security in Suharto's last cabinet even though Edi was the most qualified. Thus, both Hartas and Edi have 'axes' to grind as far as Suharto was concerned and yet, many continued to refer to them as 'Suhartoists'.

32   *The Jakarta Post*, 4 July 1998.

33   *Ibid.*

34   *Ibid*, 7 July 1998.

35   *The Jakarta Post*, 7 July 1998.

36   *Ibid*, 10 July 1998.

37   See *The Jakarta Post*, 12 July 1998.

38   'Govt denies interfering in Golkar Congress', *The Jakarta Post*, 15 July 1998.

39   Author's interview with a serving ABRI senior officer in Jakarta in December 1998.

40   *The Jakarta Post*, 24 May 1998.

41   'Wiranto in Full Control of Military', *The Sunday Times*, 24 May 1998; Author's interview with a ranking General in Jakarta in October 1998.

42   *The Jakarta Post*, 19 June 1998.

43   *The Jakarta Post*, 1 July 1998.

44   'Soldiers Held Over Abductions', *Ibid*, 15 July 1998.

45   'I'm ready to take the blame: Prabowo', *Ibid*, 18 July 1998.

46   *The Straits Times*, 19 July 1998.

231

47   "A Kangaroo Court?", *The Jakarta Post*, 28 December 1998.

48   "Call for halt to trial of 11 soldiers", *The Straits Times*, 8 January 1999.

49   *The Jakarta Post*, 12 June 1998.

50   *Ibid.*

51   *The Straits Times*, 22 June 1998.

52   *The Straits Times*, 11 June 1998.

53   For instance, Dr Nitikasbara argued that 'There should be no other institutions dictating to the national police. In turn, the national police will not run away from taking responsibility over wrong investigation practices, as have been found many times in the past'. *The Straits Times*, 19 June 1998.

54   *Ibid.*

55   *The Jakarta Post*, 8 August 1998.

56   *Ibid.*

57   See *Ibid*, 9 December 1998.

58   *Ibid*, 12 December 1998.

59   *The Indonesian Observer*, 12 December 1998.

60   *The Jakarta Post*, 12 December 1998.

61   'Habibie defends civilian-militia plan', *The Straits Times*, 7 January 1999.

62   *The Jakarta Post*, 23 May 1998.

63   *The Straits Times*, 11 June 1998.

64   *Ibid*, 26 May 1998.

65   'Breaking with the Past', *The Indonesian Observer*, 26 May 1998.

66   *The Jakarta Post*, 20 June 1998.

67   *Ibid*, 22 June 1998.

68   *The Straits Times*, 25 June 1998.

69   *Ibid*.

70   *The Jakarta Post*, 4 July 1998.

71   'SI tidak pilih President Baru', *Media Indonesia*, 8 July 1998.

72   For details, see Ridwan Max Sidjabat, "MPR Special Session will dig into meaty issues", *Ibid*, 8 November 1998; and *Ketetapan-Ketetapan Majelis Permusyawaratan Rakyat Republik Indonesia Hasil Sidang Istimewa Tahun 1998*, (Jakarta: Sekretariat Jenderal MPR RI, pp. 1-101).

73   Cited in *The Straits Times*, 12 June 1998.

74   *Ibid*.

75   *The Jakarta Post*, 20 June 1998.

76   *Ibid*, 26 June 1998.

77   *Ibid*, 12 June 1998.

78   *The Jakarta Post*, 18 June 1998.

79   *Ibid*.

80   *The Jakarta Post*, 5 December 1998.

81   See *The Philippines Star*, 28 May 1998; *The Sunday Times*, 24 May 1998.

82   *Ibid*.

83   *The Sunday Times*, 24 May 1998.

84   *The Straits Times*, 11 June 1998.

85   *The Jakarta Post*, 19 June 1998.

86   *Ibid*.

87   *The Straits Times*, 19 June 1998.

233

88   *Ibid.*

89   *The Jakarta Post*, 3 July 1998.

90   *The Jakarta Post*, 12 June 1998.

91   *Ibid.*

92   *Ibid.*

93   *Ibid*, 18 June 1998.

94   *The Jakarta Post*, 5 June 1998.

95   *The Straits Times*, 11 June 1998.

96   *The Straits Times* 25 June 1998.

97   Interview with *International Herald Tribune.* Reproduced in *The Straits Times*, 16 July 1998.

98   Cited in *The Straits Times*, 16 July 1998.

99   *Ibid.*

100 Ariel Heryanto, 'Flaws of Riot Media Coverage', *The Jakarta Post*, 15 July 1998.

101 *Ibid.*

102 *The Straits Times*, 20 July 1998.

103 Author's interview with Adi Sasono in Jakarta on 22 December1998.

104 According to Adi, President Habibie first used the term "early dirty primitive capitalism' to describe the economic system in the country in early 1998 in his conversation with then President Suharto. *Ibid.*

105 See *Laporan Akhir Tim Gabungan Pencari Fakta (TGPF) Peristiwa Tanggal 13-15 Mei 1998, Jakarta, Solo, Palembang, Lampung, Surabaya dan Medan*, (Jakarta: n.p., n.d.), pp.9-12. Also see *The Jakarta Post*, 4 November 1998.

106 *Ibid.*

107   Cited in *The Straits Times*, 5 November 1998.

108   *Ibid.*

109   Author's interview with an important member of the investigation team who prefers to remain anonymous until such time when the full facts can be made public.

110   *The Jakarta Post*, 20 June 1998.

111   *The Straits Times*, 20 June 1998.

112   See 'Skenario Cendana Menggusur Habibie', *AKSI*, Vol. 2, No. 84, 23-29 June 1998, pp. 4-5.

113   *Ibid*, p. 4.

114   *The Jakarta Post*, 20 June 1998.

115   *The Straits Times*, 30 June 1998.

116   *The Jakarta Post*, 18 June 1998.

117   Cited in *The Straits Times*, 17 June 1998.

118   *The Jakarta Post*, 18 June 1998.

119   Author's interview with leading ICMI officials between the period 1993 to 1998 and almost all of whom gained key political positions since May 1998.

120   See Max Walsh, 'Islamisation May Be the New Axis', *The Sydney Morning Herald*, 22 May 1998.

121   See Adi Sasono Defends 'Populist Policies', *The Jakarta Post*, 11 August 1998.

122   *The Jakarta Post*, 21 July 1998.

123   Muslim Group Backs Habibie's Reform Efforts', *The Straits Times*, 26 June 1998.

124   'Country will not become Islamic state', *The Straits Times*, 9 October 1998.

125 See "General accused of inciting hatred", *The Jakarta Post*, 6 January 1999.

126 The transcript of Major-General Theo Syafei's alleged speech is in the author's possession.

127 See "100 top officers in major ABRI reshuffle", *The Straits Times*, 6 January 1999.

128 See various reports as well as editorial in *Republika*, 5 and 6 January 1999.

129 For a debate on this, see "Islam vs Sekular Sejak Dulu", *Tekad*, Vol. 1, No. 1, 2 November – 8 November 1998, pp. 14-21.

7

Habibie's Foreign Policy

HABIBIE'S WORLDVIEW

Habibie's foray into international affairs did not commence with his assumption of the Presidency in May 1998. Formally, when he was elected as the country's Vice-President in March 1998, President Suharto, in naming him as the first 'executive' Vice-President, gave him, among others, responsibilities in developing and enhancing the country's external economic relations as well as forging ties abroad to upgrade the country's science and technological capabilities. Habibie was also expected to develop closer ties with the Islamic world.

Against this backdrop, President Habibie believes that there were three main factors that were uppermost for his country's approach to international affairs, especially as it prepares to enter the next Millenium.[1] First, there was the need to understand that the 'awakening of nations' have already taken place. Second, there was no escape from the fact that there was great interest in human rights and values, and where these were considered as integral responsibilities of both the people and state. Third, was the fact that for the first time, the human race was in a position to control and develop both the physical and non-physical aspects of power. In this context, Indonesia's foreign relations have to be conducted with the limits of these parameters.

The Indonesian President also has a particular 'theory of threat' as far as the behaviour of states in the international system is concerned. Habibie argued that the prime mover of any human progress was the issue of threat, or more specifically, competition. He argued that countries behaved in a particular manner, just as did the human race, because there was a perception that it was being threatened in one manner or another, or in an area or another that it considered to be important to itself. In the past, when all else failed, countries had to be prepared to face the threat of actual physical punishment. Habibie argued that even though this was still relevant and important, on the whole, this has receded some what, and instead, new kinds of threats and dangers have surfaced. This is all the more as the cost of an all-out physical war and destruction has become so great that countries are generally loathe to resort to this means. In general, there will be no real winners in such a contest. In view of this, there has been a need to look more and more into the non-physical aspects of power, partly as there has also been a rise of non-physical threats. This is primarily driven by the growing supremacy of Science and Technology and as such, the key contest emerging in international relations in the coming years will be for the supremacy in this arena. For any country to make any headway in this area, there would be the need to develop one's human resources and economy and this in turn, would affect the potential of a country, be it in the area of politics, economics and even the military arena. Hence, for any country to be successful in the coming years, the political leadership must structure itself in such a way that it can enjoy 'positive synergy' among its people and beyond so as to optimise its national development and growth.

President Habibie argued that for his country of more than 200 million to be able to meet these challenges, there was first the need to ensure that the basic needs of the people are catered for. Habibie sees the key threat facing his country being its ability to achieve the status of becoming a centre of high excellence in Science and Technology. He argued that for Indonesia to have a role in world politics in the coming years, it must produce products of the highest quality but at the lowest cost. This was the challenge which Indonesia faced and the only answer to the challenge was mastery of Science and Technology.

As far as the structure of the international power system is concerned, President Habibie also had a unique way of looking at it. While he argued that it is true that the United States has emerged as the 'sole Superpower' following the demise of the Cold War and the implosion of the USSR, yet if one looks a little more carefully, the actual power structure is far more complex and complicated. While the US may be the 'sole Superpower' militarily, yet, in reality, this does not mean much. When the non-military dimension is borne in mind, and which is increasingly becoming more and more important, then the notion of the United States as the 'sole Superpower' does not mean much. In actuality, President Habibie argued that it was better to talk of the 'United States Dollar Power', the 'Euro Power' and the 'Yen Power'. In time to come, there was also likely to be the 'Yuan Power' and the 'Rupee Power'. Presently, the American dollar, the Japanese Yen and what is emerging as the European Euro are likely to 'call the shots' and this is far more important than military power per se. In the same vein, Habibie argued that it was not apt to talk of one Superpower as when Indonesia confronts the world, especially in the light of the present economic crisis, it had to 'confront' the dollar, yen and euro world and these 'powers' could make or break Indonesia. It is these powers that mattered and hence for him, the real bottom line for Indonesia was what he called the 'economic *real politik*' .

In view of this worldview, President Habibie argued that for Indonesia to be effective and to make its mark on world politics while safeguarding the country's political, economic and strategic interests, Indonesia had no choice but to integrate with the 'real world', especially the countries with which Indonesia has close political, economic and strategic interests. He stated that he was not in favour of closing his country to the outside world and would not undertake isolationist political or economic policies, say such as the one adopted by Dr Mahathir Muhammad in Malaysia. Even though President Habibie admitted that he was not a trained economist, he professed to have read enough and may be more than most university professors as far as 'practical economics' was concerned. Hence, his basic goal as far as the national economy was concerned is to positively synergise with the key countries with which Indonesia had a trading relationship, especially since what Indonesia needs is just to pay for its trade.

In this connection, he viewed ASEAN as being particularly important for Indonesia. In his vision for ASEAN, he would like to see the bilateral trading ties among the member-states to be enhanced and where this should be undertaken in the national currency. Not only would this strengthen the national currency, but it would also allow positive synergies to take place between countries in the region. For this to be optimised, he saw the need for countries in the region to develop their respective micro and macro economic sphere. If this was successfully undertaken, President Habibie saw the possibility of a single ASEAN currency in the coming years. He also foresaw the possibility of an ASEAN Parliament but unlike in

Europe, the representation in the Southeast Asian counterpart would be on the basis of the national parliaments rather than political parties directly elected by the ASEAN-wide electorate. The Indonesian President foresaw these integrative efforts coming to fruition by 2025 and when these are actualised, ASEAN would be a major power of world standing.

While Habibie's worldview represented what can be regarded as a 'wish list', in reality, the Indonesian President was confronted with a different, far more challenging, even hostile world than what may have been anticipated. This was best evident from Habibie's foreign policy, even though by most counts, this was an area where very little was happening as all his energies were consumed by his necessity to attend to the pressing needs of domestic politics. In fact, between 21 May, from the time he took over the Presidency, right up to the early November 1998, the Indonesian President was yet to undertake a single visit overseas. Just as Habibie failed to attend the Non-Aligned Movement Summit in South Africa, he also cancelled his one-day trip to Malaysia which had been earlier scheduled. The Indonesia Foreign Minister, Ali Alatas, stated that it was difficult for President Habibie to make an overseas trip as there was no Vice-President in the country to take over state duties in his absence, indicating clearly the problems, and indirectly, the lack of priority foreign policy was given in the early months of the Habibie Presidency.[2] What little there was in this area was focused on the immediate environment, with Indonesia's immediate neighbours, Malaysia and Singapore receiving some attention and Jakarta having to respond to the growing criticisms of its policies from China.

Habibie's Foreign Policy in Operation

On assuming power, Habibie made a number of breakthroughs as far the country's foreign policy was concerned. In order to improve the country's much maligned international image on human rights, President Habibie ratified a number of United Nations' conventions on human rights on 25 June 1998, including the UN Convention Against Torture and other Cruel, Inhumane or Degrading Treatment or Punishment.[3]

In September, President Habibie signed the United Nations' Ocean Charter, committing itself to protecting the seas and using the maritime resources at its disposable in a sustainable way. The Charter was signed on a warship in Menado Bay, North Sulawesi on 26 September 1998. President Habibie also read the 'Bunaken Declaration' outlining Indonesia's commitment to manage and preserve its marine resources in line with the guidelines drawn up by the United Nations' Intergovernmental Oceanographic Commission.[4]

Another major breakthrough in foreign policy was with regard to the East Timor issue. President Habibie announced that even though he considered East Timor to be an integral part of Indonesia, he was, however, prepared to grant a special autonomous status to the province. The President also said that he was prepared to release jailed East Timorese leader Xanana Gusmao in return for international recognition of Indonesia's sovereignty over the territory. Also, he promised to reduce the number of soldiers present in the province with initial 1,000 combat troops withdrawal beginning on 28 July.[5]

Habibie's proposals were, however, dismissed by Portugal, the former colonial power that abandoned the territory in August 1975. The Portuguese Foreign Ministry argued that 'if Indonesia wants to move towards democracy, its principal aim must be to ensure the East Timorese have the right to choose how they want to live'.[6] Initially, Xanana also dismissed Habibie's proposals, arguing that only referendum on self-determination would settle the issue. Later, however, he relented somewhat arguing that he was ready to undertake some compromise as President Habibie's policies had 'already changed the direction' of the wind. He argued that he was prepared to accept Habibie's offer of 'special status' for East Timor as a transition for a period of 5–10 years before undertaking a referendum on the future of the province.[7] ABRI, whose image has been badly hurt by its military operations in the province since 1975, however, opposed moves by certain groups in East Timor for a referendum. The Army Chief, General Subaygo, for instance, argued that 'all the people of the youngest province of Indonesia continue to want integration' with Indonesia.[8]

In the meantime, while the debate within East Timor has continued as to whether the issue should be settled through a referendum or autonomy,[9] at the same time, the United Nations have been busy in working out an autonomy plan following President Habibie's initiative on the matter. On 7 October 1998, such a plan was for the first time discussed by the UN Secretary-General's personal representative for East Timor, Mr Jamsheed Marker with the foreign ministers of Portugal and Indonesia.[10] As part of the wider peace package, both Indonesia and Portugal are also expected to open 'interest sections', the lowest form of diplomatic recognition in each other's capital by January 1999.

Equally significant was Habibie's foreign policy towards his two immediate neighbours, Malaysia and Singapore. Habibie came to office, carrying with him a 'historical baggage' that was to affect, in the first instance, his relations with the two countries. As far as Malaysia was concerned, he had established close personal ties with the Malaysian leadership, especially Deputy Prime Minister Anwar Ibrahim. An important factor in this happy state of affairs was the generally positive inter-relationship between Habibie and the Malaysian leaders, especially as far as co-operation involving various strategic industries which were under Habibie's purview. Additionally, Habibie's warm ties with Malaysia, especially Anwar Ibrahim, were underpinned by the close ties between ICMI and IKD, the two Islamic-oriented think tanks in Indonesia and Malaysia respectively, whose co-operation had grown markedly in the last seven years and which were also directly being overseen by both leaders. This provided the necessary attraction and basis upon which post-Suharto Indonesia and Malaysia could develop warm ties. This was further assisted by the fact that Malaysia's distance from Indonesia was largely due to the estranged personal ties between Mahathir and Suharto and the resignation of Suharto removed the personal irritant in bilateral ties between the two countries. The fact that Malaysia was prepared to assist Indonesia in overcoming its difficulties rather than just talking about it also helped in drawing both countries closer together.

Thus, even though Indonesia was the largest country in the region and Mahathir now the 'elder statesman' of the region, being the longest serving elected head of government, both Jakarta and Kuala Lumpur were able to move quickly and establish warm ties, in part, due to the dire straits Indonesia found itself following the economic and political crisis. This warmth, and Habibie's preparedness to articulate it was made transparent in his first major foreign policy speech in early July 1998. In an interview with Malaysia's *New Straits Times* on 8 July 1998, President Habibie described Indonesia's ties with Malaysia as 'one breath, one racial group', arguing that people of both countries were very close and even looked similar. He said that 'I myself have never faced any problem with anyone in Malaysia. So I am confident that, from Malaysia, there is no problem. Even if there is, it is a misunderstanding'. President Habibie said that he was very appreciative of Malaysia's support for Indonesian efforts towards economic and political revival. In view of this, he said that 'In times of difficulty, I know who my friends are. I know that a friend in need is a friend indeed', with Malaysia's Prime Minister, Mahathir Mohamad and Deputy Prime Minister Anwar Ibrahim, named as friends of this category.[11] In the same interview, when asked whether there were neighbouring countries not comfortable with his appointment as President of Indonesia, Habibie replied that 'I don't know and I do not want to analyse, but may be they don't understand'. This was an oblique reference to Singapore, with whom President Habibie's relations started very much in frosty conditions.

Yet, at the same time, despite Habibie's positive outlook towards Malaysia, by September 1998, political developments within Malaysia let to some cooling of ties between Jakarta and Kuala Lumpur. This was brought about by Dr Mahathir's sacking and later, arrest of his deputy, Anwar Ibrahim. Anwar's arrest on 20 September 1998 led a number of prominent human right activists in Indonesia to launch a public campaign, criticising the Malaysian government for its anti-democracy and anti-human rights policies. Lawyer Adnan Ruyong Nasution, for instance, launched a Committee of Indonesian Solidarity for Anwar Ibrahim on grounds that the struggle for democracy was everyone's concern.[12]

The situation was worsened when Tun Ghafar Baba, the former Deputy Prime Minister of Malaysia and a close confidant of Dr Mahathir, visited Indonesia 'in his personal capacity' to explain the 'Anwar Affair' to the increasingly hostile Indonesian press. Wittingly or unwittingly, he mismanaged his endeavour and succeeded only in further provoking the Indonesians, leading many senior politicians and parliamentarians in Indonesia to condemn Ghafar Baba and his statements in Jakarta. For instance, Ghafar appeared upset with the growing support Anwar was getting in Indonesia and in one of his now characteristic outburst is reported to have said that 'if you think Anwar Ibrahim is so important, you can take him and make him your leader. May be he is more fitting to be a leader in Indonesia because I heard that it is okay to be homosexual here, but in Malaysia it is against the law'.[13] Ghafar's statements were described as 'arrogant', 'unethical' and 'insulting' and a leading Islamic group, KISDI argued that 'considering the statements by Baba, it is clear that he has shown contempt for the government, people and press' and hence, Kuala Lumpur should 'recall Tun Ghafar Baba'.[14]

The Head of GOLKAR's Art and Culture Department, Ais Ananta Said even suggested that 'if necessary, he should just be declared *persona non grata*'.[15] A prominent legislator, Sofyan Lubis, who also heads the Indonesian Journalists Association argued that Ghafar, as a senior Malaysian politician should have displayed greater understanding of the Indonesian press before attacking it. He argued that 'what's on the news was not Anwar as an individual but democracy that is growing recently, including in Malaysia'. He also took offense at Ghafar's statement that Indonesia could have Anwar as its leader as the country was receptive to homosexuals. Sofyan said that 'this is definitely not true. He should retract that statement and apologise to the Indonesian press'.[16] The editorial in *The Indonesian Observer* made the country's feelings towards Ghafar transparent when it argued:

> We cannot remember a time that a foreigner who has said he came here in a private capacity had the temerity to say insulting things to our face. We must therefore have patience with the likes of Mr Baba who comes from a country which, despite its modern appearance, is actually a feudal Society, which received its independence on a golden platter. This puts us in a different category from Malaysia because we are Revolutionaries who fought and died to achieve our independence. It is now the beginning of the end for feudalistic establishments which will be swept away by the new wave of reform initiated by Anwar Ibrahim.[17]

The situation took for the worst when Anwar Ibrahim appeared in a Kuala Lumpur court and where there was evidence that he had been beaten and tortured by the Malaysian police. This provoked outrage in Indonesia, as elsewhere in the world, especially against Malaysia and in particular Dr Mahathir, who is also Malaysia's Home Affairs Minister, for the manner he brutally treated a political opponent, *albeit* one who was respected the world over. The immediate fallout of this was the growing cool ties between Jakarta and Kuala Lumpur. This was made evident by Dr Dewi Fortuna, the Presidential Spokesperson and Habibie's foreign policy adviser, who argued the 'Anwar Affair' is likely to 'cloud relations' between Malaysia and Indonesia as there were very close ties between Anwar and Habibie, especially the national think tanks that both individuals headed. She argued that 'there are personal implications' as 'Anwar is close with the leadership here'.[18] What Dr Dewi hinted became a reality when President Habibie publicly expressed concern about the personal well-being of Anwar Ibrahim. In an interview with the Thai daily, *The Nation*, he stated that 'I am concerned because people should not forget that Anwar Ibrahim had contributed a lot for the benefit of his country. I am very sad to see that happen. I think it is not good. You should not introduce bad things. It's bad if you just forgot and deleted his contributions'. President Habibie also expressed unhappiness about the manner Anwar was being treated. He argued that 'you cannot just forget the Constitution of a man or a woman in this society. Because of human rights involved – and I think it is universal – people should be given the chance to defend themselves. People should not be tortured. There is a United Nations Convention'.[19]

Habibie's public response on the Anwar affair immediately raised doubts about his first official visit to Malaysia scheduled for October, as the Indonesian State Secretary, Akbar Tanjung indicated that the President was reconsidering the trip. More specifically, when asked by the *The Nation* whether he would attend the APEC Summit in Kuala Lumpur, to be held from 17–18 November 1998, President Habibie remained evasive. He argued that 'it's difficult for me. I am not coming

247

personally but coming as the President of 211 million people of Indonesia. I have to consult parliament'.[20] On 6 October, Akbar Tanjung announced that President Habibie had cancelled his planned trip to Malaysia for October on grounds of his busy schedule and that a decision was yet to be made on whether the President would attend APEC or not. Ali Alatas, the Indonesian Foreign Minister, however, dismissed the allegations that President Habibie's was cancelled due to his disdain over Anwar's arrest and treatment by the Malaysian police. Rather, he argued that the one-day visit was cancelled due to the tight state duties which required the President to remain in the country and that it was difficult for Habibie to leave for overseas as there was no Vice-President to take over state duties in his absence.[21] Following this, Dr Mahathir also announced that he had cancelled a planned visit to Indonesia where he was scheduled to address the Indonesia Forum. The organisers of the Indonesia Forum later announced that Dr Mahathir's decision had resolved a 'potentially sensitive issue' as Mahathir's presence in Jakarta could well be a liability, rather than an asset. As was stated by Bondan Winarno, the Forum Chairman, 'the bigger issue is on Anwar Ibrahim, our bigger doubts would be whether Dr Mahathir's presence in Indonesia would be an asset or liability to us'.[22] Later, even though President Habibie did attend the APEC meeting, he did not stay in Malaysia, preferring to return to Jakarta daily following the completion of the sessions, demonstrating the growing divide between the two countries.

Habibie had long experience with Singapore, especially in two main areas, the development of Batam and the aerospace industry. In both areas, there was essentially a competitive relations and where Habibie was not endeared by the Singapore side and vice-versa. More specifically, Habibie's Presidency started off rather badly for Singapore as the Singapore Senior Minister was reported to have said in early February 1998 that the 'market' did not favour Habibie as the country's Vice-

President. The blunt-talking Lee was quoted as saying that the financial markets were disturbed by President Suharto's criteria for selection of a Vice-President. President Suharto had stated that his deputy should have knowledge of science and technology, which most interpreted as a reference to Habibie. Mr Lee argued that the market believed that the criteria 'pointed to a minister whom they associated with Indonesia's high spending projects. If the market is uncomfortable with whoever is the eventual Vice-President, the rupiah will weaken again'. Yet, not only did Habibie become the country's Vice-President, but within 72 days, he took over the Presidency. On Lee Kuan Yew's part, not only were his unwelcome remarks regarded as internal interference in Indonesia's domestic politics, worst still, the Republic had to live with a leader which Mr Lee considered unfit to become Indonesia's Vice-President, even though in a typical Javanese fashion, in January 1999, Gus Dur even proposed that Mr Lee could be considered as an 'International Adviser' to the National Commission for Truth Seeking and Reconciliation which the Islamic leader was setting up to 'cool down the political climate in the country.[23]

This set the stage for cool Indonesia-Singapore relations even though from 1989 to late 1997, Singapore-Indonesian relations were excellent, due largely to the cordiality and rapport of the top leaders, especially Lee Kuan Yew and Suharto as well as Goh Chok Tong and Suharto. Many in the Habibie government viewed Singapore's close relations with Indonesia as a function of close personal ties between Singapore's top leaders with Suharto and with the resignation of the former President, a new paradigm emerged and one that was lacking in cordiality.

The first indication that not all was well in Indonesia's relations with Singapore could be gleaned from the interview Tanri Abeng gave to *The Straits Times* on 26 June 1998. While attending the Business Week 8th Annual Asia Leadership Forum in Singapore, the Indonesia State Minister for

249

State-Owned Enterprises stated the following of Indonesia-Singapore relations:

> We need to move quicker on the trade financing agreement. That's one expectation. Second, there is a need to clear the perception on both sides of what Indonesia needs and what Singapore can do, particularly in restoring confidence. I think Singapore can play an important role. If Singapore can help promote Indonesia, it will be useful. There has to be a more pro-active, open and sincere discussion. I think there is a gap in understanding. This kind of relationship is very important, because if Indonesia progresses, Singapore will also benefit.[24]

Tanri Abeng was even more critical of Singapore in his interview with the *Business Times* another daily in Singapore. There, he pointedly expressed his government's unhappiness with Singapore's promise to make US$5 million available to guarantee Indonesian trade as a prime example of this state of affairs. He argued that 'a specific example is the initial pledge for assistance in trade financing. Because, if relationship is at the best, that would have been resolved'. As Indonesian companies had difficulties in obtaining letters of credit to oil the wheels of trade due to the country's economic crisis and credit rating, Singapore announced that it wanted other countries to join the guarantee scheme but other countries preferred to do so bilaterally. Singapore's Deputy Prime Minister, Lee Hsien Loong announced in parliament in early June 1998 that Indonesia wanted more time to study the guarantee scheme. Tanri Abeng, however, felt that Singapore should be doing more to boost market confidence in Indonesia. 'Singapore', he argued, 'can help restore market confidence by giving a positive assessment of Jakarta's post-Suharto government and its policies where this was appropriate'.[25] The divide between Indonesia and Singapore became more obvious when President

250

Habibie announced plans to visit various countries in the near future but left Singapore out of his planned itinerary even though in the time honoured ASEAN tradition, visiting one's neighbours had been given priority.

Following this, the Singapore Government announced that it would be sending humanitarian aid to Indonesia, first a S$5 million assistance programme through the Singapore Red Cross and the second, a S$12 million assistance programme of rice and medicine from the government itself.[26] On 13 July, Singapore and Indonesia signed a US$8 billion gas sales agreement and where the first delivery of gas to Singapore from Indonesia's West Natuna Sea was expected to begin in 2001 and continue for another 22 years.[27] Despite this, the Habibie government continued to express its disdain for the Singapore leadership. Three days before Singapore officially handed over the $12 million humanitarian aid to Indonesia on 6 August, coinciding with the visit of Admiral Teo Chee Hean, Singapore's Education Minister and Second Minister for Defence, the highest Singapore official to visit the country since President Suharto resigned, President Habibie lashed out at Singapore in an interview with the *Asian Wall Street Journal*.

The interview published on 4 August referred to three main reasons why President Habibie was upset with Singapore: First, Singapore had not shown a spirit of friendship. Habibie argued that 'a friend in need is a friend indeed, and I don't have that feeling from Singapore, and many Indonesians did not have. It is different with the United States, and the United States is so far. Japan, Malaysia, who are so close, they are pro-active. And yet Singapore doesn't have that. They are pro-active in the negative direction, and that, I feel so sorry for'. Second, Singapore was accused of sending late its congratulations when Habibie took over as President on 21 May. The President argued that he received congratulations from many countries the day he took office or the next day

251

but Singapore did not sent its note until 'almost June, very late' even though Prime Minister Goh was said to have offered his 'warmest congratulations and sincere good wishes that under your leadership, Indonesia will restore social and political stability and start on the path of reform and recovery' on 25 May. Third, President Habibie was very upset with Senior Minister's Lee negative remarks in February 1998 about the criteria for selecting the country's Vice-President. With regard to the remarks, President Habibie said that 'I would never character-assassinate my friend...and even my enemy, I would never character-assassinate. It's against my honour and culture'.[28] While President Habibie tried to balance his unhappy perception of Singapore and its leaders by arguing that 'I have a lot of Singaporean friends. The Singaporean people are hardworking people, OK, and real good friends. I have no, no, no negative attitude, neither plan to have any. But I have to be pragmatic, to see it as it is...'. He also, indirectly cautioned Singapore by reminding the republic of the bottom line: 'It is OK with me but there are 211 million people in Indonesia.... Look at that map. All the green area is Indonesia. And that red dot is Singapore. Look at that'.[29]

Against this backdrop, Admiral Teo visited Indonesia as a personal guest of the Indonesian Defence and Security Minister, who is also ABRI Commander, General Wiranto. The visit was also an exercise in 'defence diplomacy' between the Armed Forces of the two countries. In a symbolic gesture, Admiral Teo handed packages of rice and medicine to General Wiranto at Halim airbase in Jakarta on 6 August. General Wiranto described Singapore's humanitarian aid to Indonesia as a 'milestone in bilateral ties. It is an important moment that strengthens the ties of friendship between the two nations. It urges us therefore to further maintain and develop such cooperation in the years ahead for our mutual benefit'.[30] The aid would be distributed to the needy jointly by ABRI and the SAF, an exercise that was also meant to boost bilateral military ties. In reply, Admiral Teo stated that 'relations between our countries are friendly and strong during good and difficult times. We have consistently tried to assist Indonesia within our limited means since the economic crisis started. Singapore will work with the Indonesian government to bring confidence and economic recovery back to Indonesia and the region'. At the same time, 'the close co-ordination and co-operation between ABRI and the SAF in carrying out this mission reflects the strong institutional links that Indonesia and Singapore have built over many years of co-operation'.[31]

In general, Admiral Teo's visit and the 'aid diplomacy' indicated that military to military ties between Singapore and Indonesia were still good. This was clearly made evident by Lieutenant-General Soeyono, the Secretary-General of the Indonesian Defence Ministry who argued that the aid was 'a reflection of very good relations between both countries. Singapore is our very close neighbour. In good or bad times, we are still best of friends'. He went on to say that 'despite Dr Habibie's comments [in the *Asian Wall Street Journal*], we feel that co-operation between the two countries has been strong and getting stronger'.[32] Lieutenant-General Soeyono also announced that his country was prepared to give the SAF greater access to various sites for land training exercises. He argued that 'Indonesia is very big. We have lots of space that can be used for the training needs of the SAF', signalling clearly that military to military ties were largely unaffected by the resignation of Suharto and Habibie's unhappiness with Singapore.

However, when Admiral Teo paid a 75 minutes courtesy call on the Indonesian President, the welcome was rather different. Admiral Teo, recounting his meeting with Habibie told the press that he impressed upon the Indonesian leader that 'Indonesia and Singapore are close neighbours and he looks forward to building good relations and strong ties and strengthening those ties'. Admiral Teo also conveyed Prime Minister Goh's best wishes, stating among others that President Habibie had probably one of the most difficult jobs to 'build a national consensus for political reform due to the economic, social crisis as well as restore growth to Indonesia'. Mr Goh also stated that 'the stability and prosperity of Indonesia is critical not only to ASEAN but also Singapore' and President Habibie was 'most welcome to visit Singapore at any time and at his convenience'.[33] Publicly, Admiral Teo stated that notwithstanding Habibie's negative remarks in the past, the Indonesian President 'indicated that he has a vested interest in building good relations with Singapore'.[34]

If that was all that Habibie could say about Indonesia's relations with Singapore, it was indicative of something amiss. And indeed it was. A Singapore official was later to describe Admiral Teo's courtesy call on the Indonesian President as a '75 minute monologue' with Habibie telling the Singapore visitor of all the wrongs that had been done to his country by Singapore, with General Wiranto, who was also present, 'feeling extremely uncomfortable and embarrassed'.[35] While the Singapore side did not say much about the matter, two of Habibie's close advisers were more to the point.

Dr Umar Juoro, a senior researcher at the Centre for Information and Development Studies, and an adviser on economic matters to the President stated that 'the core of the [Indonesia-Singapore] problem is a need to redefine our relationship, which for so long has been based on close ties between Suharto and Lee Kuan Yew and military ties. Giving aid is a start, but more needs to be done to improve relations'.

Dr Dewi Fortuna Anwar, Habibie's spokesperson and foreign policy adviser stated the Indonesian President was deeply hurt due to the 'inattention from Singapore to Indonesia's plight since he has taken over'. Unlike other countries which had sent senior emissaries since Habibie succeeded former President Suharto in May, Singapore had sent none until the Admiral Teo's visit, that is, 77 days after Habibie had become President. This, to Habibie, was very insulting. Dr Dewi argued that 'Singapore is one of our closest neighbours....we expected more from it than from any other country. When that was not forthcoming, the disappointment was bigger. It is because of the higher expectations that the disappointment is higher'. Dr Dewi argued that while Singapore and its leaders are fond of pointing to long-term mutual relations, the Habibie government also placed premium on symbolic gestures. In this connection, she hoped that Admiral Teo's visit will lay to rest 'President Habibie's perception that Singapore is aloof' and hoped that 'bilateral relations will continue to be as warm as it has always been'.[36]

That the state of Indonesia-Singapore political relations have remained largely cool was best evident from an interview given by Singapore Deputy Prime Minister, Brigadier-General Lee Hsien Loong, to a number of American journalists in early October 1998. According to the Singapore leader, it would take time for Singapore and Indonesia to re-establish the close ties and mutual respect they used to enjoy and this was because Indonesia was preoccupied with internal problems. The Singapore deputy premier argued that 'there is a new government, a new environment. Indonesia has many preoccupations of its own, so it will take some time to re-establish a similar basis for long-term sustainable relations'. The Singapore leader also expressed concern that developments in Indonesian could have a spillover effect, especially if there was continuing instability in Indonesia, as had happened in the 1960s before President Suharto took over. General Lee opined that Singapore was likely to face problems with illegal immigrants and piracy and there would also be a climate of uncertainty and unease affecting the region. However, he ruled out a military threat arguing that 'it is not that sort of a situation'.[37]

In the following month, early November, in an interview with Indonesian journalists, Brigadier-General Lee stated that Singapore hoped that Indonesia would be able to resume its full role in ASEAN once its economy stabilises and recovers in the next few years. He argued that former President, Suharto played a key leadership role in ASEAN during his tenure in office. He praised Indonesia's role in ASEAN and said that as the largest country in ASEAN, it had given its smaller neighbours room to grow and prosper by having a 'relaxed' relationship with them. It was his expressed hope that Indonesia would resume its full role in ASEAN, as it had been during the Suharto years.[38]

Following the above-mentioned interview, an old bilateral issue between Singapore and Indonesia resurfaced when Singapore was accused of deliberating suppressing trade statistic between the two countries. In the interview, Brigadier-General Lee Hsien Loong, stated that there were differences between the two countries in the way trade statistics were arrived at and for that reason, both countries had agreed not to publish the trade statistics as this could lead to a misunderstanding. However, the Singapore Deputy Prime Minister stated that "on a regular basis, we have prepared statistics for your [Indonesian] government".[39] However, the Director-General of External Trade, Djoko Moeljono maintained that the Indonesian Government has requested for such data but the Singapore side was unco-operative. This led the First Secretary of the Singapore Embassy in Jakarta that "Singapore has on many occasions provided bilateral trade statistics to the Indonesian Government and that this would be continued".[40] The Indonesian side, however, remained unsatisfied with this, with a new issue being added to the now growing litany of cool Indonesian-Singapore relations.

In late December 1998, in an interview with *The Straits Times*, Adi Sasono announced that he would want his government to quickly sign an extradition treaty with Singapore in order to "bring back to Indonesia economic criminals seeking refuge there".[41] On 29 December 1998, the Justice Minister, Muladi argued that an extradition treaty between Singapore and Indonesia was necessary as he suspected that a large number of white collar criminals have escaped from the law and transferred their wealth to Singapore, with many of them having become permanent residents in Singapore.[42] The Indonesian leaders, especially Muladi also noted that the high priority given to economic development and issues by Singapore "could well explain the country's lack of interest in signing an extradition agreement with Indonesia",[43] sign-posting clearly that this is likely to emerge as another bilateral issue between the two neighbours.

Between 6 and 8 January 1999, the Singapore Government undertook a major *volteface* in its policy towards Indonesia and this could be seen in its first ever assistance programme given to the two leading Islamic groups in the country. On 6 and 8 January, the Singapore Ambassador to Indonesia, on behalf of the Singapore Government, handed over food assistance to the Nahdatul Ulama and the Muhammadiyah and this was dubbed as 'humanitarian assistance' to a neighbour undergoing difficulties. Yet, in reality, according to a senior ICMI offical, it was also clear that this assistance was the first clear admission by leaders in the Republic that a new political paradigm had emerged in Indonesia since May 1998 and which the Republic had no choice but to adjust and adapt quickly.[44] This new political paradigm was the rise of Political Islam to a new privileged status and where political power was likely to be in the hands of political forces that are essentially Islamic in character, and something which 'Chinese Singapore' would have learn to live with. The 'humanitarian assistance' to the Nahdatul Ulama and Muhamamdiyah was, in many ways, the first real admission by the Singapore Government that it had no choice but as a small state, living in an increasingly perilous environment, to adjust and accept the rise of Political Islam on its door steps.

Despite this political distance, the military to military ties between the two countries continued to grow and this was

257

best testified by the introductory visit of the Chief of the Indonesian Army, General Subagyo Hadisiswoyo, who called on the top military brass of Singapore, including Dr Tony Tan, the Deputy Prime Minister and Minister for Defence on 10 October 1998. A statement released following the visit stated that interactions between the two Armed Forces 'have continued despite the economic situation' and that both forces were working closely to distribute rice and medicines that were donated by Singapore to Indonesia.[45]

Another major foreign policy issue which preoccupied the Habibie government was the growing, almost coordinated 'concert' among the Chinese communities overseas, especially in China, Taiwan, Hong Kong and Singapore in their condemnation of the Indonesian government for failing to provide protection to the Indonesian Chinese during the May riots, in which not only were Chinese businesses attacked but where Chinese women were also believed to have been raped in an 'organised fashion'. While the initial criticisms came from Taiwan and Hong Kong, with leaders from both territories threatening to halt investments in Indonesia, by July 1998, Beijing also joined in the chorus in criticising Jakarta. On 3 August, China's Foreign Minister, Tang Jiaxuan, after meeting his Indonesian counterpart, 'demanded that Indonesia take strong and effective measures as soon as possible to ensure that the safety and proper and legal rights of overseas Chinese are protected and to take measures to ensure that such incidents will never occur again'.[46] In the same vein, in a reception to mark China's National Day on 1 October, the Chinese Vice-Premier, Qian Qichen expressed Beijing's concern about violence against Indonesian Chinese and expressed the hope that 'the Indonesian side would handle the incident properly as soon as possible and prevent such things from happening again'.[47] While not responding directly to the Chinese allegations and charge, Jakarta in general has maintained that it is looking into the matter even though it has continued to maintained that no real evidence on the matter has surfaced thus far.

NOTES

1   Author's interview with President B. J. Habibie on 3 October 1998, Jakarta Indonesia.

2   'Alatas Clears Air Over Habibie's Cancelled Visit', *The Straits Times*, 9 October 1998.

3   'Indonesia to ratify human rights pacts', *The Jakarta Post*, 10 June 1998.

4   See *Jakarta Post*, 19 September 1998.

5   *Ibid*, 29 July 1998.

6   *The Straits Times*, 22 June 1998.

7   See *The New Paper*, 27 June 1998.

8   Cited in *The Straits Times*, 17 June 1998.

9   See Salvador J. Ximenes Soares, 'E. Timor Settlement: Referendum or Autonomy?', *The Jakarta Post*, 18 September 1998.

10 'UN Tables Autonomy Plan for E. Timor', *The Straits Times*, 10 October 1998.

11 See 'We are like Malaysia: Habibie', *The Straits Times*, 9 July 1998.

12 *The Jakarta Post*, 24 September 1998.

13 Cited in *The Straits Times*, 28 September 1998.

14 *The Jakarta Post*, 29 September 1998.

15 *The Straits Times*, 29 September 1998.

16 *Ibid*, 30 September 1998.

17   Cited in *Ibid*.

18   'KL-Jakarta ties may be affected', *Ibid*, 4 October 1998.

19   *Ibid*, 5 October 1998.

20   *Ibid*.

21   *Ibid*, 9 October 1998.

22   *Ibid*, 13 October 1998.

23   "Indonesian group wants SM as adviser", *The Straits Times*, 8 January 1999.

24   *The Straits Times*, 26 June 1998.

25   Cited in *Ibid* 'Jakarta Unhappy with its ties with Singapore', 27 June 1998.

26   *The Jakarta Post*, 7 July 1998.

27   'S'pore, Jakarta sign US$8 b deal', *The Straits Times*, 14 July 1998.

28   'Singapore Strain Relations with Indonesia's President', *The Asian Wall Street Journal*, 4 August 1998.

29   *Ibid*.

30   *The Straits Times*, August 1998.

31   *Ibid*.

32   *Ibid*.

33   *Ibid*.

34   *Ibid*.

35   Anonymously, this was stated in confidence to the author by a senior Singapore official.

36   'Jakarta felt abandoned by close ally', *The Straits Times*, 7 August 1998.

37 Cited in *Kompass*, 7 October 1998.

38 Cited in *The Straits Times*, 3 November 1998.

39 See "Ucapan BG Lee", in *Gatra*, 5 December 1998, p. 7.

40 *Ibid*, p. 9.

41 See *The Jakarta Post*, 26 December 1998.

42 See *The Indonesian Observer*, 30 December 1998.

43 *Ibid.*

44 Interview with a Senior ICMI official in Jakarta on 10 January 1999.

45 *The Straits Times*, 11 October 1998.

46 *Ibid*, 4 August 1998.

47 *Ibid*, 2 October 1998.

CONCLUSION

Prospects for the Future: Whither Indonesia?

O ne of the key factors determining the nature, character and content of Indonesian politics have been the
quality of its leaders. In this section, it would be appropriate to draw some comparisons between the three Presidents of Indonesia to date in order to postulate some of the
future directions that can be expected under the present regime.

Thus, instead of looking at the 'canvas' of a painting, it
may be more fruitful to examine its 'fabric' instead as this
may have more to impart than would have been the case otherwise. An evaluation of the leadership may thus be more useful than trying to examine individual policies *per se*.

SIMILARITIES

All the three men who have held the helm of national political
leadership, namely, Sukarno, Suharto and Habibie are known

to be highly dedicated to the nation and are great nationalists in their own right. While Sukarno dedicated his life to fighting national independence from the Dutch, Suharto not only crush the abortive communist-led *coup d'etat* but also brought the country to the take-off stage of national economic development. As for Habibie, building on the achievements of his predecessors, his major contribution thus far has been as Indonesia's 'father' of Science and Technology to lead the country unto this path, not only building a strong cadre of scientists but also to demonstrate that the country could be among the world's leader in the aerospace industry.

All three leaders have also been professionally trained in their respective jobs. Sukarno was trained as an engineer at the prestigious Institute of Technology at Bandung, Suharto being a professional soldier and Habibie being a German trained engineer. Also, all three had a dedicated history and background and were known as doers and not just talkers. All three operated under the same 1945 Constitution while accepting *Pancasila* as the national and state ideology. Strangely enough, all three leaders were born in the month of June.

DIFFERENCES

However, what have placed them apart is also significant. When Sukarno became President, 95 percent of the society was illiterate, and this has a particular impact on national developmental policies. According to Professor Widjojo Nitisastro, one of the key architects of the New Order's economic policies, there was hardly any intellectual core and it could have hardly filled a single bus. There were only two economists, namely Hatta and Sumitro and this weakness also played a major part in shaping the level of national confidence and outlook.

The country was also weak in infrastructural development

as it was still recovering from the underdevelopment of the Dutch colonialism as well as from the ravages of the war of independence. The weak intellectual base and poor infrastructure also meant that the political elite lacked a good information system, in turn, made worst by a nascent education system. On the whole, the country lacked a proper infrastructure of politics and economics, with Sukarno and his contemporaries having to undertake many projects through trials and errors. Sukarno was 44 years old when he became Indonesia's first President.

When Suharto became President, the illiteracy rate was about 60 percent. The intellectual core was slightly better than what Sukarno inherited. If during the Sukarno period, there were only two economists, Suharto was fortunate that he had about 200. The intellectual core of the country had also improved somewhat, with about one percent of the population qualified as such. Suharto also started his Presidency by confirming that historically the national ideology of *Pancasila*, which exhorted tolerance was the right one. Suharto was about 46 years old when he became the country's second President. As Suharto was in a slightly better position that Sukarno in terms of the literacy levels, intellectual core as well as national infrastructure, the second President could enjoy a certain degree of positive synergy with the intellectual world and this was translated into the operationalisation of a regularised electoral mechanism which elected national representatives and the leaders once every five years.

In contrast, when Habibie became the country's third President, what he inherited was a totally different world. When he became President, about 4 percent of the population was still illiterate. Compared to 2 and 200 economists of the Sukarno and Suharto era, Habibie had a coterie of more than 200,000 such skilled individuals. While the intellectual world of Sukarno was negligible and that of Suharto somewhat marginal, Habibie argued that when he became, the intellectual world had passed the critical mass, and where almost every-one acted as an expert in almost every field. Unlike his prede-cessors, who became Presidents in their 40s, Habibie was 62 when he occupied that position.

However, what has placed Habibie apart from his prede-cessors is that he may be more prepared and equipped to lead the country than was the case with the two former Presidents. This is because as an eminent engineer and scientist, he is in a position to optimise on the existing information revolution and the infrastructure that is obtained in the country. He is in an excellent position to develop a positive synergy with the various technological systems found today and his key chal-lenge is to enhance the positive aspect while containing the negative dimensions. Thus, management of the new world, which Habibie is most familiar with, is one of his key chal-lenges as President. What is often not appreciated is that Habibie actually grew up in such a society. While there was not a single computer in Suharto's office, Habibie has two in his office with another two in his house. To that extent, Habibie is not really intimidated by the brave new world of information technology that has taken the world by storm. Thus, what is obtained in Indonesia today is, in many ways, 'the state of the art President' and it is man such as this who is likely to get the job done.

In this connection, another very useful way to assess the future course of Indonesia is to examine the character of the presidents Indonesia has had thus far. Sukarno was essentially a revolutionary. He strove for power and reached the highest office of the country by launching a political offence against the Dutch colonialists. He was driven and motivated by the long sense of humiliation that was suffered by the country at the hands of the Dutch, British and Japanese, and he wanted Indonesia to stand as an equal. Hence, he fuelled the country's nationalism as that was the only way to fight and challenge the colonial power. His style of leadership was largely populist as he was also very charismatic. Somehow, he never lost this zeal and in many ways, he continued his revolutionary-populist approach to politics long after the Dutch had been driven out of the country.

Suharto, by comparison, was very much a different person. He originated from an ordinary Javanese peasantry background and being imbued with the Javanese culture and values, he strove for equilibrium, order and harmony more than anything else. Thus, by nature, Suharto could not adopt a populist approach. Rather, he behaved more like a 'prince'. To him, the country was more like a 'kingdom' and he ruled more like a Javanese king. To him, cronyism and nepotism were absolutely legitimate as he saw it as a right to reward his loyal courtiers. Thus, his vision of a leader was more akin to that of a king, being heavily influenced by the philosophy of the Javanese '*wayang kulit*'.

By comparison, Habibie's experience is far different from his predecessors and hence, his style and outlook. For some, Habibie appears to be trapped into two different worlds, the Western and the Eastern. President Habibie was educated in the West and spent many years of his adult life there. In many ways, he has adopted a Western life style and outlook and is very adept with the Western world, unlike his predecessors. In many ways too, Habibie approaches problems from the Western perspective, all the more, due to his scientific outlook and training. In this regard, adopting and accepting Western democracy and all the attendant values that flows from it is not difficult for him. Yet, at the same time, there is no doubt, that he is an 'Easterner', being of mixed Javanese and Sulawesi parentage. His early childhood and upbringing was essentially Indonesian and this has also affected him and his outlook. More important, he is very proud of his Indonesian background and views himself as an ardent nationalist who has tried to contribute to the well-being of his people and nation. For some, there would appear to be a 'clash of civilisations', between the 'rational' world of the West and the 'emotional' world of the east. Whatever may be the truth of the matter, the fact remains that President Habibie is proud of the Indonesian upbringing and is also grateful of the knowledge and skills that he had gained from the West. What he has tried to undertake is to apply his Western skills and knowledge to uplift the well being of his country and to that extent, there appears to be an attempt to bring about 'balanced development' in Indonesia, by combing the best of both worlds. This is also in line with the '*Pancasila*' state that Habibie is committed so as it preaches tolerance and synergy, values which are close to Habibie's heart.

Despite this 'fabric' of Habibie, how and what shape the dynamic of politics within and without Indonesia would take remains to be seen. Both within and without, there were particular images, many of them negative, about Habibie and how much these would hurt him remains to be seen. At the same time, in foreign relations, there were certain 'blind spots' which may be regarded as 'excess baggage' of the past. Hence, with Singapore there was essentially a competitive relations with regard to the Batam development project as well as Habibie's pet projects in the aerospace industry. With China, there were problems with regard to the Natuna development area. With Japan, Habibie was keen on technological co-operation but which was not in coming. With Australia, there were difficulties with regard to technological cooperation, especially in the aerospace industry. The point being, Habibie's past difficulties with these countries, all of which are immediate neighbours of Indonesia and with which there are strong political and economic ties, may provide the basis for continued cool ties between these countries and Indonesia.

Notwithstanding these 'blind spots', the key to Habibie's future would be the course of politics in the country in the next year or so. In November 1998, the Extraordinary Session of the MPR was held and Habibie's position was unaffected as the MPR was convened more to pass a number of laws to effect the changes that are expected in 1999. In June 1999, the country will be going to the polls and the outcome of this is going to be extremely important for Habibie's political future. With so many political parties already formed, and the number is likely to hit 150 by then, there is a very strong possibility that no single party will emerge with a clear majority. This is likely to launch the era of 'coalition politics' in Indonesia and whether the country will enter into a spiral of perpetual instability remains to be seen. Following this, in November 1999, the General Session of the MPR will be held to elect a new President and Vice President. The key question is whether President Habibie will be able to survive these key political events, especially following the June 1999 elections. While the President has been ambivalent about his future plans, what he indicated to the author would tend to signal that he cannot be ruled out as the next President. In words of President Habibie:

> I am better equipped than both Sukarno and Suharto to run the country today – not better – but better equipped to manage with the state of art available. Also, the country is in a difficult crossroads and if things are not correctly managed, there will simply be too much damage to the country and the problems will get worst. Today, if I do not do the right thing and stay on to complete the task, I will be doing a disservice to my people and country. Like most Javanese, I believe God do sent people to earth to do certain things at a certain time. May be I am the guy God sent to put the place in order. If not, the damage to this place would be irreversible. What is also not irreversible is the fact that I am already the President and what is left for me is to do the job right.[1]

Indonesia has today, probably its most democratic and

people-oriented President. Where Indonesia will head in the next century and what its role would be in the region and world at large would be largely dependent on how long President Habibie remains in power and who succeeds him. Therein lies the answer as to what the future of Indonesia, and with it, of the region as a whole, would be in the coming years.

An equally important factor that needs to be noted as far as the Habibie Presidency is the importance of political culture. Without doubt, there has been a definite shift from the Suharto to the post-Suharto era. During the Suharto era, the paradigm of the political culture was such that it gave premium of political stability at all cost. Through various measures, including relying excessively on the military, the government became very dominant at the expense of the people. A classic 'strong state' and 'weak society' model existed. This situation allowed all kinds of abuses to go on unchecked and it was this more than anything else that accounted for the rise of corruption, cronyism and nepotism in the body politic. While Suharto's political system had a 'strong government' it was extremely weak as far as accountability to the people, the electorate, was concerned. The government was the sole interpreter of all matters, including the state ideology of *Pancasila* and the 1945 Constitution and hence, the abuses prevalent in the system, especially against the regime's political opponents. In such a top-down system, there was a lack of accountability and transparency, and the rise of all kinds of abuses, which cumulatively brought the system down.

Under President Habibie, there is an attempt to introduce a new paradigm as far as political culture is concerned. Increasingly and this was stated so by the President to the author, the ideal being worked at is to create a 'small government' but where the 'society is strong'.[2] A government of this nature would be, in the true sense of the world, a 'people's government' and where the sovereignty lies with the people, with the government being nothing more than the representative of its people. As such, in order to achieve stability, the Habibie Government and through various measures, have tried to introduce the notion of a 'people's system'. In essence, this has involved the introduction of populist and people-oriented policies at all levels, in the political, economic and social system. The various policies introduced by Adi Sasono are in line with this. Even a 'civilian militia' has been set up in order to involve the 'people' in security and defence of the country. In this manner, Habibie and his government hope to project an image of greater accountability and with it, one that is largely transparent. There is also the attempt to alter somewhat the top-down system so that greater inputs are derived from the 'people'. How effective and successful the Habibie government will be in this endeavour will ultimately depend on the two key events that are scheduled to take place in the country's political agenda, namely, the general elections in June and the elections for the Presidency and Vice-Presidency in November 1999.

Some Possible Political Scenarios

In this connection, a number of political scenarios can be drawn up. The political and strategic environment in Indonesia following the Special MPR Session in November 1998 has become very complicated, with not all groups accepting the reform agenda that has been drawn up. Some groups have accepted the Special MPR Session as legitimate but not its agenda. Some have accepted the agenda as legitimate but not the Session. Some have accepted ABRI's presence in Parliament but not Habibie as the President. Some have accepted Habibie as the President but continue to oppose ABRI's presence in Parliament. There are widespread and intense divisions within society and how these issues will be resolved, will go a long way in determining the character and future of

Indonesian politics. This thus begs the question as to whether politics in Indonesia is about power struggle or the struggle for power, with many viewing it as the latter as everyone is keen to have the top political job in the country.

In view of this, what type of political architecture can one expect in the very near future in Indonesia? This will very much be determined by the political and power structure and constellation in existence at any one time. Presently, there are a number of ways one can examine this. A simple classification would be the dichotomy between the 'Status Quo" versus the 'Reformists'. Another simple categorisation would be to divide the existing political forces into either the secular or religious nationalist camps. However, in reality, the situation is more complicated than that and one good description of the political constellation was made by the Foundation of the Indonesian Legal Aid Institute. On 28 October 1998, its Chairman, Bambang Widjojanto, argued that there were four 'social forces' involved in political power struggle in the country. These were:

1. **The Restorationists group**. This referred to the remnants of the Suharto's regime who sought to revive or at least protect the former President's image and position. He argued that the strength of this group is best evident from the fact that the "law is unable to touch him and how there are still groups who give him offerings in exchange for his blessings and power".

2. **The *Status Quo* group**. This referred to the group that was interested in supporting and maintaining President B. J. Habibie in power. Here, Bambang argued that "the support [for Habibie] is not meant to build a legitimacy for Habibie per se but often because the supporters believe they can obtain their maximal political agenda and interests under Habibie".

271

3. **The Reformists group**. This group was dissatisfied with the existing conditions and has continued to campaign for a new and democratic Indonesia.

4. **The Ambiguous group**. This group, according to Bambang wanted reform "but because of certain social and political positions, cannot free themselves from political constraints and so choose to stay within the existing power structure".[3]

The author, however, prefers a three-fold typology of the political-social forces in the country and this would largely determined the prospects for stability in Indonesian in the next few months, especially until the general elections and presidential elections are held. What this typology captures is the state of 'political axes and alignments' that exist today, largely as a fallout of Suharto's resignation and rise of Habibie as the President.

The three-fold categorisation reflects the state of political alignments and the taxonomy can be divided as follows: the various radical groups, the critical groups and the realist or status quo groups. As implied, the radicals or revolutionaries would like to overthrow the existing political and even social system and in its place, install a new system. The critical group is prepared to accept the present system and power structure but is working to improve or reform it. Finally, the status quo would like to preserve the present system as they are the primary beneficiaries of the existing order.

Which are the political and social forces that would fall under the three different typology? Even though there are almost countless political and social groups in the country and they seem to be proliferating almost on a daily basis, the the following can be regarded as one attempt to categorise the main social-political forces that have the most important bearing on the political dynamics in the country today.

TYPOLOGY OF POLITICAL-SOCIAL GROUPS IN INDONESIA TODAY

Radical/Revolutionary Groups

1. *Forum Kota* -City Forum

2. *Forum Komunikasi Senat Mahasiswa Jakarta* (FKSMJ) – Jakarta Forum of Student Union Communication

3. *Aliansi Demokrasi Rakyat* (ALDERA) – People's Democratic Alliance

4. *Himpunan Mahasiswa Islam – Majelis Pembaikan Organisasi* (HMI-MPO) – Islamic Student Union – Reform of Organisation Development

5. *Front Mahasiswa Untuk Reformasi Dan Demokrasi* (FAMRED) – Student Front For Democracy and Reform

6. *Barisan Nasional* – National Front

7. *Aksi Rakyat Bersatu* (AKRAB) – The People's Joint Action

8. *Forum Bersama* (FORBES) – United Forum

9. *Koalisasi Nasional* –National Coalition

Critical Groups

1. *Forum Merah Putih* – Red White Forum

2. *Kesatuan Aksi Mahasiswa Muslim Indonesia* (KAMMI) – The Action Forum of Indonesian Muslim Students

3. *Forum Mahasiswa Indonesia* (Forum Indonesia) – Indonesian Students Forum

273

4. *Himpunan Mahasiswa Islam* (HMI) – Islamic Student Association

5. *Forum Salemba* – Salemba Forum

6. *Himpunan Mahasiswa Muslim Antar Kampus* (HAMMAS) – Inter-Campus Muslim Students Association

7. Student Union of University Indonesia

8. Student Union of Gadjah Mada University

9. Student Union of Institute of Technology, Bandung

Realist/*Status Quo* Groups

1. Ciganjur Group comprising Amien Rais, Megawati Sukarnoputri, Gus Dur and the Sultan of Jogjakarta

2. *Majelis Ulama Indonesia* - Indonesian Islamic Leaders Association

3. *Ikatan Cendikiawan Muslim Indonesia* (ICMI) – Indonesian Muslim Intellectuals Association

4. *Komite Indonesia Untuk Solidaritas Dunia Islam* (KISDI) – Indonesian Committee for Solidarity of World Islam

5. *Forum Penegah Keadilan dan Konstitusi* (FURKON) – Forum for the Promotion of Justice and Constitution.

Source: Compiled by the Author

Against this typology, the following scenarios or roadmap for Indonesia in the near future can be chartered.

Scenario One: Political Stability with/without Recovery

Some have argued that after much 'struggle' and 'infighting', the political entity would settle down, with peace and stability gaining dominance. This would be due to the success of political socialisation and the enthusiasm in implementing the various decrees that were passed by the MPR Session in November 1998. As such, the June 1999 elections are expected to proceed smoothly as would be the November 1999 MPR Session to elect a new President and Vice-President. Following this, two sub-scenarios are possible. First, the new government would be legitimate and it would be able to carry out its primary task of overcoming all the major crises confronting the country

Second, even though the new government is legitimate, it will not be able to overcome the various crises confronting the political entity. This is because recovery is not possible with political legitimacy alone. What the government also needs is capability and the new political process is unlikely to throw up politicians of this stature.

Scenario Two: Political Instability without Recovery

This scenario posits growing instability and polarisation in the country. As the country prepares for the general elections, the government is likely to lose control due to 'over-politicking', something the country has not experienced for more than thirty years. There would be the inability to cope with 'uncontrolled democracy'. There would be all-round loss of authority, in turn, leading to a number of sub-scenarios. First, the government and ABRI will try to implement the election plans according to the decrees passed by the MPR and if necessary, by force. When elections are held, some would accept the results, with others rejecting them. Second, if no elections are held, the chances are the country and its government would continue to suffer from a legitimacy crisis, where political instability would be recurrent and where economic recovery is unlikely to take place. This, in many ways, is the worst case scenario, with a 'revolutionary setting' being created in the country, which in turn, can lead to the rise of radicals to power, especially in this case, the militant 'Green Guards' or Islamic fundamentalists. A situation like this can also lead to ABRI taking over power to normalise the political situation while pre-empting the rise of radical forces that could threaten the state ideology of *Pancasila* and the 1945 Constitution.

The Likely Scenario

Of the two scenarios, the first is more likely. The elections are likely to take place with various international bodies and observers already mobilised to give the polls a gloss of legitimacy. While there will be a real 'festival of democracy', there was also a fear of electoral violence as in India. If nearly 400 people could have died in the last election in 1997 when there were only three political parties competing in a largely 'controlled environment', the death toll is likely to be much higher when there are nearly 150 political parties, competing in an almost uncontrolled, though not anarchic, setting. In this connection, Indonesia's Chief of State Intelligence Agency, Lieutenant-General Z. A. Maulani, said on 30 December 1998 that political tensions are expected to increase but "this will not manifest itself in anything as big as the mid-May 1998 rioting". The reason for this is that while in May 1998, almost all the people demanded a change in state leadership, "now there is only a small group of people that can be described as anarchists who still want a change in the state leadership".[4] In the end, there is unlikely to be a single party majority and what will emerge will be an intense polarization of political power. GOLKAR, the hegemonic party since 1971, will no longer be what it was and it would have to accept the status as one of many major parties. There will not be one major party but generally a 'grand coalition', especially of all the major Muslim parties, except for those affiliated with Gus Dur. A 'grand coalition' constituting of the following major parties is highly plausible, namely, GOLKAR, PPP, PBB, PAN, Partai Keadilan and a number of other Muslim parties. The PDI, representing the Nationalists and PKB, representing the Traditional Muslims, together with the Nahdatul Ulama will become the key 'Opposition' force in Indonesia following the elections in June 1998.

As for the Presidency, the consensus is fast emerging that Habibie will remain as the country's President. This is mainly due to the backing he has from almost all the key political groups in the country, which constitutes the legal majority as well as from ABRI. In the post-Suharto political paradigm, there is no one who is more capable and acceptable than Habibie, and political democratisation will ensure that the Presidency goes to Habibie. The more interesting question and contest would be with regard to the Vice-Presidency and here, there are three main contenders, General Wiranto, Adi Sasono and Amien Rais. Despite the non-Muslim and international media attempt to project Megawati Sukarnoputri as a possible Presidential candidate, the limited nature of political support the PDI and PKB are able to garner and the 'structure' of the electoral system will mean that unless these two political parties are prepared to join the 'grand coalition' of largely Islamic parties, they stand the chance of being increasingly sidelined from political power.

Yet, at the same time, the Islamic forces, mainly ICMI-led, Muhammadiyah and Masjumi in orientation, are also conscious that Megawati Sukarnoputri do have a populist appeal, especially in Central and Eastern Java, where the majority of

277

Javanese live. As such, ICMI and modern Islamic strategists have concluded that the single biggest threat to the Islamic game plan to gain power is the Megawati factor. She is a threat due to her popular appeal, especially among the Javanese, who view her as a symbol of victimisation by the New Order. There are also many Javanese who support Megawati as she is the daughter of Indonesia's first President, Sukarno. For many, Sukarno is viewed as a great leader, almost God-like, and Megawati has inherited this positive resonance towards her father. The non-Muslim media has played this up, further boosting Megawati's image.

It was this 'Megawati factor' more than anything else which convinced ICMI stalwarts like Adi Sasono that a new political force needed to be establish if the Islamic forces were to retain power. Campaigning for GOLKAR was regarded as 'politically suicidal' as it was a political party that was associated with too many abuses in the past. Adi and the ICMI leadership would also like to distant themselves from the old Suhartoist political vehicle.[5] Privately, Adi has mentioned that even if GOLKAR nominated Habibie for the Presidency, it would be one of the many 'great misfortunes facing the country'. As such, a new political party needed to be established and this first began as a movement. The basic idea of this movement was to undermine and undercut Megawati's support, especially in Java, where more than 60 percent of Indonesia's population live. The new movement and party was not Islamic, appeared populist, appeared cultural, not religious and appeared to represent the interest of the 'small people'. The object was to undercut the romantic notions the Javanese had of Megawati and Sukarno. If successfully implemented, the new political force could act as an effective block force to stop popular support from swinging towards Megawati's PDI and the Gus Dur's group, which appear largely sympathetic towards the former.

Regardless of the outcome of the political competition, the

278

June 1999 elections will most like usher in a democratic Indonesia with the presence of a strong Opposition. This will be good for democracy while ensuring a more accountable government. To a large extent, if President Habibie remains in power, there will be no problem for the functioning of a viable opposition as he believes that this is good for the country as a more democratic, people and public oriented government would come to power and at the same time one that is responsive to the dictates of democracy. Indonesia would emerge as a normal and functioning democracy even though one must be sanguine that democratisation will take roots but with a great deal of growing pains, especially in the initial years. Many of the Indonesian political elites believe that this is a phase of politics the country must go through, no matter how difficult and painful it may be so that a legitimate political order emerges and with that, its economy will improve, once credible and legitimate governance return to the country. This process will also assist in building national reconciliation and consensus, which in turn, would assist in the crafting of a social contract for the country so that it make effectively make its presence felt in the region and beyond in the next Millennium.

NOTES

1   Author's interview with President B. J. Habibie in Jakarta on 3 October 1998.

2   Interview with President B. J. Habibie on 3 October 1998 at the Presidential Palace, Jakarta, Indonesia.

3   See "Four Forces seen vying for power", *The Jakarta Post*, 29 October 1998.

4   Cited in *The Jakarta Post*, 31 December 1998.

5   Adi Sasono's decision not to campaign for GOLKAR, even though he is one of its key leaders was made public on 1 January 1999. See "Adi Sasono Tidak Mau Jadi Juru Kampanye Golkar", *Merdeka*, 2 January 1999.

279

SELECT BIBLIOGRAPHY

'Adi Sasono Defends Populist Policies', *The Jakarta Post*, 11 August 1998.

'Alatas Clears Air Over Habibie's Cancelled Visit', *The Straits Times*, 9 October 1998.

'Breaking with the Past', *The Indonesian Observer*, 26 May 1998.

'Calon Presiden Mendatang Tidak Harus Calon Tunggal', *Suara Karya*, 13 April 1989.

'Country will not become Islamic state', *The Straits Times*, 9 October 1998.

'Detik-detik Yang Menegangkan', *Gatra*, 30 May 1998.

'Govt. denies interfering in Golkar Congress', *The Jakarta Post*, 15 July 1998.

'I'm ready to take the blame: Prabowo', *The Jakarta Post*, 18 July 1998.

'Indonesia to ratify human rights pacts', *The Jakarta Post*, 10 June 1998.

'Jakarta felt abandoned by close ally', *The Straits Times*, 7 August 1998.

'Jakarta Unhappy with its ties with Singapore', *The Straits Times*, 27 June 1998.

'KL-Jakarta ties may be affected', *The Straits Times*, 4 October 1998.

'Menko Polkam Sudomo Minta Maaf Kepada Presiden: Sehubungan Ucapannya Tentang Konsensus Nasional', *Kompas*, 13 April 1989.

'More Candidates for Presidency Will Be Allowed', *The Jakarta Post*, 13 April 1989.

'Muslim Group Backs Habibie's Reform Efforts', *The Straits Times*, 26 June 1998.

'New Bill Reduces Habibie's Powers', *The Straits Times*, 9 July 1998.

'No Split within ABRI', *The Sunday Times*, 17 May 1998.

'Not Grooming a Successor', *The Jakarta Post*, 16 March 1994.

'Perlukah Membicarakan Suksesi Sekarang?', *Forum Keadilan*, No. 23, 3 March 1994.

'President's Suharto's Wish', *The Jakarta Post*, 22 February 1994.

'SI tidak pilih President Baru', *Media Indonesia*, 8 July 1998.

'Singapore Strain Relations with Indonesia's President', *The Asian Wall Street Journal*, 4 August 1998.

'S'pore, Jakarta sign US$8b deal', *The Straits Times*, 14 July 1998.

'Skenario Cendana Menggusur Habibie', *AKSI*, Vol. 2, No. 84, 23-29 June 1998.

'Soldiers Held Over Abductions', *The Jakarta Post*, 15 July 1998.

'Succession, No Problem: Suharto', *The Jakarta Post*, 24 February 1994.

'Suharto's downfall was engineered', *The Indonesian Observer*, 27 June 1998.

'Military Must Be Ready to Ensure Smooth Succession', *The Jakarta Post*, 4 March 1994.

'The Succession Issue', *The Jakarta Post*, 17 March 1994.

'UN Tables Autonomy Plan for E. Timor', *The Straits Times*, 10 October 1998.

'We are like Malaysia: Habibie', *The Straits Times*, 9 July 1998.

'Wiranto in Full Control of Military', *The Sunday Times*, 24 May 1998.

A ranking General, *Interview by author*, October 1998.

A ranking General, *Interview by author*, September 1998, Jakarta.

Amien Rais, 'Keterbukaan Dan Suksesi', *Editor*, No. 45, 15 July 1989.

Ariel Heryanto, 'Flaws of Riot Media Coverage', *The Jakarta Post*, 15 July 19998.

Benedict R. O. G. Anderson, *The Idea of Power in Javanese Culture, Language and Power: Exploring Political Cultures in Indonesia*, Ithaca, New York: Cornell University Press, 1992.

David Jenkins, *Suharto and His Generals: Indonesian Military Politics, 1973-1983*, Ithaca: Cornell Modern Indonesian Project, 1987.

Donald W. Wilson, *The Next 25 Years: Indonesia's Journey Into the Future*, Jakarta: Yayasan Persada Nusantara, 1992.

Dr. Afan Gaffar, 'Trends in Contemporary Indonesian Politics: Preparing for Succession', *Seminar Paper in Seminar conducted by the Institute of Southeast Asian Studies*, Singapore, 28 November 1995

Editor, No. 23, 3 March 1994.

Edward Aspinall, 'The Broadening Base of Political Opposition in Indonesia', in Garry Rodan (Ed.), *Political Oppositions in Industrialising Asia,* London and New York: Routledge, 1996.

282

Far Eastern Economic Review, 7 May 1998.

Forum Keadilan, No. 23, 3 March 1994.

Forum Keadilan, Vol. 7, No. 5, 15 June 1998.

Gatra, 30 May 1998.

Geoff Forrester and R. J. May, eds., *The Fall of Soeharto*, (Singapore: Select Books, published in association with Regime Change and Regime Maintenance in Asia and Pacific Project and North Australia Research Unit, Research School of Pacific and Asian Studies, Australian National University, 1998).

Interview with *International Herald Tribune*, reproduced in *The Straits Times*, 16 July 1998.

John McBeth and Michael R. J. Vatikiotis, 'Indonesia: The Endgame', *Far Eastern Economic Review*, 28 May 1998.

John McBeth, 'Indonesia: A Warning Shot', *Far Eastern Economic Review*, 2 April 1998.

John Mcbeth, 'Indonesia: Shadow Play', *Far Eastern Economic Review*, 23 July 1998.

John McBeth, 'Indonesia: Suharto's Way', *Far Eastern Economic Review*, 26 March 1998.

Margot Cohen and John Mcbeth, 'A 'Disappeared' Speaks Out and His Testimony Implicates the Armed Forces', *Asiaweek*, 8 May 1998.

Margot Cohen and John Mcbeth, 'Indonesia: The Vanishings', *The Jakarta Post*, 7 May 1998.

Margot Cohen, 'Indonesia: Campus Crusaders', *Far Eastern Economic Review*, 26 March 1998.

Max Walsh, 'Islamisation May Be the New Axis', *The Sydney Morning Herald*, 22 May 1998.

Michael R. J. Vatikiotis, 'Consumers Caught in the Middle', *The Jakarta Post*, 9 April 1989.

Michael R. J. Vatikiotis, 'Succession Scenarios', *Far Eastern Economic Review*, 28 September 1989.

Michael R. J. Vatikiotis, *Indonesia under Suharto: Order, Development and Pressure for Change*, London: Routledge, 1993.

Michael R. J. Vatikiotis, *Indonesia under Suharto: Order, Development and Pressure for Change*, Revised Edition, London: Routledge, 1994.

President B. J. Habibie, *Interview by author*, 3 October 1998, Jakarta, Indonesia.

Richard Mann, *Plots and Schemes That Brought Down Soeharto*, (Singapore: Gateway Books, 1998).

Richard Robinson, 'Indonesia: Tensions in State and Regime' in Kevin Hewison, Richard Robison and Gary Rodan (eds.), *Southeast Asia in the 1990s: Authoritarian, Democracy and Capitalism*, Sydney, Allen and Unwin, 1993.

Salvador J. Ximenes Soares, 'E. Timor Settlement: Referendum or Autonomy?', *The Jakarta Post*, 18 September 1998.
Suara Pembaruan, 20 November 1997.

Soeharto: My Thoughts and Deeds: An Autobiography (as told to G. Dwipayana and K. H. Ramadhan), Jakarta: PT Citra Lamtoro Gung Persada, 1991.

Susan Berfield and Jose Manuel Tesoro, 'A Nation Asserts Itself', *Asiaweek*, 5 June 1998.

The Australian, 22 May 1998.

The Indonesian Observer, 26 May 1998.

The Indonesian Observer, 8 June 1998.

The Jakarta Post, 22 February 1994.

The Jakarta Post, 21 March 1994.

The Jakarta Post, 30 August 1997.

The Jakarta Post, 20 October 1997.

The Jakarta Post, 3 December 1997.

The Jakarta Post, 15 December 1997.

The Jakarta Post, 1 March 1998.

The Jakarta Post, 11 March 1998.

The Jakarta Post, 16 March 1998.

The Jakarta Post, 16 April 1998.

The Jakarta Post, 8 May 1998.

The Jakarta Post, 10 May 1998.

The Jakarta Post, 14 May 1998.

The Jakarta Post, 15 May 1998.

The Jakarta Post, 16 May 1998.

The Jakarta Post, 17 May 1998.

The Jakarta Post, 18 May 1998.

The Jakarta Post, 19 May 1998.

285

The Jakarta Post, 21 May 1998.

The Jakarta Post, 22 May 1998.

The Jakarta Post, 23 May 1998.

The Jakarta Post, 24 May 1998.

The Jakarta Post, 26 May 1998.

The Jakarta Post, 4 June 1998.

The Jakarta Post, 5 June 1998.

The Jakarta Post, 6 June 1998.

The Jakarta Post, 12 June 1998.

The Jakarta Post, 18 June 1998.

The Jakarta Post, 19 June 1998.

The Jakarta Post, 20 June 1998.

The Jakarta Post, 22 June 1998.

The Jakarta Post, 26 June 1998.

The Jakarta Post, 29 June 1998.

The Jakarta Post, 1 July 1998.

The Jakarta Post, 2 July 1998.

The Jakarta Post, 3 July 1998.

The Jakarta Post, 4 July 1998.

The Jakarta Post, 7 July 1998.

The Jakarta Post, 10 July 1998.

The Jakarta Post, 12 July 1998.

The Jakarta Post, 21 July 1998.

The Jakarta Post, 29 June 1998.

The Jakarta Post, 8 August 1998.

The Jakarta Post, 19 September 1998.

The Jakarta Post, 24 September 1998.

The Jakarta Post, 29 September 1998.

The New Paper, 14 May 1998.

The New Paper, 16 May 1998.

The New Paper, 20 May 1998.

The New Paper, 21 May 1998.

The New Paper, 27 June 1998.

The Philippines Star, 28 May 1998.

The Straits Times, 20 May 1998.

The Straits Times, 25 May 1998.

The Straits Times, 26 May 1998.

The Straits Times, 28 May 1998.

The Straits Times, 1 June 1998.

The Straits Times, 11 June 1998.

The Straits Times, 12 June 1998.

The Straits Times, 13 June 1998.

The Straits Times, 15 June 1998.

The Straits Times, 17 June 1998.

The Straits Times, 19 June 1998.

The Straits Times, 20 June 1998.

The Straits Times, 22 June 1998.

The Straits Times, 25 June 1998.

The Straits Times, 26 June 1998.

The Straits Times, 30 June 1998.

The Straits Times, 16 July 1998.

The Straits Times, 19 July 1998.

The Straits Times, 20 July 1998.

The Straits Times, 22 July 1998.

The Straits Times, August 1998.

The Straits Times, 28 September 1998.

The Straits Times, 29 September 1998.

The Straits Times, 30 September 1998.

The Straits Times, 5 October 1998.

The Straits Times, 9 October 1998.

The Straits Times, 13 October 1998.

The Sunday Times, 17 May 1998.

The Sunday Times, 24 May 1998.

TIRAS, 31 December 1997.

INDEX

A

Abdurrahman Wahid, 87, 90, 93, 120, 210
Adi Sasono, 2-3, 6-8, 10, 13-14, 17, 21, 25, 27, 40-49, 32, 40-50, 52, 55, 58-59, 61, 65, 67, 68, 82, 86-88, 92, 94, 102, 104, 106, 110, 120-121, 123-125, 127, 131, 134-135, 146, 154-155, 171, 183-184, 187-197, 204, 210, 216-222, 224, 227-228, 231, 243, 252-253, 270, 275-277
Amien Rais, 6, 16, 18, 51, 55, 57, 81-82, 85-87, 90, 92-93, 97, 115, 117-118, 120-121, 123-125, 130, 135, 139-142, 144, 148, 163, 169, 209, 274, 277
Anti-government, 81-83, 119, 136, 194, 217
Anti-Suharto, 78-81, 83, 90, 116-117, 134, 139, 163, 222
Army, 5, 9, 12, 38-39, 41, 44, 50, 52, 57, 87-88, 102, 118, 148, 188-190, 193, 216, 228, 243, 258
ASEAN, 3, 22, 75, 240-241, 251, 254, 256

B

Bambang Yudhyono, 41, 43, 48, 50, 52, 183, 188, 195, 204, 219, 221
Brawijaya, 46-47

C

Chinese, 74, 84, 101-102, 108, 118-119, 148, 179, 209, 211-214, 216, 222-223, 226-227, 257-258
Collusion, 66, 102-103, 108, 125, 133, 162-163, 165, 200, 203, 226
Conspiracy, 78-79, 110, 116-117, 137, 150, 152, 189
Constitution, 4-5, 7, 12, 15, 17, 22, 25-27, 30, 53, 68, 75, 84, 89, 92, 94,-95, 106, 109, 126, 128, 143, 151-152, 156-158, 200-201, 205, 221-223, 247, 263, 269, 274, 276
Corruption, 66, 91, 103, 108, 112, 118, 133, 162-163, 165, 200, 203, 220-221, 226, 269
Crisis, 4, 13, 18, 50-53, 59, 62-63, 66-69, 74, 78, 80-81, 83, 87, 91, 103-104, 107110,

W